SHE'S JUST SPIRITED

SHE'S JUST SPIRITED

*Parenting a Neurodivergent
Child and the Diagnosis
That Changes Everything*

NEFERTITI AUSTIN

BLOOMSBURY ACADEMIC
NEW YORK · LONDON · OXFORD · NEW DELHI · SYDNEY

BLOOMSBURY ACADEMIC
Bloomsbury Publishing Inc, 1359 Broadway, New York, NY 10018, USA
Bloomsbury Publishing Plc, 50 Bedford Square, London, WC1B 3DP, UK
Bloomsbury Publishing Ireland, 29 Earlsfort Terrace, Dublin 2, D02 AY28, Ireland

BLOOMSBURY, BLOOMSBURY ACADEMIC and the Diana logo are trademarks
of Bloomsbury Publishing Plc

First published in the United States of America 2025

Copyright © Nefertiti Austin, 2025

Cover images: © istock/Prostock-Studio

All rights reserved. No part of this publication may be: i) reproduced or transmitted in any form, electronic or mechanical, including photocopying, recording or by means of any information storage or retrieval system without prior permission in writing from the publishers; or ii) used or reproduced in any way for the training, development or operation of artificial intelligence (AI) technologies, including generative AI technologies. The rights holders expressly reserve this publication from the text and data mining exception as per Article 4(3) of the Digital Single Market Directive (EU) 2019/790.

Bloomsbury Publishing Inc does not have any control over, or responsibility for, any third-party websites referred to or in this book. All internet addresses given in this book were correct at the time of going to press. The author and publisher regret any inconvenience caused if addresses have changed or sites have ceased to exist, but can accept no responsibility for any such changes.

Library of Congress Control Number: 2025942485

ISBN: HB: 979-8-8818-0555-5
ePDF: 979-8-7651-6518-8
eBook: 979-8-8818-0556-2

Typeset by Deanta Global Publishing Services, Chennai, India
Printed and bound in the United States of America

For product safety related questions contact productsafety@bloomsbury.com.

To find out more about our authors and books visit www.bloomsbury.com
and sign up for our newsletters.

Parents, caregivers, and educators of neurodivergent children:
"They will never forget how you made them feel."
—*Dr. Maya Angelou*

CONTENTS

Abbreviations viii

Preface x

Introduction 1

1 She's Just Spirited 9

2 Recognizing Neurodivergence 31

3 The Assessment Rabbit Hole 49

4 Diagnosis in Hand, Now What Do I Do? 61

5 Try, Fail, Repeat 83

6 Overcoming Stereotypes 105

7 Comorbid Symptoms in Neurodivergence 123

8 It's a Family Affair 139

9 Growing with Your Child 151

10 Educational Trauma and Triumph 163

11 Dream a New Dream 183

Resources and Recommended Reading 191
Educators' Reader Guide and Discussion 197
Parents' Reader Guide and Discussion 202
Acknowledgments 206
Notes 208
Bibliography 220
Index 229
About the Author 240

ABBREVIATIONS

2E	twice exceptional
ABA	applied behavioral analysis
ADA	Americans with Disabilities Act
ACNB	American Chiropractic Neurology Board
ADHD	attention-deficit/hyperactivity disorder
AFAB	assigned female at birth
APIDA	Asian Pacific Islander Desi American
ASD	autism spectrum disorder
BIPOC	Black, Indigenous, person of color
CBT	cognitive behavioral therapy
CCPT	children-centered play therapy
CT SCAN	cranial tomography scan
DM	direct message
DSM	*Diagnostic and Statistical Manual of Mental Disorders*
EOP	educational opportunity program
FAPE	free appropriate public education
FASD	fetal alcohol syndrome disorder
FDA	Food and Drug Administration
HTP	hand, tree, person

ABBREVIATIONS

IDEA	Individuals with Disabilities Education Act
IEP	individualized education program
IQ	intelligence quotient
LAP	learning accommodation plan
LD	learning disability
LGBTQ+	lesbian, gay, bisexual, trans, queer or questioning, and more
MRI	magnetic resonance imaging
ND	neurodiverse or neurodivergent
NICU	neonatal intensive care unit
NPS	nonpublic school
NVLD	nonverbal learning disability
ODD	oppositional defiant disorder
OT	occupational therapy
PDA	pathological demand avoidance
PT	physical therapy
PTSD	post-traumatic stress disorder
SDP	special day program
STEP	Support Team Education Plan

PREFACE

After *Motherhood So White: A Memoir of Race, Gender, and Parenting in America* came out, I was asked what my next book would be about. Kate McKean, my amazing agent, suggested I write the story I didn't want to write. That was an intriguing idea and I considered writing about my relationship with my mother. We discussed it and reached the conclusion that books about narcissistic moms had been done and to think of something else. Briefly stumped, I thought of my kiddos. My teenage son was growing up nicely and would head off to college in a few years. Although *Motherhood So White* was specifically about my coming of age as a Black mother in the early twenty-first century, it was also a love letter to him and my grandparents, whose Black adoption of me and my brother set the stage for me to adopt August and Cherish. I had my topic. I would write about my sweet and spicy daughter, who took up residence in my heart when she was six months old.

Cherish's diagnosis literally changed everything, and I am a better parent and human for it. Still, I hesitated because I am not a therapist, school counselor, psychologist, psychotherapist, or psychiatrist. I am a mom who loves her children fiercely and recognize the need for a simply phrased tool kit for parents. I am also keenly aware that neurodivergence respects no geographic boundaries, socioeconomic levels, race, gender identity, or religion. It is the gift that keeps on giving, whether we like it or not, which is why I agreed to share our lives (again).

As you flip through the pages of *She's Just Spirited*, may you feel stronger and grow more confident in your parenting advocacy of your neurodivergent child.

You're doing a great job,
Nefertiti

Introduction

From the first day my son called me Mama, to the day I held an angel in a blue dress, I have enjoyed every happy stressful moment of motherhood. My children, born six years apart to the same mother but different fathers, are night and day. August, whom I wrote about in *Motherhood So White: A Memoir of Race, Gender, and Parenting in America*, is a thriving lacrosse-playing senior in high school on his way to college. Still reserved but fun, I will turn him loose in the world fortified with the love, joy, and support of his village that coparented with me in various capacities as coaches, play aunts and uncles, mentors, and family. August eased me into motherhood, paving the way for his little sister Cherish, whose boundless energy and girl-boss personality flipped me inside out. Sweet, affectionate, and a force to be reckoned with, Cherish challenged who I thought I was as a mother, bringing up old wounds and uncharted waters for our family. I owe her a debt of gratitude for teaching me how not to hold a grudge, how to lean on others for support, and how deep my well of love actually is. I suspect this is the journey of all parents of neurodivergent children; we just don't know it at the outset.

Now a tween, Cherish keeps me on my toes. She is creative, resilient, capable, and prone to tantrums, big emotions, and self-doubt. Cherish is her harshest critic and feels with an intensity beyond her years. Her desire to be "normal" has been heartbreaking, as she has attempted to rebel against her unique brain. Witnessing her journey through attention-deficit/hyperactivity disorder (ADHD) and sensory processing disorder (SPD) is humbling. There is only so much I can do. This is Cherish's water to carry, though I do my best to lighten her load.

On this road, I have turned to friends, administrators, the Internet, therapists, and trusted teachers for help with Cherish. I've read books, listened to podcasts, and even written short articles about parenting a neurodivergent child, and have yet to find a parenting book, written in plain English, about how to support my daughter. I have visited schools that specialize in special education and those who have services to support neurodivergent children with push-in and pull-out services. There is so much information that it is overwhelming at times. I, however, will not stop. As her steadfast advocate and number-one fan, I am confident that if I keep pushing, Cherish will come out the other side, kinder to herself, independent, and a productive member of society.

Neurological differences are common among children and there is lots of research that explains who, what, when, why, and how neurodivergence occurs. While I will tread some of that same ground, I will take parents by the hand and walk them through the process. How do you get an assessment? Who do you ask? How much does it cost? Why does my child need one? I will explore the various treatment plans for children across the neurodivergent spectrum and share what I learned about the autism community's reconsideration of one controversial type.

Despite the treasure trove of information that exists on neuroscience, neurodivergence, and learning disabilities, there are three major holes that need to be addressed.

First, most of the books are written by psychologists, psychotherapists, school counselors, and educators. The jargon is intimidating, and disputes among experts add to an already precarious situation for parents and caregivers. Parents need easy-to-follow books describing their lived experience of loving and raising neurodivergent children, not another theoretical tome that requires a dictionary and a glass of wine to get through the first chapter. Brain images and the proverbial volcano sticking out of the ocean with emotions listed beneath the surface are fun, until the explanations descend into *Diagnostic and Statistical Manual of Mental Disorders* (DSM) lingo and medical verbiage. Nerd that I am, I personally love all of that but also know that when Cherish is having an epic tantrum or is inconsolable because she felt wronged by a friend or teacher, I don't have the bandwidth to wade through dense pages. I need a short snippet to calm my nerves so I can help my daughter and I bet you do too.

Second, race, culture, gender identity, and socioeconomics are barriers to successful treatment plans for children of color. Black and brown children are negatively labeled first: aggressive, uncooperative, and the like, then punished, and, finally, helped. In some cases, it is too late. The damage has been done. The young person does not trust adults or the system. Adults have to be careful with their words, as kids are always listening. Referring to or calling a child aggressive for behaviors beyond their control or because the educator is unable to see past their own unconscious bias directly alters a child's trajectory toward incarceration. The 2016 Survey of Prison Inmates revealed that two out of five inmates reported at least one disability: hearing, vision, cognitive, ambulatory, self-care and independent living.[1] Many of these men and women had never been formally diagnosed but were told by a teacher or doctor that they had a disability. I think about young and old people who are incarcerated or unhoused. I wonder if a diagnosis and consistent treatment would have spared them their current circumstances. Parents and caregivers of Black and brown children recognize the significance of appropriate mental health interventions, even when our educational system holds fast to racism and stereotype. White children are given more leniency in school and in society, which maintains their forward trajectory. They are forgiven over and over and given room to fail forward. We have got to do better.

Third, gender matters. I am struck by stories shared by women in their mid-twenties who blog and vlog about their fraught youth. They wished their parents had given them meds, taken them to counseling, or had them assessed when they were young. They write about feeling "spacey," of academic struggles in high school and college, and later, having trouble maintaining employment and gravitating to toxic relationships. For many of these women, anxiety and depression are constant companions. While the Black community is slowly coming around to acknowledging and addressing mental health challenges, suicide among neurodivergent Black people is on the rise. This information is missing from most parenting books.

Additionally, the intersection of mental health and neurodivergence has LGBTQ+ Gen Z teens and young adults fired up. They are open about their neurological status, and create content on TikTok, Snapchat, and YouTube in defiance of their parents' cisgender notions about who is male or female. Gender fluid, curious, and confident enough to include their diagnosis as part of their identity, I suspect these young people have lots to teach us about our own children.

So, I'm back with a new book, *She's Just Spirited: Parenting a Neurodivergent Child and the Diagnosis That Changes Everything*. This is not a memoir like my previous book. Then, I was meditating on what it meant to be a Black mother. How it felt to be at the bottom of the motherhood hierarchy, even though America had been nursed at our teats. I shared uncomfortable truths about loving and rearing a Black boy in racially charged America, building community, and how my Black adoption by my maternal grandparents primed me to adopt two children I did not know many years later.

While I do not know the whereabouts of the neurodivergent Rosetta stone, I have done the heavy lifting of speaking with therapists, psychologists, administrators, and lots of parents who have generously shared their parenting strategies. Ultimately, it's all trial and error.

She's Just Spirited is my "two cents," as a fellow parent, forced to shed all that I thought I knew about parenting to wade deep into the trenches of raising a neurodivergent child, and the lessons I've learned along the way. Neurodivergence is not new to me, though we didn't call it that back in the day. For most people, mental health was a taboo subject. Their lack of normalcy reflected negatively on the family. Relatives were hospitalized for having a "spell" or kept out of sight when company visited. Unless they were a prodigy with explainable idiosyncrasies, it was easy to be erased within one's own family. I don't recall elders speaking of their challenges as caregivers, making my generation unprepared to pick up the heritable mantle of neurodivergence. Even with my background as a trainer for prospective adoptive parents, I was surprised by the heavy lifting having a child with a different learning style presented. It would have been lovely to have had an example to follow when Cherish's diagnosis made itself known, but oh well.

My crash course in parenting a child whose sensitivity and unique way of being in the world is far from over. And, even if I blow your mind with my "two cents you didn't ask for," which you'll find at the end of every chapter, I'm not sitting on high laughing at the peons who are still getting their sea legs in the neurodivergent space. I am still learning and growing as a parent.

My foray into the ocean of how-to parenting books was not without deep consideration. With every page I wrote, I thought of Cherish. Would she be comfortable with me sharing scenes from our life? Would she want people to know of her triumphs and struggles? I checked in with her and promised not to embarrass or exploit her neurodivergence. I explained that I want to help parents and think that by sharing broad strokes of our experience as a family, we can make sure another little spirited girl got off to the right start. Cherish agreed though she doesn't fully understand the seriousness of the gift she is giving.

She's Just Spirited is for parents and caregivers knee-deep in the overwhelming throes of raising, teaching, and loving a neurodivergent child. It will illuminate, in parent-friendly terms, spectrum disorders like autism (ASD), attention-deficit/hyperactivity disorder (ADHD), and ocular issues like dyslexia. Numerous tips on parent advocacy, teen engagement, psychological hits and misses, and raising children of color will be offered, as well as insight into what culturally relevant care looks and feels like.

She's Just Spirited is also for educators tasked with shaping young minds. You hold a tremendous amount of power over our children and families. How you connect, praise, punish, and guide children in your care can make or break a child, especially a neurodivergent one. Our kids are sensitive, resilient, fragile, funny, creative, and learn differently. It is critical that those of you who work in mainstream and special education love the profession and sprinkle that love on all of the children you welcome into your classrooms. Parents are aware that you are underpaid and underappreciated, but we need you to remain open and up to date on the latest pedagogy in supporting diverse learners. Our children's lives depend on it.

Where relevant, I have included cool charts and visuals to do a better job of explaining overlapping diagnosis, comorbid challenges, sample individualized education program (IEP) forms, and parents' rights. These are documents parents don't typically see until their child is in crisis: one too many emails, suspensions, tantrums, or an announcement to do self-harm. At that point, parents need to quickly digest information and complete lengthy forms to get their child a therapist or additional supports. I hope the inclusion of these forms will alleviate a little stress, should you ever need them. I also included interviews with a therapist, a counselor, and a head of school. The latter oversees more than two hundred neurodivergent children whose differences range from dyslexia to dysgraphia to dyscalculia. She has a fascinating story and heartfelt approach that supports children, teachers, and their parents. August even indulged me and allowed me to ask him a couple of questions about being the sibling of a neurodivergent person. His perspective on having to grow up faster tracks with other glass children who felt ignored in households where neurodivergence ruled the roost. At the end of this book, you will find references in all formats: books, blogs, podcasts, social media, news articles, and even television shows to add to your collection of things you were going to read or watch, if only you had time. Finally, there is a study guide for parents and educators. It's always good to compare notes and try new strategies when you run out of ideas or need a different perspective.

She's Just Spirited will front-load parents and caregivers with pertinent information about neurodivergence and special education in easy-to-digest chapters. Educators and clinicians will come to appreciate the stress parents operate under as they navigate their new reality with a diagnosis that changes everything.

1

She's Just Spirited

A lot of thought goes into starting a family. Is this the right time? Can we afford another mouth or two or three to feed? Is this the best neighborhood/city to raise a child? How much space will we need? Will our family and friends help us with childcare or financial support? Are my eggs healthy? Is my sperm count high enough? What if we can't get pregnant? Do I even want to be pregnant? And my personal favorite, because this was my thinking in 2006—my eggs are fine and thirty thousand[1] children in my backyard are in foster care. Since Black boys were overrepresented, I wanted to give at least one baby boy a forever home, no need to increase the population. However the decision to curate a family is reached, the thought of bringing a new life into the world is exciting.

Instinctively, partners set about dreaming about their baby or older child, if adoption is the choice. Will it be a boy or a girl? Whose nose or height will she have? What should we name her? As future parents wrestle with nursery color schemes, requests for maternity or paternity leave, interviewing nannies or finding quality day care, we plan for every eventuality, except neurodivergence. Adoptive parents have a slightly different mindset, as we are advised during parenting education classes that children in out-of-home care will have special needs. The specificity of that information, however, does not hit home until later.

The day a baby is born, data comes at parents fast, starting with the routine physical examination. The baby's sex at birth, height, weight, Apgar evaluation for heart rate, breathing, muscle tone, reflexes, and skin color[2] are determined. Medical staff measure head circumference, conduct a hearing test, and take a sample of blood to check for sickle cell anemia, phenylketonuria, and hypothyroidism. They receive their first shots and within twenty-four to forty-eight hours, maybe longer if delivery was via an uncomplicated C-section, mother and baby are discharged. If there are complications: preeclampsia, prematurity, jaundice, or lack of oxygen (asphyxia), injuries to the baby during or after birth or brain bleeds due to pressure from the delivery, the baby and mother may remain in the hospital for an extended stay. This was the case with Cherish who was six-weeks premature, jaundiced with a low Apgar score, weighing only four pounds eleven ounces, and not expected to survive. Before being discharged into the care of her foster mother, Cherish spent thirty days in the neonatal intensive care unit (NICU).

Did her birth trauma lead to an increased risk for developmental delays and neurodivergence? Yes, says the Cleveland Medical Clinic which studied birth trauma (perineal tears, post-traumatic stress disorder, significant blood loss, postpartum depression, etc.) in mothers and concluded that environmental factors, like exposure to drugs or asphyxia raise the possibility of developmental delays[3] in children. Kaiser Permanente researchers have found that babies who experienced certain birth complications, before and after birth, were at a 44 percent greater risk of developing autism later.[4] Birth asphyxia increases risks for ADHD,[5] and birth injuries that result in cerebral palsy up the ante for children to develop along the autism spectrum. Birth trauma isn't the only avenue to neurodivergence. Even when the birth mom does everything right—she doesn't drink or smoke, exercises, keeps stress to a minimum, and maintains prenatal appointments, participates in birth classes and yoga, opts for a home-, water-, or Doula-assisted birth, and has a normal pregnancy and birth, neurodivergence appears anyway.

Even with all of this information a keystroke away, we keep it in the deep recesses of our brains, because the baby we pray and plan for is about to arrive. Post delivery via stork or the social worker, our new main concern switches to how much love, care, and protection we will give our new addition.

Signposts

During the first year, parents and caregivers are bombarded with statistics about what is normal and what is not. These early goalposts are plastered on the walls of pediatricians' offices, growth calculators on parenting websites, and comments from grandma. Although these milestones reflect the *average* age a child smiles (three to six months), waves (seven months), and crawls (seven to ten months), it is the bar by which developmental success is measured. Pediatricians aren't the only voice in a parent's head. Words of wisdom from veteran parents, siblings, and friends converge to confirm or contradict what parents have learned from the Internet, with its endless links offering unsolicited advice. As time goes on, who our child is or is becoming gets lost in unconscious comparisons on playdates and offhand remarks from family and friends. A slow burn of anxiety ignites when other children are seemingly on schedule and ours is not. Secretly, we scheme to make our child smarter, faster, and healthier to avoid even considering the obvious: our child is different.

How did this happen? What did I do wrong? What do I do now? And a thousand other thoughts and questions arise, but the truth is that neurodivergence is an umbrella term for a diverse set of developmental differences that derive from a combination of genetic and environmental factors. No one did anything wrong, it just is.

A spectrum disorder, neurodivergence encompasses broad categorization and symptoms. In this book, I will focus on four: attention-deficit/hyperactivity disorder (ADHD)—an umbrella term for attention deficit disorder (ADD)—dyslexia, autism spectrum disorder (ASD), and nonverbal learning disorder (NVLD). By no means an exhaustive list, neurodivergent people make up 15 to 25 percent of the world's population.[6] Knowing that neurodivergence is an international occurrence should offer relief and serve as a great conversation starter for parents, caregivers, and educators who are nurturing a neurodivergent child. I wish this relief extended to my own tribe of adoptive parents, who took their babies home at birth or adopted them under the age of two. There is a prevailing belief that infants do not suffer from trauma. The mere fact that a child has been separated from her first mother, father, and siblings, possibly exposed to drugs in utero, and is in foster care implies trauma is present. Adoption and birth trauma plays out similarly: sleeplessness, irritability, neurological differences, cognitive and/or physical delays, behavioral issues, and so on. Depending on how many disrupted placements a child has experienced and the type of care she received, her adoption trauma may include acting our sexually, engaging in risky behavior, or running away from home. The list is long, and we eventually learn that nurture cannot—will not—override whatever biological wiring our child is born with.

Without question, my interest in neurodivergence is personal. My daughter, Cherish, who is adopted, was diagnosed with ADHD and SPD at six years old. And while some may feel that kindergarten is too young to have a child assessed, when I share her story at the end of this chapter, you'll understand where my head was when I made that decision.

Like most parents, I was concerned about my daughter being labeled in school. Well aware of the stereotype tightrope walk, BIPOC, LGBTQ+, and trans youth already engage in at school and in the world, I was hypersensitive to how she would be perceived by white teachers. Later, this concern expanded to include educators who were not trained to support girls with ADHD. Assumptions about a child's motive or ability are tied to labels, which can trigger devastating consequences. The most egregious are suicides of youth unable to deal with the crushing weight of negative stereotypes and the murders of Black kids, mostly boys like Trayvon Martin, who are assumed to always be up to no good. I will cover suicide in a later chapter but bring it up here because untreated mental illness coupled with labeling forces our kids to exist in little boxes, delineated by race or gender identification or socioeconomic status or how their brains function. The truth is, everyone is a living, breathing, intersectional experience of all of the above, and more, elastic in our ability to grow and thrive. This holistic approach to who a child really is resides with parents. It is up to us to dismantle labels and eliminate the boxes society uses to pigeonhole our kids.

Before I dive into spectrum disorders, I'd like to examine how parenting trends create blind spots for parents. In American culture, we adhere to rules around how to parent, who should parent, and what successful parenting looks like. These points of entry to parenthood are grounded in upbringing, their generation, birth order, whether they were rich or poor, and so many other factors. We over- or undercompensate for what we did or did not get in our family homes and subscribe to one road map, believing that is *the* path to raising a well-adjusted, happy, successful child.

Admittedly, it is hard to drown out the chatter about parenting styles. Am I a slacker mom? Authoritative, gentle, or a laissez-faire parent? Will I helicopter, snowplow, lighthouse, or let my child figure it out? All of these are necessary and important questions, although the answer changes as a child matures. New parents think they need to know what type of parent they will be and feel cheated when those trends don't apply to their family. The important thing to remember is that a trend or a style is not one size fits all. You may try on many hats or wear several hats simultaneously, depending on the needs of your child.

As a proud member of Generation X, I have fond memories of being a latchkey kid who drank out of the water hose and didn't see a grown-up for hours on Saturdays. We brag about being adults before the invention of personal computers, smartphones, and Google, and are forever grateful to have come along before social media, where all of our fails would have been on full display. The soundtrack of our youth was old-school hip-hop, New Wave rock, actual breakdancing (not that hoppity disgrace at the 2024 Paris Olympics), and never-ending comparisons between Prince and Michael Jackson. Our parents were baby boomers, raised after an Allied victory in Europe and Japan. Their world was one or the other: democracy or communism; right or wrong; straight or gay; black or white. There was no room for gray.

The fantasy of an American nuclear family—Father as the head of the household; Mother as the head of the home; Junior, Sissy, and a dog—was the guiding principle of many households. Suburban life was the dream sold on television and magazines, and any configuration outside of this societal familial norm was met with skepticism and derision. Children were expected to conform to the rules of home, school, and society, because that is how order and happiness are preserved in a patriarchal society. Our behavior, academic success, and careers reflected our parents. Many caregivers still hold this perspective and remain in denial about their child's needs longer than necessary. No judgment. I was raised by my maternal Depression-era grandparents and had to work hard to change my ideas about what good parenting looks like.

Loving and conservative, my grandparents raised three kids during the 1950s and 1960s. My mother was the wild one, so I took my parenting cues from my grandparents, determined not to follow in my mother's negligent and drug-addicted footsteps. I am easily the embodiment of a tiger mom with Western mom tendencies.

Tiger moms have roots in Asian culture where strict schedules, high standards, and respect for authority produces successful children. Western moms, on the other hand, are looser about raising perfect citizens and amenable to negotiating with their kids on things like how much time is spent practicing the piano.

Therapy for children wasn't a thing when I was growing up. We Gen Xers rolled with the consequences, even as we lived lives of quiet desperation. There was no social emotional learning or time-outs or grace for kids who were defiant, unable to focus or sit still. In the 1970s, they were labeled *bad, incorrigible, freaks, or dumb* and left to the margins of society. They were held up as how not to be, as if they had control over how their brain worked or their gender identification. This limited perspective was not helpful for kids of my generation who existed in the gray.

When I became a parent, I wanted to be less authoritative and more nurturing, open, and understanding. I was determined to treat each child according to his, then her, strengths, rather than the one-size-fits-all approach my grandparents used. However, my idea of the type of mother I would be was interrupted by the murder of Trayvon Martin. His death shook me and made me realize that being a Black mother came with an extra layer of stress. I would make choices about his trajectory based upon keeping him physically and emotionally safe. I traversed this topic in my memoir, *Motherhood So White: A Memoir of Race, Gender, and Parenting in America*. Cherish's neurodivergence sent me back to the parenting drawing board.

While race is still the cornerstone of our lives, Cherish lives in the gray. She requires an incredible amount of empathy, lots of affection, and patience. The tiger part of my parenting style didn't work for her, because being overly demanding or punitive with a neurodivergent kid got us nowhere. The Western half of my parenting philosophy was too loosey-goosey for Cherish. She would exploit extra playtime and extra snacks, and play on her iPad for hours, if I let her. I would go to bed and wake up early thinking about the day ahead at home, at school, or dance rehearsal. I worried about friendships and if her medication was at the right dose. I struggled to find a neat instruction manual for raising her and learned the hard way that no matter how many articles or parenting books I read, Cherish lived in the margins. Unlike her brother who operated more predictably, she existed at many intersections: identified as female, athletic, girly, feisty, fast learner, neurodivergent, creative, sweet, and sensitive. She defied my parenting logic, and I didn't always know where to begin.

Adoption added another layer of confusion to work through. Information about first parents or other relatives is hard to come by, and people who adopt are truly taking a leap of faith that they can handle whatever comes their way. What many of us did learn through hours of parenting classes before obtaining a certification to become foster and/or adoptive parents is that children enter foster care due to abuse and neglect, and almost all are considered special needs. This designation is due to their age, ethnic heritage, need to be placed with siblings, and physical, mental/cognitive, and emotional problems that may be genetic, the result of abuse and neglect, or the result of multiple moves in foster care.[7] The special needs label does not automatically presume a child will need special education, but the classification is necessary to support children in finding temporary or permanent homes. Foster children, even those placed at birth, experience trauma that can and does present at different stages of their lives.

Cherish is the youngest of ten and shares a mother with August. Other than both being tall and lanky, they are total opposites in temperament. I have no information about her deceased father, but know that their birth mother was athletic, a good student, and suffered from mild depression and addiction. One of the brothers has ADHD, a learning disability, and all other labels Black boys are saddled with. While I was not dismissive of this intel, nor did I ignore the social worker's warning that ten-month-old Cherish would have *all of the labels*, I did not see evidence of this in her and went about my parenting duties. I saw no red flags, only a ball of energy who was not stereotypically docile or girly, though she insisted on wearing a dress every day of preschool.

If I sound like I missed the writing on the wall, I saw it in capital letters a few years later.

All the Labels

Starting with the most overused label ever, ADHD/ADD is the typical go-to for educators, family, and friends who are not clinicians. They see an overactive child who is silly, rambunctious, unable to sit still or engage in the lesson and automatically assume the child has a behavior problem. This label follows a child his whole life and impacts his social and educational trajectory. Hardly a new disorder, ADHD was written about as far back as 1775. It was, however, Sir George Frederick Still's observation in 1902 of children who were uncooperative, emotional, easily agitated, and morally abnormal that yielded the damning declaration that hangs over youth today: "These children had problems with concentration and sustained attention, as well, and could not learn from the consequences of their actions."[8] Later in this book, I'll dive into the role gender plays in how girls are understudied and boys are overstudied in relation to ADHD, the range of ADHD types, and what parents can do to support their children.

While ADHD is personal to me, dyslexia is the most common neurocognitive disorder.[9] According to those brainiacs at the Yale Center for Dyslexia and Creativity, 20 percent of the population has dyslexia.[10] A language-based disorder, dyslexia occurs in the region of the brain where language is processed and is responsible for 80 percent of learning disabilities in children and adults.[11] In short, the brain has trouble matching sounds with letters or words, thus creating problems with reading ability, writing, and numbers. Imagine trying to read and the letters do their own word scramble, every time. It is exhausting and embarrassing for youth who see kids around them reading or adding or counting with ease. Some kids with undiagnosed dyslexia act out. They might be the class clown or bully. They *know* they are behind their peers, assume classmates and teachers think they're dumb, and feel shame. The shame cycle can mimic hyperactivity, behavior issues, task avoidance, and so on, which leads to misdiagnosis and delays in support.

Unfortunately, dyslexia may not be discovered until a child reaches kindergarten or even later, when it is expected that she can follow nursery rhymes or recognize rhyming patterns[12] like "bat," "sat," "cat," while those on the autism spectrum disorder (ASD) may have symptoms in infancy. Food texture sensitivities, poor eye contact, or lack of muscle control are early indicators that a child may fall outside stated norms of physical, psychological, or social development. ASD has many faces, and early intervention will go a long way in improving outcomes for children and their families.

Like other neurological differences, ASD is hereditary. The environment also plays a role in who presents on the autism spectrum, but genes are the most dominant cause.[13] As there are many forms of ASD, I would like to praise the autism community for being on their shit. Well-financed advocates and research continue to improve outcomes for kids on the spectrum, and many go on to lead productive lives.

The last neurological difference I will tackle in this book is nonverbal learning disorder (NVLD). Although children with NVLD share symptoms with the autism spectrum and dyslexia, they are not the same.[14] The "nonverbal" part of the name is confusing, so I will clarify that in this instance. Kids with NVLD can speak. They may not be social butterflies, but their verbal ability is fine. For example, comedian Chris Rock, whose career is based on speaking, has NVLD, but one would never know it. NVLD tends to rear its head late in a child's life with pattern recognition in reading and math, messy handwriting, and visual-spatial and coordination challenges. While the intellectual ability of these students can be impacted by this learning difference, they often have great memories, amazing attention to detail, and other extraordinary coping skills. Unlike kids on the autism spectrum or those with dyslexia, a diagnosis may not occur until middle or high school, because this is when the limits of their ability to memorize or parrot instruction gives out.

Most likely, NVLD flies under the radar because the symptoms look, sound, and feel like ADHD, dyslexia, or autism, or simply like a child who is emotionally immature or academically delayed. Given the light shined on this disorder thanks to the openness of Minnesota Governor Tim Walz, whose son, Gus, has NVLD, ADHD, and anxiety, I will share what I have learned and provide suggestions on asking care providers about this specific disorder to help parents avoid a misdiagnosis long before a child reaches their teenage years.

Speaking of getting older, neurodivergent children grow up to be neurodivergent adults. If, somewhere along the way, an intervention is made, tools are learned, and they figure out how to maximize their strengths, that individual will experience success and happiness. This is the goal of parents, and I am confident that everyone will get to the other side, but getting there is a process: a series of starts and stops; dreams realized, then dashed, then realized again. Keep the faith.

Baptism by Fire

My family's windy road to learning that Cherish had ADHD and sensory processing disorder (SPD) began in 2017. Until this point, our little trio was moving and grooving. I thought I hit the educational jackpot because both of my kids attended the same school. One drop-off, one set of school rules, and vacations that aligned, I was winning. Cherish would benefit from the Reggio Emilia–inspired philosophy practiced at the school, which was light-years from the traditional curriculum at her previous school, where kids were expected to sit still and not talk out of turn. The student-centered and experiential learning with teachers who documented each child's development meant less emphasis on testing or grades, which made the learning environment relaxed and individual. Teacher Sean, handsome with a twinkle in his eyes, had taught at the school for almost two decades and was highly recommended. I was so excited to send Cherish to a preschool with a 12:1 ratio plus a teacher's assistant. Her new classroom had an attached atelier, a sandpit, play structure, tricycles, bikes, paint, dramatic play, and so many other cool things. The kids walked around barefoot and had freedom to move. I was grateful for Teacher Sean's wisdom and expertise, plus he was aware that Cherish was adopted and we had a great rapport.

But over the course of the school year, the emails describing Cherish's behavior as disruptive arrived with more frequency. Her reactions did not match the size of the problem. The emails prompted lots of meetings with him and the director of the preschool. My adjunct professor job allowed me to be more present at the school, joining in for sing-a-longs, coffee with other parents, and, sometimes, the head of school. I interpreted Teacher Sean's observations as reflective of Cherish's excitement about her new environment. I agreed that she was immature and assumed her learning curve would last longer than the other children who needed less redirection. Most of her classmates were able to complete their projects and explain why they chose purple or how gravity pulled the marble through the tube. Cherish was having fun and seemed less interested in articulating how pulleys worked, though she shined when it came to creating menus or filling the role of the shopkeeper during dramatic play. I thought she needed the entire school year to feel secure and understand that the wilds, clay, marbles, books, teachers who adored her, and makerspace were hers to enjoy. Cherish just needed more time.

By midyear, the tone of the emails changed. The subject expanded to include concerns about her social skills. In other words, Cherish had trouble during social confrontations and expressing herself when she became upset. I would talk to Cherish, roleplay even, then send her off the next day, fingers crossed that this day would be better than the previous. I looked within to see if anything was different at home. We had moved because the home we lived in was being sold. In our beautiful duplex in Leimert Park, Cherish got her own room and so did I. Her bedroom was a *Trolls* extravaganza: Poppy and Branch dominated her comforter with twin sheets to match. She had miniature groceries, place settings, and her artwork taped to the wall. Cherish was a fashionista at an early age and owned multiple pairs of Disney princess heels. She was also incredibly active.

While August played baseball, with basketball and lacrosse sprinkled in, Cherish's ability to keep rhythm led us to ballet and tap for toddlers. The duration of the classes was about an hour, and she loved wearing tutus. I was out of my depth with all of the frills and lace but enjoyed buying mustard leotards, fairy-pink tights, black patent-leather tap shoes, and buff toe shoes for my daughter. She was so adorable; I could just eat her. Cherish learned to plié, leap, and stand in first and second positions with ease. After class, she'd arrange her Black ballerina doll into the same positions. I showed her pictures of Prima Ballerina Misty Copeland, the first Black female principal dancer for the American Ballet Theatre, proud that my daughter might follow in her footsteps. The truth was, for all of Cherish's grace and dance acumen, the lessons weren't going well. She kept running off the shiny wood floor to sit with me or play with her brother in the waiting area. Sometimes, she'd sit down or wander in the opposite direction of the other tiny dancers. Her ballet instructors were tolerant, at first. They would redirect Cherish or work with her independently. They let her skip ballet and work solely on tap. Cherish used that time to make as much noise as possible, giggling in delight. August and I even tried waiting in the car, thinking we were distracting her. Nothing worked.

Eventually, I canceled her lessons. I could not pay for classes she was not participating in, plus she was distracting the other children. The teacher suggested two years old was too young and to try again when she was four. We tried again at five, and then eight and nine years old, and had the same result.

Figuring ballet was too slow and tap was akin to playing the drums with reckless abandon, I redeemed a coupon for Euro soccer to see if chasing a ball was more her jam. As soccer balls rolled in her direction, she would sidestep them like she was playing dodgeball. The coach gently explained how she had to return the ball with a kick or run alongside the ball and kick it away from her. Cherish would nod in understanding and then continue to not only sidestep the ball but move completely off the field.

"I'm hot," she complained.
"Five more minutes, sweet girl."
"I'm tired."
"You can do it. Kick the ball. That's all you have to do."
Arms folded across her bony chest—"I'm hungry."
And just like that, soccer was a bust.

For the moment, I let sports go. Cherish had lots of options during and after school, so I let her take gymnastics and a cooking class. Those were a better fit. As preschool drew to a close, the emails about how Cherish would shut down instead of trying to compromise with friends continued. I worked with her at home and accepted that my spirited girl might experience regular consequences for calling the boys "losers" for not climbing to the top of the apparatus faster and might have to sit next to Teacher Sean when she broke classroom agreements. I knew her to be stubborn, even defiant, but drew the line at his characterization of her as angry.

"Sean, Cherish is the only Black girl in this class, and you may not describe her as angry."

I was shocked that a seasoned teacher would call a Black girl angry. His remark confirmed that the work I was doing around supporting Black children in independent schools with fellow parents, teachers, and administrators was needed. Small words like *angry* lead to huge disparities in how Black children were treated in school. Monique W. Morris wrote *Pushout: The Criminalization of Black Girls in Schools*[15] to illuminate the high incidences of disruptions in Black girls' education. A core and human right, education created access to a higher standard of living, including better health outcomes and happiness. Misunderstandings related to tone, attitude, or unladylike behavior[16] has too often resulted in the arrest and abuse of Black girls by law enforcement and school officials. There has been a clear and present double standard where white girls are given the benefit of the doubt, and their sass is spunky or courageous. I needed Teacher Sean to understand that his default description of Cherish reinforced a stereotype specific to Black girls and women.

Embarrassed, Sean apologized. "I am so sorry. That was not the right word. Cherish is a kind and loving child. She was not ready to put the blocks away and became angry."

"That makes sense," I responded. Once she was engaged in an activity, it was hard to get her to switch to something else, let alone time to clean up. "As you know, she's had issues with transitions all year. Cherish has the same issue at home."

Teacher Sean and I continued communicating, and preschool came to an end. Cherish had mastered the appropriate pencil grip, phonics, uppercase-letter recognition, and counting and was academically ready for kindergarten. Again, Teacher Sean expressed concerns about her social and emotional development, which I noted but chalked up to immaturity. In fact, I often described Cherish as a pit bull in a skirt and never once considered that her birth trauma— premature birth, low birth weight, and jaundice—or being in foster care were indicators that something was amiss. I forgot that by virtue of being adopted, Cherish would be part of the 30 to 60 percent[17] of kids from foster care who have special needs; this includes physical disabilities. I mistakenly believed that our nurturing, stable, and loving environment would override whatever birth trauma or first family trauma she experienced in utero or received genetically. I was thinking with my heart and unaware that our whole lives were about to change.

The following school year, Mr. Willie Jamal Jackson—it doesn't get any Blacker than that—greeted Cherish on the first day of kindergarten. I was thrilled that my daughter, who did not have a father in the home, would have a Black father figure she would spend time with every day. Mr. Jackson was a gentle but firm giant. His co-teacher, Mrs. Monroe, was from Orange County, an affluent area south of Los Angeles County. Total opposites, they were both experienced public school teachers, though new to teaching at an independent school. The rules of engagement were very different in private school.

The year Cherish joined kindergarten, the school added a third class, which created an 18:2 student-teacher ratio, plus an aide who floated between classrooms. Her teachers were part of a sextet who comprised a blend of veteran and new teachers and those coming from working in public education. Both of Cherish's teachers were former LAUSD (Los Angeles Unified School District) teachers, with a range of expertise working with children of different socioeconomic backgrounds, academic abilities, different learning styles, races, ethnicities, and religions. We hit the teacher jackpot, right?

August primed Cherish for kindergarten. He shared his wonderful experiences having explorations (choice activities) in the afternoons, playing in the creek outside the classroom, making a birdhouse, and observing Shelly, the class turtle. Cherish was so excited. On her first day of school in September, she wore rose gold tennis shoes, flamingo-pink pants, a striped black-and-white shirt, and matching pink ribbons in her hair.

Within weeks, emails and sidebar comments began in earnest:

Cherish has trouble remaining on her square.
She gets frustrated easily.
Cherish randomly walks around the room.
She wants all of our attention.
We gave her a wiggle seat.
Cherish needs a lot of re-direction, like fifty to sixty times per day.
She won't remain in her reading group.
Cherish takes items that do not belong to her.
She was unkind to a friend.
Cherish sat on the bench during snack time.
Can we meet?

In October, I googled the National Institute for Mental Health for a definition of attention-deficit/hyperactivity disorder. I had a general sense of what it was but wanted to see if Cherish's behavior tracked with known markers for inattention, hyperactivity, and impulsivity. Bingo. I shared my Internet sleuthing with Mr. Jackson and Mrs. Monroe. They couldn't say for sure if she had ADHD, as they were educators not psychologists or psychotherapists. They wanted to give Cherish more one-on-one time, more wiggle breaks, and incentivize her with additional playtime, if she could stay on task a little longer each day. They felt that she was too young to be assessed for any neurological difference. I disagreed. We had tried everything and something was wrong. Cherish did not have the stamina or ability to regulate herself. She needed help.

I called her pediatrician who suggested that I contact Vista Del Mar Child and Family Services. It took about three months to get an appointment, and payment would be on a sliding scale. Dr. Goldstein, middle-aged mother of one son, was working as a fellow in the Reiss-Davis Child Study Center at Vista Del Mar. Once per week for six weeks, she used a battery of tests to assess Cherish and me. I had to complete a thick stack of papers self-evaluating our home, parent–child relationship, sibling relationship between Cherish and August, and note which milestones she had achieved by age six. The testing window was long, and I felt sorry for Cherish, who sometimes sat underneath the table and refused to answer Dr. Goldstein's questions.

It was a grueling but necessary process, intended to help me help my daughter. While I waited for results, it was time to figure out which summer camps would be right for Cherish. She was far too active to stay home, and I didn't have time to play camp counselor. Another trip around the World Wide Web produced the Child Success Center in Santa Monica, founded by Melissa Idelson, OTR/L. They offered a special needs summer camp for rising kinder and first graders. In order to attend, each child had to be evaluated. The director, an Aussie with two adult children, asked if Cherish had been assigned occupational therapy (OT). I admitted that I thought OT was for kids with food and touch sensitivities and had not considered OT as an option. At that point, I did not know that ADHD was a spectrum disorder and had compartmentalized ASD, ADD, and ADHD. I thought those neurologic differences were separate entities. Prior to Melissa's suggestion that Cherish receive an OT assessment, no other professional—not the pediatrician or the psychologist who diagnosed her—even hinted that she would need a secondary evaluation. This would have been a significant miss, considering interventions for neurodivergent youth required a combination of treatments to be effective.

Melissa directed me to her website, where I swore I saw a life-size photo of Cherish in flashing neon lights on the sensory processing disorders (SPD) page, adapted from *Learn to Move, Move to Learn!* by Jenny Clark Brack.[18] The disorders were broken into eight categories: tactile, proprioceptive, auditory, vestibular, arousal and attending, vision, social consciousness, and olfactory/gustatory.[19] I learned that children with SPD were easily overstimulated and emotional and had trouble in school and with friendships. Cherish had no trouble forming attachments or making friends. Her dance card was typically full with invitations to birthday parties and playdates. Her friends found her to be fun and silly though there were times when she would shut down or become overly frustrated by minor slights.

I paid the Child Success Center to assess Cherish for SPD. Within two weeks, I received both results: Cherish had ADHD and SPD. By this time, neither diagnosis was a surprise. A few of Cherish and August's multiple siblings were neurodivergent, so the odds of Cherish being in the same boat was high. I accepted that there was nothing I could have done differently from ten months to six years old to change the birth trauma to have caused a significant impact on her cognitive and emotional development. And there was no time to wallow. Cherish had one parent and that was me. I would do what I always did: keep it pushing and support my baby.

No matter the origin of Cherish's neurodivergence, her diagnosis opened the floodgates for out-of-pocket expenses for assessments; disclosure of intimate details about our homelife repeated over and over on forms, to teachers, school counselors, and psychologists; being honest about Cherish's feelings about herself and her behavior; weekly appointments for OT and therapy; haggling with the insurance company over the limitations of coverage for neurodivergent children; and juggling the emotional and physical needs of August. I was suddenly on a roller coaster that went from zero to sixty miles per hour, without warning.

At least now I had an answer for why Cherish was so spirited. The knowledge begot new questions like, How long will this last? I naively thought OT plus therapy for a few months would give her all the tools she'd ever need and, by first or second grade, Cherish would be like the other kids. I missed the memo that raising a neurodivergent child was a marathon, with peaks and valleys. While I was quick to get her assessed, I was slow to realize that my new village would grow to include an occupational therapist, psychiatrist, and psychologist—plus the school psychologist and nurse. My beautiful, friendly, capable, spirited, neurodivergent daughter changed my whole world in one fell swoop. There was no going back. I could not unlearn that her brain received and processed information differently. I could not pretend that socially and emotionally there would be challenges at each developmental milestone. I could not unsee her tears and confusion about why she was singled out in class. And I could not unfeel her heartbreak when kids and teachers did not understand her. I was under a new mandate and willing to do whatever it took to help my sweet girl blossom into her fullest self.

Reflection

Neurodivergence is usually not top of mind for prospective parents. We are swept up in getting pregnant or approved to foster/adopt and then plan for their life once they arrive. Barring any physical disability or obvious birth trauma, parents and caregivers are often surprised to learn their child has ASD, ADHD, dyslexia, NVLD, or other invisible differences and are stumped by the prospect of having a child who may always need them. This may trigger sadness and confusion in parents and that is understandable. Time, however, is not on your side, because early intervention is key. Now that the curtain has been pulled back, learning everything you can about your child's neurodivergent brain takes center stage. Just know that neurodivergence will challenge everything you thought you knew about yourself, your partner, who you are as parent, your family values, and beliefs.

Buckle up for the ride of your life.

Not that you asked, but here are my two cents:

Trust your instincts.

> If you think something is *wrong* or *different* about your child, contact the pediatrician.

Request a referral.

> Make an appointment with a psychologist or therapist who can administer assessments or occupational therapy.

Be honest.

> Minimizing symptoms leads to delays in treatment.

Neurodivergence is genetic and/or a result of birth trauma.

> Parents, you did nothing wrong.

2

Recognizing Neurodivergence

Between learning that Cherish needed to be redirected fifty to sixty times per day to receiving her diagnosis six months later, I sprang into action. Cherish went to occupational therapy (OT) once per week to work on social skills and build her stamina for nonpreferred tasks—writing, sitting still for longer than five minutes, and interacting with children her age with a similar diagnosis. The children mirrored her energy and would refuse to play with her if she wouldn't share toys or agree to the rules of a game. Their brutal honesty helped her see that she had to be flexible or wait her turn, even when it was hard to do so.

Cherish also saw Dr. Lori Baudino, PsyD, BC-DMT, an author and expert child psychologist who uses dance/movement therapy as an "integrative approach." She believes that "movement is a universal way to relate that helps children connect and learn."[1] I liked Lori, whose homey clinic was in her converted garage. An author and mother, she learned to read through playing basketball and was confident that through behavior modification she could help Cherish have success at home and school. Dr. Baudino observed Cherish at school and made a house call to see Cherish's room and how we related as a family. A persistent issue I had was the jumbled mess that took up residence in Cherish's bedroom. While she could make her bed, every toy, book, ball, Lego, rock, and any other thing she found interesting was everywhere. Her messiness offended my sensibility of order and, try as I might, I couldn't get Cherish to understand that each item had a home. I was constantly organizing her room and fussing at her as I went to put her things away or I'd throw the stuff in the trash. I didn't know how to handle the attendant disorganization that came with ADHD. I leaned toward being punitive by withholding certain toys, which had the opposite effect. Instead of order, I got tantrums and a bigger mess.

Dr. Baudino helped me realize that Cherish's spatial awareness prevented her from seeing that the tangled mass of Barbie dolls with missing limbs stacked upon each other, markers, and Play-Doh should not all live in the dollhouse. It was not on purpose. Cherish was not trying to get on my nerves. Dr. Baudino made a game of cleaning up by enlisting Cherish's dolls to put things away. Genius! My daughter enjoyed this approach and unstacked the dolls, giving each their own space. She even organized them for tea and bedtime. From that moment on, I used the same technique with the understanding that I had to remain in her space to assist with cleaning rather than dictate: *clean your room, hang up your jacket.* It felt like micromanaging, something my Type A personality hated. No doubt it would have been faster for me to clean her room or the bathroom after she bathed, but being organized is a life skill that Cherish would need in school, on a job, in her own home, and out in the world.

One of the skills I learned from Dr. Baudino was how to be on Cherish's team. In the above scenario, Cherish was on one team and her dollhouse was on the other. "When you complained about the dollhouse being messy, you placed yourself on the opposite team. You and Cherish became adversaries," Dr. Baudino told me. "When you became the doll, you joined Joy's team. You became her ally and removed the blame and overwhelm at the mess." I get chills at the simplicity of a strategy she employed in my home five years ago. "Cherish could climb through the struggle because the team was stronger than just one person." There was no way I could have gotten to that on my own.

Being forced to slow down and spend more time with Cherish reaffirming her efforts would be one of many changes in my parenting style. I really had no choice but to accept that Cherish was not a self-starter nor able to remain on task without supervision and short breaks. She would eventually grow into this skill, but at seven years old, it was on me to keep the guardrails in place.

The therapeutic interventions Cherish was receiving were amazing; however, there was one small problem: the weekly costs of therapy were unsustainable. I was paying a couple hundred dollars per week for OT and Dr. Baudino. Neither accepted insurance and there was no way I could pay either for months on end. In hindsight, the timeline for her diagnosis would have been shorter if I had chosen a private agency where I didn't have to wait for a psychologist to be assigned to her case, but I went with our pediatrician's recommendation. In the end, Cherish's diagnosis came at the end of kindergarten with a note to have her reassessed every three to four years. I took this information to her school and continued private OT and sessions with Dr. Baudino until I found services that were covered by our insurance.

Invisible Differences

Unless electrodes are connected to a person's brain, it is impossible to see what is happening inside one's mind. This holds true for children, teens, and adults who are neurodivergent, because their difference is often *invisible*. Think about the hours you've spent explaining why your child covers his ears when the music is too loud or gets cranky if their space is invaded or needs to be reintroduced to friends over and over. People will respond to behavior that is occurring *outside* the body, not understanding that a neurodivergent brain might be responding to an overstimulating school assembly or bright lights in the grocery store. Neurodivergence also operates on a spectrum and the symptoms your child is exhibiting serve as crucial information to help you and your partner make an informed decision about going forward with an assessment and other interventions. But first things first, let's take a look at typical characteristics of ADHD, ASD, dyslexia, and NVLD.

What Does ADHD Look Like?

As I mentioned in chapter 1, ADHD is a spectrum disorder with three varieties: inattention, hyperactive, and impulsivity,[2] which will manifest differently depending on the person and their stage of development. A child's experience with ADHD is varied. She may look inattentive or hyperactive, fall behind in core educational skills like reading or writing, have poor social relationships and suffer in quiet or loud, ugly desperation. Impulsivity, the lack of ability to control one's actions, may also be present or show up later in the form of lying and stealing. Teens with ADHD are less hyper but still fidgety. Untreated, they may have poor academic performance, cut themselves, self-medicate by vaping, smoking marijuana, or stealing pills from parents, and engage in risky behavior such as stealing from stores or acting out sexually. As adults, ADHD interferes with the ability to maintain employment, because the ability to stay on and complete a task was never developed. They may be volatile, unpredictable, and have low tolerance for stressful situations.

For kids who experience inattentive-type attention deficit disorder (ADD),[3] their symptoms are much quieter. They are peaceful, reserved, not overly active. In fact, you might forget they are in the room. In school, they seem invested in the activity but likely couldn't repeat the directions because their mind was elsewhere. Their grades may start out solid and then slide without warning. These kids do not disrupt the classroom, are benignly ignored by everyone, and throw up no red flags. Parents, caregivers, and educators assume a tutor is needed or the child is shy and miss the anxiety, depression, and inattentiveness lurking just beneath the surface. They dismiss neurodivergence as a culprit, in favor of describing the cooperative child's habitual careless mistakes, misunderstanding of directions, disorganization, failing grades, inability to keep track of her stuff, and forgetfulness as spacey or immature. In fact, ADD may not be caught until tenth grade or later, when the coping mechanisms—staying up really late working on homework assignments that should have taken a fraction of the time; hiding clutter to appear organized; obsessive behavior like checking three times to make sure the door is locked—give out. The assumption is that she will grow out of or into skills that will turn her into a productive member of society. Wrong. She will grow up confused, anxious, and possibly engaged in unexpected risky behaviors that lead to disappointment, failure to launch, and unnecessary struggles throughout adulthood.

On the other hand, the impulsive bunch like Cherish who experience ADHD are unable to sit still, even in the wobble stool or chair; have epic tantrums beyond the age of five; elope during nonpreferred activities; and are laser focused on preferred activities, which makes them gold-medal-winning athletes or inventors. They are easily distracted and have trouble maintaining eye contact because their purview is 180 degrees, rather than the person or object right in front of them. They are easily aroused and excitable; have trouble transitioning between tasks or remaining on task, which leads to poor academic performance despite their brilliance with numbers; have mood swings; and have trouble with social relationships. Rounding out the diagnosis are anxiety, insomnia, low self-esteem, depression, and poor self-regulation.

Another aspect of impulsivity manifests as lying and stealing. The lack of executive function means they have trouble planning and executing a plan. Even when they know it is their turn to feed the dogs, they may lie and say they fed them, as you both stand before an empty bowl. Chances are, they forgot because they became distracted by a preferred activity or remembered they were hungry. They don't know how to backtrack to complete the first directive, and rather than admit the obvious—the dogs did not get fed—they lie. This dovetails with children who have short-term memory issues, who really believe that what they're saying is true. They will double down on the lie because they forgot but blame you for blaming them for lying. Before you know it, your child is angry and yelling (you might be too) because it feels like manipulation and selective memory being passed off as truth.

As for stealing, shiny pretty objects or random items may come home in cargo pants pockets, backpacks, jackets, or little hands. Want or need is not the objective, so I'm not talking about children who are unhoused or food insecure. I'm speaking of kids who want for nothing but take six bottles of glue home from school or toys from a friend's house and then claim they "found" it. As parents, this behavior is scary because we begin to worry our child is destined for a life of crime. We are embarrassed and frustrated because now we have to explain that our child has impulsive type ADHD and swiped their child's item before they could pause long enough to remember that the item was not theirs. Even when adults understand, kids can be cruel. They will call out the offender in front of everyone, creating a cascade of big emotions for your child who wasn't trying to steal, they just couldn't help it.

Therapists suggest that parents and educators refrain from getting angry or calling the child a *liar* or *thief*. Shaming does not help, nor does it mitigate the behavior. Our child feels worse, adding another layer to their anxiety and depression. Parents, caregivers, and educators should casually note: *That is not the truth. This item does not belong to you. You have to return it.* Getting into, *Why did you lie?* or, *Why did you steal?* is another form of shaming. Through learning about empathy, our impulsive kids will begin to think about how sad a friend feels when their money or body spray is missing. Parents can implement a reward system to purchase those desired items so they won't feel a need to take someone else's property. Front-loading them about leaving Jake's things at Jake's house or dressing them in clothing without pockets is another option. Finally, do not assume they will grow out of this behavior. While all children leave some things in childhood, unwanted behaviors like stealing can morph into huge problems when they become teenagers and young adults.

Cherish, whose picture emerges as I write about the symptoms, yielded a lot of negative attention from teachers, classmates, friends, her brother, and me. It was hard to keep up with what was happening in her brain, making for stressful interactions almost everywhere she went. I was hypervigilant and constantly hosting sidebar conversations with her, insisting that she apologize when she was wrong and trying to educate adults around her that her behavior wasn't her fault. Cherish didn't wake up hoping for a challenging day. It was the low levels of dopamine in her brain, coupled with an overstimulated amygdala, that prevented her from being able to self-regulate, read a room, or stop hoarding markers. I would learn many of these lessons along the way, so please do not assume that I had all of the answers at the beginning of our neurodivergent journey.

Children, adolescents, and adults will typically have more than one neurodivergent attribute, so ADHD or ADD is not likely to appear by itself. It may accompany ASD, dyslexia, NVLD, a learning disability, anxiety, and depression, even if it isn't the dominant neurologic difference.

Autism Spectrum Disorder

Whereas Cherish's behavior in kindergarten forced me to take action, parents of kids on the autism spectrum often respond before things get out of control, because ASD symptoms can present within the first eight to twelve months of life. Some kids hit all developmental milestones through age two and ASD isn't discovered until the toddler stage and even later. With regard to ASD, race matters. Black children often aren't diagnosed until three years after their parents have raised concerns.[4] Attendant implicit bias, racism, and parental mistrust of the medical system contribute to this significant delay. According to the Child Mind Institute, "[Black] families feel their child's doctor is dismissive of their concerns, blaming disruptive behaviors on poor parenting or the harmful stereotype of Black children having a propensity for misbehaving. Other parents have described being accused outright of exaggerating to game the system and receive free government-issued services."[5] Further, research has tended to focus on middle-class white children, effectively marginalizing Black children and those from lower socioeconomic backgrounds, whose symptoms must match those of white children for consideration of ASD. Asian Pacific Islander Desi American (APIDA) children suffer from the model minority stereotype, enforcing the idea that APIDA people are at the top of the racial hierarchy, brilliant at math, and musical prodigies. This myth coupled with delays in treatment due to traditional cultural values, language barriers, fear of outsiders serving their community, stigmas, and misinformation about disabilities make APIDA vulnerable to untreated ASD.

The number of children diagnosed on the autism spectrum grows every year. According to the Centers for Disease Control (CDC), one in thirty-six children have ASD and boys are four times more likely to be diagnosed than girls. In the last chapter, I gave a short list of tells in infants and toddlers that may signal ASD and think it's worth mentioning that some kids are able to mask symptoms well into their teens. Josefina, a mom friend from Chicago, believed her thirteen-year-old son, who has ADHD, was on the autism spectrum. Josefina and her husband were aware of his ADHD, having been told when he was in kindergarten that he was not learning because his mind was constantly racing. Brand-spanking-new adoptive parents at the time, they weren't sure what that meant. They were aware of the fetal alcohol syndrome disorder (FASD), an invisible physical brain-based condition[6] both he and his sister had, but thought that was it. "We got both kids on the same day, and poof, we were parents," Josefina said.

ASD was not part of their vocabulary until Blake became a teenager. In fact, autism never came up during annual physicals, individualized education programs (IEPs), or weekly sessions with his therapist, but Mom always thought something was a little off. She would describe him as socially awkward, unaware of invading other people's personal space. Blake also perseverated about slights and had a stubborn streak a mile long. If ever he was rushed to get dressed so they could leave for school or hurried by a teacher to complete an assignment, Blake did the total opposite. He'd work at a snail's pace or not do anything at all. He had low tolerance for multistep directions and would be annoyed that he was being rushed or yelled at. On the other hand, Blake was a gifted artist and mannerable. He maintained eye contact and was very charming. Josephina said, "I never knew there was a name for his symptoms. I thought Blake was being Blake," although she did flag her concerns with his pediatrician and therapist. Both clinicians seemed unfazed by his behavior, preferring to stick with the narrative that his improper social behavior was a result of fetal alcohol syndrome disorder, exhibited by impulsivity, acting younger than his chronological age, overwhelmed by sensory input, and so on.

At first glance, there were no outward displays of ASD. A victim of bullying and being left out of playdates and social gatherings by classmates, he learned to mask his authentic self so they would stop calling him weird. After numerous meetings with teachers and school counselors, Josefina decided to have him and his sister reassessed for autism. She would learn about the overlap between ADHD, FASD, and ASD (see Figure 2.1).[7] Her instinct that something was up with Blake was spot on, but clinicians were still dismissive of her concerns. Josefina had to take matters into her own hands, "I am always thinking about his future. What's his life gonna be like? I'm scared for him because Blake will always need services." Now, with college looming, Josefina and her husband know that Blake will not attend a university. He will take modified classes to graduate and go to trade school. They hope that with their support, Blake will learn a skill that will enable him to have his own money and possibly live independently.

Demand Avoidance

Driven by anxiety rather than rebellion, demand avoidance or pathological demand avoidance (PDA) is present in ASD and ADHD. Seeking to not switch up routines, kids will go to great lengths not to do what is asked. Parents and teachers on the receiving end of the avoidance often read their actions as defiance or disrespect. Actually, it's a hypersensitive response to expectations, so they avoid the directive. Although the United States does not recognize demand avoidance, ask a parent of a child on the autism spectrum if they've witnessed their child shut down, have a tantrum, or refuse a command to brush their teeth and wait for a lengthy response.

Fetal Alcohol Spectrum Disorder

Diana Malbin, the leading authority on fetal alcohol spectrum disorder (FASD), developed the Neurobehavioral Model[8] to address issues related to FASD. Figure 2.1 demonstrates overlap with other forms of neurodivergence.

RECOGNIZING NEURODIVERGENCE

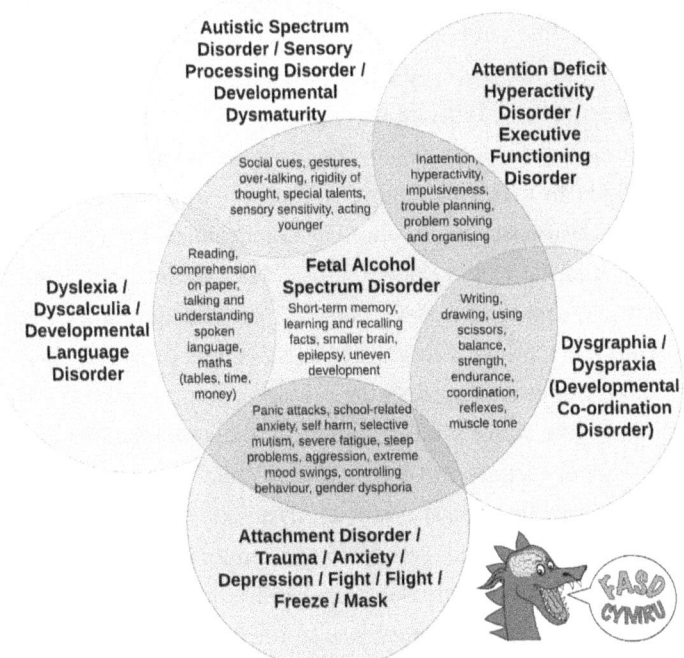

FIGURE 2.1 *Fetal Alcohol Syndrome Disorder. FAS relies on the presence of facial features, but FASD is a broader term (only 10 percent of those with FASD have the facial features and so have FAS, but all with FASD have the effects on the development of the brain). FASD affects each individual in a unique way. Its effects can overlap with a wide range of other forms of neurodivergence, including ASD, ADHD, SPD, dyslexia, dyscalculia, dysgraphia, dyspraxia, anxiety, and depression. Source: Catherine Griffiths.*

Dyslexia

Like other neurologic differences, dyslexia is an inherited trait. One in five people (not just kids) have this condition, which has nothing to do with eyesight. Dyslexia is a language-based impairment that impacts the three Rs—reading, writing, and arithmetic—which is why it tends to show up during the lower elementary years. It is also neurobiological, meaning the brain processes written and spoken information differently. For example, your child sees the word "left," sees the letter sequence l-e-f-t and reads "felt."[9] Many kids mix up their letters, see words backward, invert words (remember pig Latin?), or make up words, so that's not the problem. What is problematic is the inability to match the sound (phoneme) with the letter, making phonemic awareness a challenge. In this instance, if "left" was read to your child, he would know that the word is "left" not "felt." This strategy may sharpen a dyslexic person's memorization skills, but that's an awful lot of work for a child who has a language processing disorder.

Speaking of processing disorders, dyslexia isn't the only one. There's dysgraphia (the act of writing is difficult, poor motor skills, inability to use organize letters and words); dyscalculia (poor number sense, trouble with mathematical symbols); dyspraxia (lack of control over motor skills, trouble with self-dressing); auditory processing disorder (unable to keep pace with words spoken leading to memory issues); and scotopic sensitivity syndrome, also referred to as Irlen Syndrome or visual processing disorder (bright light sensitivity or the sensation of watching a 3D movie without wearing the 3D glasses).[10] These disorders may accompany dyslexia, which is why a specific screening for dyslexia is important to distinguish which processing disorder your child has.

If your child refuses to read aloud at home or in school, feels embarrassed about his lack of ability to read or write, is disinterested in books, and/or is called "dumb," "slow," or "stupid" by other kids (and adults, let's be real), then he may have dyslexia. If you know your mom or a cousin has dyslexia and your son is struggling or avoiding the task altogether, consider dyslexia as the reason he shuts down or acts out during reading. Disruptive behavior will hide signs of language processing disorders. Adults will get stuck on labeling him the class clown, causing numerous emails, meetings with teachers, and punitive action to take place. He may bully other kids, avoid reading, or memorize passages without understanding the meaning in an effort to hide his disability. He may conveniently need to use the bathroom for the duration of the reading circle. It will take an observant adult to get to the root of the behavior to understand that the child is in distress and needs an intervention.

Adoptive parents, this information applies to you too. Pay attention to the signs, because the social worker may not know to clue you in about dyslexia as part of your child's DNA. For educators who may spot the breadcrumbs of dyslexia before parents, don't forget that Black kids are misdiagnosed for dyslexia. In fact, professor and dyslexia expert Dr. Sally Shaywitz states in a February 2024 Yale School of Medicine article, "New Study Highlights Potential Missed Diagnoses of Dyslexia in African American Students" that the

> National Assessment of Educational Progress (NAEP) releases a report on reading and math scores from thousands of students across the United States. NAEP data have consistently shown that 20 percent of White and 50 percent of African American students are shown to read at a level considered "below basic," which good evidence indicates represent children with dyslexia. Results of the current study and the many decades of NAEP reading data indicate that high numbers of African American students have dyslexia but are currently undiagnosed and do not receive evidence-based interventions for their reading difficulties.[11]

Nonverbal Learning Disability

I'll admit that I had not heard of nonverbal learning disability[12] until the day after the Democratic National Convention in August 2024, when a conservative commentor made a disgusting remark about a child. She vilified teenager Gus Walz's exuberant pride for his dad, Minnesota Governor Tim Walz, and then deleted her post. Her ugliness made me take a closer look at NVLD. The first person who popped up on my Internet search was comedian Chris Rock, who was diagnosed with NVLD at fifty-five years old. A friend suggested he had Asperger's syndrome, and he had himself assessed. While ASD was not his diagnosis, NVLD was. Rock sees a therapist as part of his treatment plan.

So, what exactly is NVLD? Contrary to the first part of its name, it does not mean that a person is nonverbal, as in mute. In fact, people with NVLD are great with words, hence Chris Rock's success with spontaneous verbal jabs, storytelling, and making jokes. The problem resides with the interpretation of nonverbal social cues like tone and facial expressions, which can land people with NVLD in hot water with friends. The other person may perceive her as being rude or not listening, when it's actually NVLD at work blocking her ability to process what is being said to her. If this sounds like a person with low support needs, a variation on the autism spectrum, you'd be correct. NVLD also impacts focus, fine motor skills (tying shoelaces), and gross motor skills (jumping), as well as organization and planning. Hmm, this sounds similar to ADHD. When it comes to reading comprehension, writing, and math skills, NVLD mimics dyslexia, dysgraphia, dyspraxia, auditory, and visual processing disorders.

Because there is so much overlap, it is easy to see how neurodivergence plays along the spectrum. Every child is unique in their response to their disability, so comparing kids, even siblings with a learning difference, is never a good idea. Over time, as children grow from elementary years to tweens, teens, and young adults, their neurodivergence will present differently. Reading, which was a challenge in second grade, might not be an issue in fifth grade, but lying is now a thing. Self-regulation, bike riding, chewing, and other milestones will be achieved, and your child will still have a learning disability. Your child will grow taller, gain weight, mature emotionally, and have better social skills. They may finally have a bestie or friend group and still have anxiety. Neurodivergence does not go away, but kids, parents, caregivers, and educators can learn to recognize the signs and be ready to pivot when new challenges arise.

Denial

There's an old saying, *Denial ain't just a river in Egypt.*

Even with all of the available information about neurodivergence, denial is real. Sometimes a delay is enacted by well-meaning educators and family members who don't see anything wrong. *She'll grow out of it* is not helpful or accurate. This is especially true when a child is well behaved. People often mistake well-mannered kids as "good" or "fine," totally missing the turmoil that child is experiencing on the inside. Sometimes the cog in the wheel is one of the parents. I have several friends who had a hard time getting their partners on board. They just couldn't fathom that anything was wrong with their child. Or feedback from others is that the child is spoiled, faking it, the parents don't want to parent, parents are too permissive, parents are clueless, the child eats too much processed food, spends too much time on an iPad, ad nauseum. The shaming of parents is endless. While the intentions of others may be good, they are not brain specialists or trained professionals who can diagnose or recognize neurodivergence.

Delays are also driven by cultural or religious beliefs or distrust of the medical establishment. Black parents have all kinds of receipts about how racism, outright neglect, and disparities in health care to never go near a physician. Immigrants, LGBTQ+ families, APIDA, and Latine communities have legitimate concerns about how they will be perceived and how their children will be treated, and they are not willing to risk religious or cultural betrayal. All of these concerns are valid; however, a child's mental health cannot withstand dithering by parents or caregivers. The price of denial is high and includes lifelong struggles, suicide, depression, anxiety, homelessness, incarceration, sexual violence, drug addiction, and self-harm in the form of cutting or burning oneself. No one brings a life into the world or adopts a child into their world just to watch her suffer.

Reflection

There is no one way to prepare for a neurodivergent child. Even when neurodivergence runs in families, the next generation is often surprised and not sure what to do. Boomers often handled neurodivergence in whispers; hiding loved ones in sanitariums; ignoring the issues; disowning or kicking their kids out. But you have to make a choice.

If you are planning to adopt or have already adopted, all agencies have resources for children with special needs. Remember, love does not conquer all and it behooves adoptive parents to do their homework. In Los Angeles County, for example, UCLA TIES (training, intervention, education, and services) for Families offers a range of services from weekly therapy sessions, to parent education classes, support groups, psychiatric needs, educational support, and referrals. The training is free and optional for prospective foster/adoptive parents. I earned this certification in 2007 when I adopted my son but didn't use it until 2017. Who knew?! I am so grateful I took advantage of this free service, which is what I switched to after paying for services.

The bottom line is this: if *you* think something is wrong or if you are being urged to get an assessment by your partner or child's teacher, you are morally obligated to do it. It is your responsibility to overturn every stone in the quest for answers and support. Until your child can advocate for herself, make the call to your child's pediatrician or ask the school for a referral for an assessment.

Not that you asked, but here are my two cents:

Neurodivergence is an invisible disorder.

Learn to recognize the signs of neurodivergence.

Neurodivergence is a spectrum issue.

Every child presents differently, so comparing your child's progress to siblings, your nephew, or a coworker's daughter will only hurt your feelings.

Tune out negativity from family and friends.

They mean well but do not live with your child and have no idea what your day-to-day is like.

3

The Assessment Rabbit Hole

It would be disingenuous of me to tell you the mountain of forms parents and caregivers need to complete are not overwhelming, confusing, and, at times, frustrating. But be frustrated and complete the forms anyway. If you are partnered, divide and conquer. Whoever is stronger, let them do it. Have the other partner bring water or wine or coffee, wipe your brow even. Take breaks, refer to emails from teachers or coaches. Compare notes with your partner about concerning behaviors at home, during extracurricular activities and on playdates. If your child is quiet and withdrawn, note that. If she flaps her arms, is nonverbal past the age of two, is still having difficulty reading or writing as a third grader, has tantrums that do not fit the situation, is inattentive, expresses that she is dumb or stupid, feels like she doesn't fit in socially, is depressed or anxious, or wishes she wasn't around, write it down. When you reach the self-reporting section of the psychological assessment, no detail is insignificant.

You can expect to complete a variety of tests, depending on your child's symptoms, because rarely is a diagnosis one thing. For example, kids who have NVLD will sometimes also have ADHD, so a combination of assessments is necessary. The Woodcock-Johnson III Tests of Cognitive Abilities;[1] Wide Range Achievement

Test 5 (WRAT 5);[2] Conners4 Feedback Handout for Parent Ratings; Comprehensive Test of Phonological Processing, second edition (CTOPP-2);[3] and/or the Shaywitz DyslexiaScreen[4] for learning disabilities are common. The CTOPP-2 essentially measures reading—oral and silent phonological abilities and processing skills; reading fluency; rapid naming of colors, objects, letters, and numbers; as well as short- and long-term memory storage. There are many tests designed for preschool through adulthood, and my very short list with its oversimplified explanation is an example for caregivers new to the process.

Filling out the above forms and countless others takes denial off the table. There is no reason to lie or minimize symptoms. If your child is biting her nails, licking classmates, eloping, and having epic tantrums, check the corresponding box. While all questions may not perfectly match your child's behavior, many come very close. The goal is to paint as detailed a picture of your child as possible. The clinician typically doesn't know your family dynamic and will make an assessment based upon the information you provide and how the child self-rates. Kids may be asked to draw a picture of their family or a house. The latter is called the HTP technique and measures personality traits and potential psychological problems.[5] They will be asked how they handle stress, disappointment, achievement, and failure. Questions about bedtime, toilet routines, and a bunch of other questions that feel redundant because you answered that on page 1 and it's showing upon again on page 7. It may feel like they are trying to trick you into revealing something embarrassing, but asking the same questions different ways will ensure accuracy.

Finally, make a hard copy or save the forms to a digital file. I keep a folder on my computer desktop and in my file cabinet, just in case there's a flood, fire, earthquake, or other force of nature, or the assistant didn't receive the forms I spent hours completing. Even if the point person quits, I won't have to re-create the wheel.

Having Your Child Assessed

Neurodivergence will be determined through an assessment. Depending on where you go and how much money you are willing to spend, you can get a full profile or a baseline summary of how your child's brain works. A full profile may include an MRI; CT scan; interviews with parents, caregivers, and teachers; observations of strengths and weaknesses in home and/or school; test scores; appetite; child's ability to regulate; self-reported questionnaires by parents about beliefs and attitudes about neurodivergence, as well as their psychological and/or psychiatric history; and much more. In cases where a child is in foster care or has been adopted, this information may be scant. The clinician will then rely upon the adopted parent's impressions, home environment, other caregivers, and/or teachers to draw conclusions to gain insight into a child's psycho-emotional interior. A baseline profile includes much of the above, although with expensive tests like an MRI, biometrics may not be requested or necessary to determine neurodivergence. Parents should expect to do the legwork of requesting reports from educators, doctors, and the like, and then submit those documents to the person administering the neurologic exam.

As your child's profile is being compiled, get ready to peel back the layers of your homelife. The questions are endless, repetitive, and intrusive. There are no wrong answers, so be honest about family history, environmental stressors, and your feelings about your child's behavior. Lying only delays the inevitable. Transparency is crucial, so make sure your partner is on board with the information you share. If your partner is not on board, you will have to have hard conversations about their reluctance—is it a religious or cultural objection? Is there post-traumatic stress disorder (PTSD) from a previous experience? Are they neurodivergent and in denial or shock about passing it to the next generation? Could it be that a diagnosis will make the situation real, which then requires action? You might have to enlist the teacher or a third party who has already been through it for help. Or even table the discussion and reapproach when feelings aren't so raw or confusing. Ultimately, the earlier your child is assessed the better.

What Is Being Assessed?

Determining how our brain functions is the goal of the assessment. Parents, caregivers, and educators need to know what we are working with. If a child defies neurotypical standards of behavior or language processing, we need to know that. We need to know that their brains work beyond socially constructed boundaries and only a licensed clinical therapist, psychologist trained in neurodiversity, or psychiatrist can tell us what that means. Hence, neurologic tests are formatted to determine "mental status, cranial nerves, motor function, sensory function, and reflexes."[6] Each section takes a different measurement to build a complete profile. For example, in the mental status exam portion, "questions [are] designed to assess your level of alertness, orientation, mood, and cognition."[7] The results reveal learning disabilities, cognitive abilities, strengths, and neurologic differences that require behavioral or medical interventions, occupational therapy (OT), physical therapy (PT), therapy, and accommodations at school. Nothing is 100 percent, and how a child shows up at age seven will be different at twelve and sixteen years of age. The bottom line is that you work with the diagnosis in front of you, knowing that maturity, tutors, adapted gymnastics, and other interventions may solve one issue and not another in the short term. As parents, educators, and caregivers, we are playing the long game, so lace up your walking shoes, put your big-girl panties on or man up, and get your child assessed.

Why Is This Step Necessary?

Assessments have a lot of value. They are the first line of defense for parents and caregivers, who are usually playing catch-up because we missed symptoms when they were very young. Or we secretly knew and hoped that by changing schools or finding the right therapist or using the just right dose of Risperdal or Vyvanse, our kid would magically fit in. The crazy thing is, we wouldn't hesitate to use an inhaler if we couldn't breathe but somehow get tripped over admitting that our child needs help beyond our abilities. Having your child assessed is not an admission of wrongdoing or imperfection. It is the start of a path forward. Your child needs to know why letters float, why they have face blindness, or why they are having trouble focusing or retaining directions given five minutes earlier. If you do nothing, nothing will change. In fact, things will get worse. Grades will plummet, friendships will be negatively impacted, tantrums will be unmanageable because she has never learned to self-soothe. Quality of life for everyone in the household goes down and your child will fail to thrive socially, emotionally, physically, and academically. Grades are not everything, but social relationships are very important. By age four, kids have generally moved on from parallel play and seek a bestie or friend group. To achieve this aim, children will lie, play to the crowd as class clown, endure bullying, or lash out in confusion to get their peers' attention and approval. They want to know that someone, other than their parents, thinks they're funny or cool. They need a person, their person, to affirm them.

Whether your child invents a flying car, they need tools on how to advocate for themselves, interact with their neurotypical peers and siblings, and organize themselves and learn to love the brain they have. An assessment starts this process.

Making the Request

Start with your pediatrician. They will give you a referral to a clinician who specializes in psychological and psychoeducational evaluations. You can also go to your local school. If you do, Sonya, my school psychologist friend, suggests putting the request in writing and hand delivering it to your home school. Even if the school psychologist is not available, ask the secretary or student worker to time-stamp your request and make a copy. This way, you have proof that your request was received. You can also email your request, just make sure you send it to the right person. Requests for an assessment that leads to an individualized education program (IEP) should go to the special education coordinator or assistant principal. Adding a "read receipt" tracker on your Gmail account is another way to keep track of when and how many times the recipient opened the email. It also autogenerates a receipt for you and starts the special education clock, giving the home school fifteen days to respond to you or be out of compliance. If you don't hear from anyone within two weeks, follow-up with a direct phone call and/or email. I'm not trying to overwhelm administrators or suggest they would lie about not getting your email, but being an advocate for your child means being a squeaky wheel.

Learn from my mistake. Because Cherish was assessed when she was in kindergarten, I decided to have her reassessed during third grade. I emailed a request to our home school. I was informed that since the school year was ending, someone would get back to me at the beginning of the next school year. There was no urgency on our end, and we went on with our lives. The public schools returned to school, the parochial schools went back, the private schools started in fall 2022, and I contacted our home school about the ETA of Cherish's IEP. I was informed that the school had not "purchased" a psychologist for the school year and that the assistant principal was covering three elementary schools. Public school principals use their discretion to budget line items for school psychologists, nurses, and other personnel. They are working with tight budgets and doing the best they can with limited funds. My patience was requested and Cherish was added to the list of children needing IEPs. An entire school year passed with intermittent communication from the assistant principal. She was so kind and overwhelmed by the volume of cases on her desk. By this time, I casually mentioned to Sonya what I needed, and she immediately explained Cherish's rights for a timely IEP: fifteen days to respond to request and a completion of the IEP within sixty days. These are calendar, not business, days. The school we were zoned for was out of compliance. I had the option to complain but chose not to. However, armed with a full understanding of our special education rights, I walked in a request for an IEP and followed up with an email alerting the assistant principal that I was aware of the ticking clock. This time, she moved quickly, and Cherish was granted an IEP on schedule.

How and Where to Get Assessed?

There are two ways to get the ball rolling. One is free and the other may cost up to $18,000. If you go the private route, it is super important that the person administering the assessment is *certified* to do so. You can use Google, contact your insurance company, or get referrals from friends or your child's school. If you go the public school route, you must first contact the local school. Believe it or not, your neighborhood school may not be the school at the end of the block. Your address may be zoned for the elementary or middle or high school several miles away. How will you know? You can go to your local school and ask if they are your home school or go to website of your local school district and plug in your physical address to get the answer. Following Sonya's advice, contact either the assistant principal, special education administrator/counselor, or whoever is in charge of starting the process.

Once you speak with the administrator, express your concerns. Again, this is the time to be explicit about emails from teachers, other caregivers, and life at home with your neurodivergent child. Chances are, the behavior the teacher reports mirrors what happens at home. You will then be sent caregiver forms and later receive a date for the psychoeducational section of the IEP, administered by a school psychologist. Your child's teachers will also receive forms that they will complete and return to the administrator. Under the Individuals with Disabilities Education Act (IDEA),[8] the IEP is used to formulate a plan for kids who need special education accommodations. Many factors determine the length of the process. Is it winter, spring, or summer break and school is not in session? Is the administrator on vacation or only at the school once per week? How many cases is the administrator overseeing? In my daughter's case, it took several weeks and then several more before I received the preliminary IEP. While you wait, alert counselors and administrators at your child's current school that an IEP is forthcoming and that, when you receive the results, you'd like for someone from the school to be present during the IEP meeting.

What Time of Day Should My Child Be Assessed?

The time of the test is important. I opted to test Cherish after school. I knew that she was spent but wanted the results to accurately reflect who she was. If I had taken her in the morning, the results may have been skewed and not representative of a child who had trouble self-regulating, misread social cues from friends, hoarded food, and was easily aroused and hyper-focused on tasks she liked. She also scribbled rather than formed letters properly because the energy it took to write words was exhausting. The psychologist was able to experience her avoidant behavior, when she sat under the desk and refused to answer another question. This was my world and who Cherish *actually* was at home and school when she didn't want to do something.

Individualized Education Program

Serving K–12 students, an IEP is a comprehensive report of the emotional-social behavior and psychological assessments of your child, compiled with data from educators, the school counselor, psychologist, a therapist's report, if applicable, physical examination, and a caregiver self-report. It will determine if a child has learning disabilities, emotional issues, and behavior problems and is used to set or review academic, social, and behavioral benchmarks. It is used to adapt curriculum, adjust content delivery by chunking assignments, incorporating breaks when needed, and resets teacher and student expectations around work completion. The objective is to ensure equitable access to the curriculum for children with short attention spans, reading challenges, short-term memory deficiencies, and sensory and processing issues.[9] An IEP is also for children on the autism spectrum or who are blind, hearing impaired, or deaf. This document, which can run up to thirty pages, is crucial for her current educational setting and may include recommendations for public schools with special day classes or nonpublic schools (NPS) that serve neurodivergent students. More on this in chapter 10.

The IEP is a federal document that travels with your child, regardless of in which state you reside. If your child switches school, moves up to middle or high school, the IEP also travels with her. It carries weight at all educational institutions—public, nonpublic, private, parochial, and religious. A good rule of thumb is to have your child reassessed every three years if she attends private school and obtain a new IEP annually, if your child attends public school. Continuity of support is necessary to ensure that all stakeholders are on the same page and your child's educational experience remains an appropriate fit. Although an IEP carries no weight beyond twelfth grade, kids who are delayed can maintain services until they are twenty-two years old. For those who matriculate to university, the IEP can be given to the educational opportunity program (EOP) office, college counselor, or office of student disabilities, who structure a realistic class schedule and notify professors for accommodations under the Americans with Disabilities Act (ADA).

Attending an IEP can be daunting, and parents should never, ever, show up or Zoom alone. I repeat: *Do not go into the meeting solo.* Bring an educational advocate, teacher, or friend who can ask questions or take notes. Parents are too close to the situation and need an advocate to ask questions, fill in blanks about learning, social and emotional successes or challenges, and even translate acronyms to help devise a plan to move forward with accommodations. As I mentioned earlier, the actual IEP can run up to thirty pages. Essentially, parents can expect the meeting notice, list of those in attendance, reason for IEP, observation forms from caregivers and teachers, recommendations, accommodations, and even suggestions for appropriate educational placements and schools that may fit your child's needs. There is a signature page that parents are asked to sign; but be warned, once your "John Hancock" is on the line, the IEP is locked, and changes cannot be made until the next IEP. Of course, there are exceptions, but if you disagree or have more questions, do not sign the IEP. Request a follow-up meeting and ask questions until you understand what is happening.

504 Plan

A 504 Plan, named for Section 504 of the Rehabilitation Act of 1973,[10] guarantees free and appropriate public education (FAPE) for people with disabilities. Youth receive accommodations based upon their disability and/or neurodivergence, and parents are required to submit forms to support a diagnosis of dyslexia or autism spectrum disorder. Sounds like an IEP, right? Although both documents[11] ensure that physically and neurodivergent children receive appropriate education in the least restrictive environment, and allow for FAPE, an IEP "specifically provides FAPE through tailored *special education services*, supports, and measurable goals to meet the unique needs of a child with a disability."[12] In other words, an IEP offers special education either at a traditional public school or a nonpublic school, which is free to parents but school districts foot the bill. A 504 Plan is not mandated to provide special education services and works for kids who need accommodations within a generalized education setting. Both the IEP and 504 Plan grow with your child as her strengths and weaknesses change.

Reflections

Realizing that your child operates left of center and having her assessed are the building blocks of an accurate diagnosis. Learning how your child's brain functions and how she processes information is life changing. Parents who are armed with details about their child's neurodivergence are in a better position to advocate for appropriate services and accommodations.

Misdiagnosis does occur, and if that happens, it is easier to narrow down mistakes if every T is crossed and every I is dotted. In fact, the biggest mistake is not having your child assessed. While you wait weeks or months to get a diagnosis, begin to build bonds with clinicians, educators, or others who spend time with your kid. As long as everyone is on the same page, your child's best interests will be met.

Not that you asked, but here are my two cents:

Have your child assessed for neurodivergence.

Be organized and present all documents at once.

Sending items piecemeal will cause delays and confusion.

Never attend an IEP meeting or Zoom alone.

There are different types of educational plans. Please note:

Not all kids qualify for an IEP.

All kids qualify for a 504 Plan.

An IEP and 504 Plan should be revisited annually.

4

Diagnosis in Hand, Now What Do I Do?

During the assessment portion of the program, you poured your life out to complete strangers on paper, in Zoom meetings, and/or in person. You laid bare intimate details of your daily existence that even close friends may not be privy to. You had to. Your child needs help and the path forward required vulnerability.

Your child, if old enough to complete a self-assessment, will be asked a series of questions or given a rating sheet to digitally complete. If the child is in lower elementary or unable to read, the clinician may read the question aloud and mark their answer on the form: Obtaining information about emotional IQ (intelligence quotient) is derived from open-ended questions that measure a child's:

feelings about school;

feelings about himself or herself;

feelings about place in family;

feelings about academic ability;

feelings about social interactions; and

feelings about being able to self-regulate.

The format of the questions may sound similar, but there are subtle differences that yield different markers. For example, "Doesn't seem to listen or pay attention," versus "Does not follow verbal directions."

The first question is assessing focus. Is the child clued in that someone is speaking to her? Is she tracking with her eyes? Is she aware of her surroundings, or off in another world?

The second question is assessing auditory processing. Did the words match the sounds? Did the child understand what was being asked of him? From a behavioral point of view, the teacher may think he is being defiant, but the clinician knows that his processing speed may slow his response.

Next, the psychologist may ask your child to draw a house, tree, or person. The H-T-P[1] test indicates social behavior, place (in a family), emotions, and attitudes. Home represents the relationship with family and environment. A tree signifies the depth of relationships in the person's life, stability, and emotional health. The person is used to determine cognitive development.[2] The Draw-a-Person test was created in 1926 and remains an integral part of determining cognitive, developmental, and emotional functioning, as well as how a person perceives himself.[3] Details are important and a trained professional may see isolation in a house with no windows; attention-seeking for the child who draws himself overly large; or worry about the future if the picture is to the right side of the page as opposed to a centered picture. Interpretation is subjective and viewed through the lens of the clinician who may lack cultural competence to appropriately interpret a child who is BIPOC or LGBTQ+. Parents should keep that in mind when receiving results.

There are more ratings scales, and the number of assessments turns on whether your child is getting a comprehensive psychoeducational evaluation or a basic one. The difference is cost and timing. A short assessment may be needed right away to get services started or for an application for school. Many occupational therapists (OT), public mental health outpatient centers, and private agencies that specialize in autism spectrum disorder (ASD) or other neurodivergence require their own assessment and will not accept previous assessments. I wish there was a database to house the numerous evaluations your child will endure. My advice is to stay loose as you snatch the Band-Aid off, over and over, and repeat yourself ad nauseum.

Interpreting Results

After weeks of self-reporting, self-assessing, completing a ream of forms by hand, and taking your child back and forth to appointments, you wait. In the meantime, you continue to parent and pray that the results will yield answers to what is happening with your child and how best to support her. Make sure that everyone in your child's network—caregivers, educators, coaches, and pediatrician—are aware that a diagnosis is forthcoming.

At last, the email arrives. Typically, an in-person meeting occurs between parents or caregivers and the psychologist who administered the test. They will review their findings, go over each rating scale, share their interpretation of your child's self-rating scale, or, if applicable, attention/executive functioning test, teacher rating form, sensory profile, Rorschach Inkblot Test, among others, and render a diagnosis. Designate a partner or friend to take notes and don't be afraid to ask for clarification from the clinician with a PhD or certification to administer the psychological evaluation with many years of experience assessing children and working with parents and educators. The doctor has language and an understanding of terms, treatment plans, and interventions that you may be unaware of. Their job is to deliver their findings, and your job is to be open to the results. Chances are your child will be evaluated many times over the course of their childhood, but the first cut is the deepest.

This is also the moment of truth. If you or your partner have been in denial about your child's development or behavior, the time to face the music is now. The evaluation, which is the first step in the new trajectory of your child's life, is in black and white. There is no place to hide. Even caregivers who have been in denial know that their intuitive sense of their child's neurodivergence—ASD, ADHD, or dyslexia—was just confirmed by the psychological evaluation. What might catch parents off guard are the multiple diagnoses the psychologist lists in the evaluation. Up until this moment, you might not have known that neurodivergence run on a spectrum that overlap with one or more differences. For example, I suspected Cherish had ADHD but never heard of sensory processing disorder (SPD), nor did I know that there were three types of ADHD. I can see it so clearly now.

Although the psychologist has reviewed the psychological evaluation with you, read it again when you get home. Go to a quiet room, grab multiple highlighters, a dictionary, and a tissue as you read it again. As you wade through pages and pages of *DSM-5* jargon and confusing psychological speak, the most important section is the diagnostic impression. All of the pages leading up to this point, usually twenty-plus pages, are incredibly important; but in practical terms, the summary specifically itemizes the diagnosis, special education eligibility, and recommendations for home and school.

You will take this document and share it far and wide. While teachers should not receive the psychoeducational evaluation directly from you, the school counselor, special education director, administrator, and pediatrician should receive a copy. If OT, psychotherapy, medication, and/or behavioral support is needed, those providers will request the evaluation. These professionals need as much information as possible to implement strategies to support your child's neurodivergence at home and school.

Therapies

Even kids with the same diagnosis will present differently and the evaluation will assist parents, caregivers, and educators with information to craft a treatment plan curated to your child's specific needs. What could that look like? The short answer is it depends. Treatment should factor the child's age, symptoms, social and emotional development, physical development, cognitive and behavioral levels, and possibly recommend an appointment with a psychiatrist to determine if psychotropic medication is appropriate. Here is a breakdown of possible home interventions:

Psychotherapy. Aimed at helping a child see how her behavior is impacting learning and/or relationships with friends. Sessions may start weekly and escalate to multiple sessions per week or slowly taper off to biweekly. These one-to-one sessions are between the child and her clinician. Parents can meet separately with the therapist or request family therapy. Before selecting a therapist, do your homework. Read the doctor's reviews, ask around about that person. Expect to be placed on a waiting list and know that private insurance may only cover a few sessions when indefinite psychotherapy is needed. The therapist who is assigned may be a different race or gender from your child. They may not have training or experience working with trans or LGBTQ+ children who are neurodivergent, and this lack of cultural competency may not be the best fit for your child. You have the right to interview the therapist who will be working with your child. And, if after a few sessions, your child expresses, either verbally or through body language, that they are uncomfortable, stop the sessions and try another therapist. It's okay to shop around. For adoptive and foster parents, psychotherapy is free through regional centers, Medicaid, or Medi-Cal, if you live in California. Ask the social worker for resources.

The therapist not only works with your child and your family but also works with your child's teachers and administrators. Her job is to act as a liaison between you and the school, explain new behaviors that may crop up, assist teachers in crafting praise charts, and make referrals if your child needs additional therapy. This is a two-way relationship where parents feel heard and respected.

Using different methods of engagement, many therapists use play therapy as an effective means of communicating with younger children. Through role play, therapists teach empathy and create a safe space for children to reveal anxieties, attachment issues, and cultural dynamics at home and school. The therapist's observations provide crucial insight for parents of children who do not always share their true feelings or insecurities. There are several types of play therapy, though these four are the most common:

Child-centered play therapy (CCPT)[4] is one-on-one therapy where the child leads the session. The "play" aspect is the language by which the therapist and child communicate to build a strong connection. CCPT is great for kids three to eight years old.

Cognitive behavioral therapy (CBT)[5] seeks to replace distorted or negative thought patterns to help with problem-solving, emotional regulation, coping strategies, emotional regulation, and awareness.

Family play therapy[6] is for families with a neurodivergent child. It improves family dynamics that are impacted by stress due to the diagnosis by helping parents with new or improved parenting skills manage conflicts and uphold the family unit as integral to a child's successful functionality.

Group play therapy[7] builds social skills for children with similar challenges. The small group provides a safe space for kids to practice what they learned in CCPT and work on social anxiety, inattentiveness, and poor communication. Group therapy is also great for kids who need to process trauma, bullying, depression, and grief.

Art therapy is not a "play" therapy, per se, but is very effective in eliciting information from children who have experienced trauma or have behavioral challenges or speech impediments due to ASD, nonverbal learning disability (NVLD), or inattentive type attention-deficit/hyperactivity disorder (ADHD). A certified art therapist is trained in psychological theory and uses the creative process to help children with mental issues.

Dance/movement therapy is an "integrative therapeutic approach to movement that supports the emotional, cognitive, physical, and social integration of the individual based on the empirical premise that the body, mind, and spirit are interconnected," says Dr. Lori Baudino, PsyD, B-C, DMT. Her use of DANCE as an acronym—*d*ifferentiated movements; *a*ttach the movements (rituals, patterns, preferences) together; *n*arrate to bring words to movement, mood, and emotion; *c*onsciousness; and *e*ngagement—is a lens that gives us an understanding of what someone is going through.

With the exception of OT, which is typically covered by insurance, parents have other options that are often not covered:

Neurofeedback or biofeedback[8] provides computer-based immediate feedback that helps with self-regulation of brain waves. Kids wear a special cap with electrodes attached to their scalp that allows them to see how their brain responds to stimuli. Over time, behavior that has impaired communication or socialization will be eliminated by the child who learns to regulate their central nervous system. This type of treatment ranges from $800 to $4,000 for thirty to forty sessions or more. Although neurofeedback is FDA (Food and Drug Administration) approved, it is not covered by insurance, and some believe it to be a placebo.

Yoga helps with concentration, calmness, and relaxation for kids who are easily aroused and unable to sit still. It increases body awareness, helps kids with ASD by way of social and communication skills and regulation of their vestibular and proprioceptive systems. Translation: yoga helps with balance, movement, strength, and coordination.

Occupational therapy (OT) is great for fine- and gross-motor skill development, sensory issues with food or spatial awareness, movement, handwriting, and social and emotional skills. OT is covered by insurance; however, the quality of care and duration of each session is tied to whether insurance is covering OT or if you are paying out of pocket. When Cherish went from receiving private OT to OT covered by Medi-Cal, there was an immediate stepdown in care. The sessions were shorter, the gym was significantly smaller, and there was no option for group therapy or a chance for her to work with someone her size with whom she shared a diagnosis, which would have helped improve her social skills.

Chiropractic neurology is a niche specialty of chiropractic medicine. The therapy is holistic in its approach, requiring input from the child's psychologist, occupational therapist, nutritionist, and other members of the child's medical and mental health team. The focus is on rewiring the nervous system through specific chiropractic manipulations to help with balance, developmental delays, and other neurological issues. If you go this route, ask to see proof of certification from the American Chiropractic Neurology Board (ACNB).

We tried CCPT, group therapy, yoga, and gymnastics. CCPT was and is a staple for Cherish, who has had four out of five great therapists. The outlier was too young and inexperienced to be working with neurodivergent children. Cherish made it her mission to run circles around her every week. All women, her therapists ranged from married with children to married without children to single, never married. They were white, Latine, and Black and culturally competent. The non-Black therapists were aware of the role respect plays in Black families and the importance of strict boundaries that govern most of our households. I had individual sessions, too. Ordinarily not super forthcoming with strangers, I felt strangely at ease discussing my parenting style and receptive to suggestions to man-down when Cherish needed tenderness not punishment. I guess the moment called for it, and I use many of the tools they shared with me today.

Cherish was seen and loved by each one of them, who were conscientious enough to write kind notes and give her tokens once their rotation was over. She still has these items. Of the movement therapies, gymnastics was the best. Cherish attended two times per week, learning back flips, front somersaults, and stretching her long limbs on the colorful mats. She had a lot of friends she looked forward to hanging out with. The coach was gentle but firm. He had a way of encouraging her to jump back in the mix when she was tired. Instead of hovering, I could sit in the car and wait for class to end. I was so happy Cherish had an activity she truly enjoyed. Then the COVID-19 pandemic came and ruined all the fun.

Parents have options when it comes to choosing different therapeutic models. As you investigate which type fits your budget, child, and family, be thorough and ask questions of the adults who might work with your child.

> What type of experience do you have?
>
> How many years have you worked with [fill in the blank] children?
>
> What is your therapeutic process?
>
> What are the goals?
>
> Will my child have a voice in the type of treatment you offer?
>
> When can parents expect to know if treatment is working?
>
> Are you comfortable working with a LGBTQ+ family?
>
> Do you have experience working with adoptive families?
>
> Have you worked with families of different races or religions?

The answers to these questions should guide your choice. You are never stuck with a therapist. If the first, second, or third clinician isn't a good fit, keep looking. Your child's mental health is too important to turn it over to just anyone.

Educational Settings

All children—even elite athletes, dancers, and actors—spend more time with nonparental adults than parents, grandparents, aunts, uncles, siblings, and caregivers. School is basically their home away from home. Their teeth are lost, menstrual cycles begin, voices drop, crushes happen, besties emerge, social media trends are acted out, and cliques form. For some kids, school is a sanctuary away from judgy parents who don't understand or approve of emo, an outgrowth of punk and grunge music with attendant fashion statements consisting of dark clothing, silver stud accents, black makeup, and jet-black hair, or LGBTQ+ youth lifestyle. These young people find kindred souls anyway. The academically strong proudly make themselves known through academic decathlon wins and debate championships. Star athletes experience the kind of glory that propels them to reach for heights that they likely won't achieve, since less than 1 percent will go pro—but they don't know that yet. And, if there are enough Black kids at a mixed-race school, they are likely to sit together at lunch. Author Beverly Daniel Tatum noticed this self-segregating pattern of Black youth in her seminal work, *Why Are All the Black Kids Sitting Together in the Cafeteria? And Other Conversations About Race*. Racial identity may start at home but is shaped outside of it by friends and other adults, especially during the crucial middle school years.

During my brief stint in law school, we studied a case about *in loco parentis*, Latin for "in place of the parents," for a moot court competition. As far back as 1859, the law established that teachers, tutors, coaches, and other adults in charge of children unofficially serve in place of parents. They are obligated to supervise, attend to, and look after the children in their care. This provision gives administrators authority to drug test students, discipline bullies, and expel those who bring weapons to school. Educators agree that "[f]or both educationally pragmatic and moral reasons the *in loco parentis* duty of care K–12 schools owe their students includes supporting the psychological well-being of children."[9] Protecting a child's mental health falls *in loco parentis* and is mostly covered under the Individuals with Disabilities Education Act (IDEA), but given the broadness of what constitutes mental illness, an IEP is used to ensure a child who needs accommodations or special education receives a free appropriate public education (FAPE). Private, parochial, and religious schools[10] have the same responsibility but not FAPE, which applies to public schools. During that competition, I was given a window into my future. Essentially, my parental stand-in during the school day would be the school. I would entrust them to educate and care for my kids physically and emotionally.

Most parents and caregivers have never heard of *in loco parentis* but assume that their child's educational setting is prepared to support their needs. The reality is that educators' plates are full, resources vary from school to school, district to district, and all teachers are not created equally. Some know just what to do when a child is struggling to read, and others need guidance on how to engage a neurodivergent child or those with different learning styles. Enter the treatment plan in the form of accommodations, crafted from the psychoeducational report to fill these gaps. Here are a couple of recommendations therapists may request on your child's behalf:

Differentiated instructional strategies: chunking assignments; giving tests in a different classroom away from distractions; and use of a classroom aide who works with a small group of children who need a different pace are a few examples. Differentiated learning is revising standards of success or completion for neurodivergent learners. Perhaps they are required to master 80 percent of the lesson within a longer time frame and their test reflects what they have learned, not what the entire lesson entails. Teachers can be creative and work with parents to identify key aspects of each lesson and share how they are scaffolding information in a way that is accessible to all learners.

Shadow: also known as a para-educator or co-teacher. Hired by parents, the shadow works in a mainstream classroom with a child with special needs. Her job is to help with task initiation, task completion, emotional regulation, and communication. The shadow confers with teachers and parents on how to do their job without disrupting the flow of the classroom. Parents can expect to pay upward of $4,000 per month for this individualized attention. Splitting the fee with another family is a cost-effective way to provide support to multiple children in the same class or at the same school.

Avoid multistep directions: for kids with working memory issues, auditory, and language processing issues, multistep directions are useless. Your child will spend emotional capital trying to match what she heard to the expected action and fall behind or be accused of not listening. The child may be embarrassed and/or look for ways to avoid the task. Directions should be repeated at macro (to the entire class) and micro (directly to the child) levels. Teachers should individually ask the kid (not publicly humiliate them) to repeat the instruction to ensure that she actually heard and understood what the teacher said. For those with ADHD and processing challenges, repeating directions is essential to their ability to attend to and stick with the assignment. Is this an extra step for teachers? Yes, and well worth the thirty additional seconds of instructions.

Take breaks: helps manage stress, improve focus, and reset the central nervous system. Like the calming effects of yoga, breaks help kids relax, build resilience, and complete tasks. Asking a child to sit at her desk for an hour or longer is a recipe for disaster and educators need to be consistent about allowing short breaks: allowing a child to stand, take a sip of water, or do crab walks or jumping jacks to get their wiggles out throughout the day. Breaks are also useful at home for kids struggling to finish chores or homework.

Goal setting: should reflect the learner. If a spelling test requires matching words to definitions or writing sentences, the child with dyslexia will need a different measurement of success. Maybe she can orally recite the definition to receive credit. Setting attainable goals sets a child up for success and encourages them to stretch to the next milestone.

Technology: can be effective. Children can use talk-to-text software, use a calculator, or use apps like Speechify, Dyslexia Quest, and Learning Ally Audiobooks, which are great for kids with dyslexia and reading challenges. ModMath, Magrid, and others support dyscalculia. Not always free, these apps are worth the subscription and can be used at home too. If you're like me and worship at the altar of Google and YouTube, you will find short videos that enhance learning and reinforce school lessons. Some K–12 education systems provide iPads, Chromebooks, or tablets for free during the school year. Touch screen or use of a stylus are handy for tactile learners and helps to forge a connection between the material and the learner because the physical act of touch feels hands on, even though the lesson is virtual. Typing also reduces fatigue. The amount of energy needed to copy from a whiteboard onto paper or read sheet music and then check fingering during piano lessons is exhausting.

Home and School Overlap

Because treatment occurs at home and school, parents must be diligent in their roles as facilitators of their child's education. You cannot expect the school, *in loco parentis* or not, to do everything. Parents and caregivers have to have some skin in the game. Throwing money at tutors, shadows, and fancy technology is not enough. You are the glue for both environments. If that statement stresses you, it stresses me too. I could not wrap my mind around having to do one. more. thing. and was emotionally and financially tapped out. Cherish's therapist came through for the win. She helped me narrow down several low-stakes activities Cherish and I could do together once or twice per week. Starting with everyone's favorite, Monopoly. Just kidding. Here are the suggestions:

Board games: teach children how to take turns, count, read, concentrate, focus, and improve memorization. Parents can be creative with the length of time by using an hourglass filled with colorful sand for games like Monopoly, which can go on for hours (without intervention).

Card games: Uno, Speed, and Mother May I provide short bursts of fun and can be played solo when you have to get back to work or tend to your other child or partner. I'll add dominoes here as a sneaky way to enforce addition and the five times table.

Organization: is critical. Our children's brains are already different and adding confusion to a disorganized central nervous system is not a good idea. Having designated spaces for markers, shoes, money, Legos, backpacks, pajamas, toothbrushes, and the like minimizes stress in the morning and at bedtime. Being organized assists a child's growing independence and boosts their self-esteem when they can complete tasks on their own. I'm not going to pretend that announcing "Today, we will organize your room" ever went over well. It was always a fight; but Cherish loved the outcome and ease of being able to locate items when she needed them.

Role play: is essential for neurodivergent children, who tend to miss social cues, are unable to read facial expressions, or have trouble communicating. A basic script can be used to help with conflict resolution over sharing, misunderstandings, teasing, or mean-girl behavior. Role play is effective in building confidence, managing anxiety, encouraging new skills, and teaching empathy. Empathy is embedded in role play to help your child understand how the other person felt to avoid the same situation cropping up again. Role play is never one-and-done, nor is it solely for little kids. Teens, young adults, and grown folks use role-play strategies to ask for raises and promotions and improve interview skills when seeking a new job.

Quiet corner: is a designated area for kids who need a moment in a safe space. Your child may need to calm down away from their desk, friends, or siblings. This area should host quiet activities like reading, drawing, building blocks, knitting, and/or soothing music. This is not the space to rock-out and should be a tech-free zone. At home, the quiet corner could be a cozy space in their bedroom with stuffed animals, a bean bag, or large fluffy pillow. If they share a room or their bedroom isn't big enough for more furniture, identify a different area to be used for a reset. *Note*: this is not time out or a punishment and your child, siblings, and others who live in the home should clearly know they are not in trouble.

Positive reinforcement: is more than saying, "good job." Praise must be timely and specific. If she kept her seatbelt on during the bus ride to and from school, note how cool it was that she was able to control her body. If she mentored a friend during a tough emotional moment, tell her how empathetic she was. The more praise she hears the more likely she is to repeat positive behaviors. For kids with ADHD, there is a ton of research that credits positive reinforcement with allowing them to learn faster.[11]

Validate her feelings: creates a judgment-free zone. Students will know that they are heard by their teachers and caregivers. They are more likely to be open to problem-solving and taking an adult's advice if they know that their feelings and perspective matter. Validation helps a child calm down and brainstorm ways of avoiding a similar situation in the future or have tools to navigate the situation without having a meltdown. Kids need a designated safe person. At school it could be the counselor or nurse. At home, it could be a caregiver, a sibling, or a relative.

Incentives: for completing nonpreferred tasks. Some kids are motivated extrinsically. If you dangle stickers, points, Robux, extra playtime, or treats, they will rise to the occasion. I'll admit that I struggled with bribing kids to do stuff they are supposed to do. Growing up, I never received money for grades and believed the reward was in the doing. I passed this along to August, who, like me, is not extrinsically motivated. We do things because we are supposed to. Well, Cherish cured me of this old-school mindset. She is 100 percent good with a bribe, and now. . . . I am here for all of it. Cherish taught me to pick my battles. Also, given her short attention span and propensity for anxiety, incentives didn't always work. Recently, she had a chance to spend the night with her great aunt. This was a big treat that Cherish had been looking forward to. The deal was that she would fold, put away her laundry, and wash the dishes before she left, since it was her week. Oh, the attitude and standoff that ensued lasted two hours. I was surprised that she'd risk losing a fun activity over chores. Eventually, Cherish admitted that she was afraid to sleep alone in the guest bedroom. (OMG, we could have saved so much drama and time!) In this instance, the incentive could not override her anxiety about sleeping in the dark in a bedroom that wasn't her own. I told her that I understood. She did not have to spend the night. Cherish's entire disposition improved. We also compromised over her chores. I agreed to fold her laundry, and she would put her clothes away and wash the dishes when she returned later that night. It was a win for everybody.

Incentives may not work every time; however, consistency, frequency, mixing up the rewards, and compromise may be the push your child needs to start and complete nonpreferred tasks.

To Medicate or Not

The last but most charged part of the treatment plan is psychotropic medication. So much is at stake: comorbid struggles with anxiety and depression, race, culture, religion, and the opinions of close friends and family factor into the deeply personal decision to medicate a child.

Caregivers get a lot of conflicting information about how extended use of medicine will set their child up for drug addiction in their teens and twenties. We don't understand the formulations, and don't want to further stigmatize our child. It's like if a child takes medicine, the parent has failed at managing her behavior or supporting her different learning needs.

I was never against using stimulants. I understood that the type of medication Cherish needed would stimulate the part of the brain that could not regulate on its own. I was more concerned about her self-medicating when she entered the teen and young adult years if she didn't learn to focus and regulate when she was younger. I had drug addicts for parents and knew that when mental illness went untreated, people used whatever means necessary to cool themselves out. I did not want this for Cherish. As a Black mother, I had to weigh historical medical abuses against my community and the exigent need for a stimulant medication for her neurodivergent brain. Although I chose behavior modification therapy first, I was at peace with contacting a psychiatrist to prescribe meds for Cherish. Ironically, white children are more likely prescribed psychotropic drugs than Black or Latine children[12] but because BIPOC children are singled out for bad behavior and poor academic performance at greater rates, most Black parents assume our kids are offered drugs *before* comprehensive treatment plans.

Without question, the stimulant medication was a game changer. Cherish was in lower elementary school and finally able to get through the day. She stopped sitting under the table and scribbling her work and responded to directions better. Most importantly, she felt better. That said, psychotropic medicine is not magic, nor does it replace therapy, OT, or accommodations in school. All of these modalities were needed to support Cherish and, as she grew, her meds changed. I'll go into more details about switching meds in the next chapter.

Assessments

All of the above treatment plan suggestions are just that, suggestions. There is more than one way to support a neurodivergent child, whose personal journey will look different at each level of development. Although schools function as *in loco* parents to protect kids and support their mental health, an IEP or 504 Plan is the surest way these accommodations reach your child. As you may recall, an individualized education program is federally mandated to provide accommodations to be used by educators. Even if your child attends a religious, private, or parochial school, an IEP must be utilized, if the child has one. If not, schools may use alternate accommodation plans. In Catholic schools, the accommodations are referred to as a Support Team Education Plan (STEP); private schools call it a 504 Plan or Learning Accommodation Plan (LAP). The STEP, 504 Plan, and LAP do not have to be updated annually but an IEP does, as long as a child attends public school. These documents are also built using the psychoeducational evaluation and the IEP, if available. If you went the free route and had your child assessed through your neighborhood school, the psychologist will have observed your child at school, even if she attends a private school. The psychologist will use these observations, teacher assessment, parent ratings, report cards, and impressions from your child's therapist, if they have one, to generate the IEP. Even if you have a privately obtained psychoeducational evaluation, your child might have to be assessed by her local school district's psychologist. Each educational system is different, but if a second evaluation is needed, think of it as getting a second opinion for free. Parents and caregivers are entitled to receive any and all assessments of their child. Just be sure to put the request in writing.

With diagnosis in hand and a treatment plan, the train has officially left the station. You may feel like you are running behind it, because the information you've learned about your neurodivergent child could fill a bookshelf. The assessment process is overwhelming, and it may take years to fully understand what your child is experiencing. With such high rates of neurodivergence in the world, you are not alone. Millions of us are slogging through mountains of paperwork, looking for clues about our children's invisible disabilities. Instead of perseverating (ASD parents know this word) or blaming your partner or the foster care system, get educated. I know that the parent section of the treatment plan is written in invisible ink, so don't look there. You can read a book like this or check the Internet for reputable websites on the latest treatment models for dyslexia, ASD, and psychotropic medications. You can sign up for webinars dedicated to your child's diagnosis. One of my favorite parent education websites is *ADDitude Magazine*. This online resource has short articles and videos that get to the heart of whatever challenge I am experiencing, as I parent Cherish.

After learning how challenging it was for parents to obtain services for children on the autism spectrum, attorney and media expert Areva Martin founded the Special Needs Network in 2005. The organization was born of love, as her son, Marty, met all early developmental milestones and was diagnosed with ASD at two years old. She writes of coming to terms with his diagnosis in *The Everyday Advocate: How to Stand up for Your Child with Autism and Other Special Needs*. In her work, Martin realized that parents weren't always aware of their educational and health rights, which was an impediment to seeking and facilitating appropriate therapeutic interventions. Her book guides parents on how to advocate for quality care for their child.

Parent education is necessary because having a neurologically different child affects the household. Neurodivergence is not just happening to your child; it's happening to everyone, and treatment requires buy-in from siblings, grandparents, godparents, and whoever else helps with caregiving. Partners must be on the same page or everything to this point was a waste of time, emotion, and money.

Even with all of this information, there will be parents and caregivers who will drag their feet. They will hire an expensive shadow to sit in class with their child. They will take their child to school early to give her time to get her wiggles out, send noise-canceling headphones and weighted blankets, and apologize one thousand times for their child's behavior. They will purchase fancy vitamins, spend many hours meeting with teachers and administrators, and keep them home from school. All the while, their child is not getting better. Neurodivergence does not go away.

The value of a psychoeducational assessment and treatment plan cannot be overstated. Learning that Cherish had SPD, on top of ADHD, explained why carpool rides with her brother's friends were excruciatingly uncomfortable. She would be squeezed in the middle seat of my aging Toyota Prius with big smelly boys on either side. Without language to communicate that she felt claustrophobic and that her personal space was being violated, she would throw a tantrum. Months passed before I figured out what was happening in her brain. First, it was the end of the school day, and she was already tired and hungry. Second, her meds had worn off and she was dysregulated. Third, the length of the car ride didn't matter. Cherish felt hemmed in and her fight-or-flight instinct kicked in, which added another block to her churning tsunami of emotion. Because I was part of a carpool, there was nothing I could do. But then, I came up with a strategy. I'd front-load her with information.

"Cherish, we are taking John and James home. You will sit in the middle and keep your hands, feet, and arms to yourself."

The not-touching part was hard because she felt trapped. Or she wanted to play and continued snatching their hats when they told her to stop. Unable to respond to social cues, Cherish was being annoying.

"I don't want to sit in the middle."

"I understand, but the smallest sits in the middle seat. It's a short car ride and I'll let you choose the music."

I brought extra snacks or other items to occupy her hands. It wasn't perfect, but the tantrums lessened. I share this experience because without the comorbid SPD diagnosis, I would have assumed Cherish was being a jerk. I could not have learned this on my own because I had never heard of sensory processing disorder. No amount of Internet sleuthing, TikTok videos, or Instagram posts would have yielded this invaluable intel. I owe it all to the early assessments. Yes, there were more, but the first psychoeducational evaluation coupled with the OT assessment from the Child Success Center gave me a lens to really see who my daughter was at that time. Cherish's issues with spatial awareness have improved, but it's still a thing. I allow her to sit in the front seat whenever possible and limit the number of kids we transport to avoid tripping the high alert button on her central nervous system.

Reflections

You have a diagnosis and the mystery of why your child bangs her head or can't read as a third grader has momentarily been solved. Enjoy this victory. Then, tighten your seat belt because your child's diagnosis may change over the course of their life, and comorbid issues like anxiety and depression may join their dominant neurologic difference later on. For this reason, having your child assessed as early as possible will give parents and caregivers a baseline for determining an initial treatment plan. The treatment plan is for home, school, and anywhere your child spends a significant amount of time. This includes Grandma's house. If possible, all of her environments should mirror each other, as consistent expectations are key for children who are neurodivergent.

Communicate with your partner, caregiver, psychologist, therapist, and child's teacher regularly. There is no such thing as overcommunicating or asking too many questions of adults who interact with your child on a daily or weekly basis. Your desire to understand your child's neurodivergence makes you a stronger advocate and better equipped to help her help herself.

Knowledge is power. Such is the gift of the assessment and diagnosis.

Not that you asked, but here are my two cents:

- Take notes and ask questions whenever meeting with psychologists and other medical professionals.
- Read and re-read the psychoeducational evaluation.
- Skip to the summary of the psychoeducational evaluation and work backward.
  - Match the diagnosis with the symptoms for a more direct understanding of the report.
- Have a team mindset knowing you cannot support your child alone.
- Become an expert on your child's diagnosis.

5

Try, Fail, Repeat

Weeks have passed since you acted on instinct or a nudge from a partner or suggestion from a teacher to have your child assessed for a neurological difference. After numerous assessments, the diagnosis arrived informing you that your daughter falls into one, maybe two, spectrum categories that include a comorbid condition that needs to be addressed stat. The psychologist has handed you a treatment plan and wished you godspeed.

There is no practice, only starts, stops, and do-overs for the foreseeable future, but you don't know this yet. You think the recommended treatment plan will make your child normal. Whether we admit it or not, parents and caregivers seek normalcy for our children. No one wants to be the parent of the "bad" kid, of the child with no friends, of the child who is struggling academically, or who isn't athletic. We accept the treatment plans hoping and praying that after checking all of the boxes, our child will miraculously be able to respond to directions on command, have no food or spatial sensitivities, read no later than first grade, have no melt downs or tantrums beyond age four, and get along with everyone. This is unrealistic to accomplish in a short window because our neurodivergent children experience and interact with the world through their lens not everyone else's. I can be all preachy about it now because a lot of time has passed. I've grown as the mother of a neurodivergent child and learned to stop trying to fit a square into a circle.

Back then, I jumped in feet first and signed up for everything. Because kindergarten was just okay, I searched for a summer camp for kids with special needs. Cherish was transitioning to first grade and the online flyer was for her age group. I couldn't have planned that any better. If Cherish got some self-regulation skills, her new teachers wouldn't have to coax a six-year-old to sit still, remain in the classroom, write neatly, wait her turn to speak, use the scissors, or go to the bathroom.

I was open with Cherish's teachers about her ADHD diagnosis, sensory processing disorder, weekly OT, and sessions with her therapist. This was still new territory for me as a parent and I relied on the treatment plan from the psychologist who made her diagnosis. I was aware it would have to be tweaked along the way and felt confident about the new school year. Having been an advocate on behalf of my neurotypical son, who had experienced microaggressions and unfair treatment as a Black boy in a white educational setting, I was comfortable being a presence at school. Now, my firecracker of a daughter was stretching me into the realm of neurodivergence, and though unexpected, I was up for the challenge.

I wanted Cherish to be ready. Ready to sit in her chair, not under the table, ready to seamlessly rotate through stations, follow directions, recognize social cues from friends, and eat her lunch. To achieve these lofty goals, I partnered with her teachers and connected her occupational therapist, psychologist, teachers, and administrators to form Team Cherish. We came up with lots of strategies to keep Cherish focused. We positioned her to succeed socially and emotionally, because as long as her behavior was unmanageable, she could not learn. I was incentivized to do whatever it took to support Cherish, because her private school education was not cheap, and neither was OT or therapy.

As per the treatment plan, I regularly met with her teachers. Cherish is extrinsically motivated, so a reward system to encourage self-regulation was put in place. Ideally, earning stars or happy faces would also keep her on task. Like most schools versed in social emotional training, posters of the zones of regulation[1] were in each classroom and scattered throughout the hallway. Children were encouraged to match the size of the problem with the size of the reaction. Caregivers were also taught about these zones and asked to use the same language at home for consistency. It's a brilliantly simple chart that everyone can relate to. Everyone except children who are neurodivergent. Their arousal levels, the speed at which they process information, and their reaction time varies based upon their difference from neurotypical students. This chart should have stopped Cherish in her tracks when she overreacted to a minor slight like a friend cutting in front of her in line, but it didn't always have the desired effect. After a big reaction, she could reflect on how and why she reacted a certain way and vow to have an appropriate reaction next time. But next time, and the time after that, and the time after that, she was unable to self-regulate or think before speaking. Half a decade has passed and Cherish is still working on this skill.

At the time, I was still operating under the assumption that if she could *just* regulate, everything would be fine. I globbed on to the next suggestion, which was Cherish needed to burn energy before school to help with regulation. This required us to arrive at school a little earlier so she could go to the sensory room to jump on the small trampoline, crab walk through the hallway, jump some more, and then crash on the bean bag until it was time to line up with her class. While in class, she used a wiggle chair, because remaining on a square invited sensory issues with someone violating her bubble or something else catching her eye compelling her to move around. She had multiple fidget spinners to occupy her hands, and a list of daily tasks printed on bright pink paper taped to the upper corner of her desk. The list was supposed to reduce the number of prompts needed from the teacher and serve as a motivator to earn a reward for remaining and/or completing tasks. It was a great idea that worked sometimes, but not consistently.

I researched activities that matched Cherish's personality and high energy. I bought a trampoline off Nextdoor and signed her up for tap dance, rhythmic gymnastics, European soccer, ice skating, and T-ball. I didn't know if she would thrive in a solo sport or needed a team environment to learn how to work well with others. A friend told me about a digital subscription to classical music, using headphones with a strong neutral sound profile for an immersive listening experience. If we used it fifteen minutes per day on the ride to and from school, the soothing music would aid her self-regulation. My friend's son took to the soft sweet tones and found the music relaxing. Cherish would unplug the headphones or fall asleep before using it.

Already a helicopter mom, I morphed into a snowplow to ensure Cherish was getting her needs met. I answered every email, showed up to every parent–teacher conference, conferred with her therapists, and educated myself on ADHD and sensory processing disorder. When I finally pulled the trigger on allowing Cherish to take psychotropic medication, I pulled up an online medical dictionary to learn the types of stimulants and the differences between Adderall and Ritalin. Why would she need stimulants? How did stimulants impact her brain? What were the side effects? How long did it take to work? Would she take medication her whole life? I asked friends what their kid took and if the meds worked. I was doing my part and expecting educators to do theirs. I was crazy busy and needed Cherish to attend to her lesson, require less redirection, and stretch into a healthy social and emotional relationship with peers.

The timing of all of this life happening could not have been worse. I was writing my memoir, *Motherhood So White: A Memoir of Race, Gender, and Parenting in America*, and then traveling around the country to promote it. I leaned on my aunt and friends to take care of my kids while I was away. August had a busy schedule—baseball practice, Saturday science classes, after-school enrichment classes, and playdates. Cherish was dragged to every practice and game, and we spent hours sitting in the car waiting for him. I zigzagged all over Los Angeles, depending on others to get August to the baseball field and staring down a marathon of occupational therapy (OT) and therapy appointments for Cherish. Anything I needed to do for our home or myself, like grocery shop, get a pedicure, or walk the dogs—oh and work—I did during the school day. I was running on all cylinders with nerves on fire anticipating an email, text, or phone call about what Cherish did or did not do that day. The school treatment plan was ever evolving, and I appreciated the effort on behalf of her teachers, who truthfully, didn't stand a chance with Cherish.

At home, the treatment plan looked a little different. I took stock of my daughter's room to see how her space contributed to her ability to self-regulate. Like most little kids, she had too much shit. Too many stuffies. Too many crayons. Too many dolls. Too many toys. Cherish also had too many broken items she refused to part with in her LOL! Surprise Doll–themed, cozy but junky bedroom. All shades of pink, bold teal, and her artwork decorated the walls. Cherish also had a weighted blanket, fidgets, mood lighting, and a snuggly bodysuit to wear while she watched television or played with her dolls. The suit was stretchy and designed to tire her out so she could relax enough to fall asleep. One major side effect of the stimulant medication was that it impacted her sleep. Some nights she'd be up very late and super cranky in the morning, which set off a spiral of dysregulation, tears, and refusal to go along with the plan at home or school.

Remembering Dr. Baudino's advice, we'd use toys to clean her room. At that point, I was unaware of Cherish's short-term memory issues. I was constantly repeating myself and finally purchased a whiteboard. I hung it in her room, under her calendar, and made a short list of manageable chores:

make up bed

place dirty clothes in hamper

take a bath

In theory, the whiteboard should have been an easy go-to. She had control over placing a check mark beside, drawing a line through, or even erasing completed tasks. Cherish could earn stars, Happy Meals from McDonald's, park visits to ride the swings, and extra TV or tech time. At that time, she was into Minecraft and Subway Surfer, and craved playing video games on an iPad or phone. Instead, she would erase the list, draw flowers on the whiteboard or ignore it altogether and ask me what she needed to do. I considered giving her agency over this process and had her write out the chores list. While she liked deciding what went on the whiteboard, it did not always translate into tasks being completed without redirection. A tween, Cherish still needs encouragement to finish tasks, but I have noticed that as long as the information is there, she will follow it, just in her own time. I've learned to recognize the overall victory of chores being accomplished at some point during the day versus complaining that they aren't finished according to my timeline.

I was faithful to both treatment plans and then 2020 arrived like a tsunami. Kobe Bryant, his daughter, and others died in a helicopter crash; the COVID-19 pandemic shut the world down; Ahmaud Arbery, Breonna Taylor, and George Floyd were murdered; and remote learning was a revelation.

While I could trust August to independently log in to his middle school classes, Cherish needed all of my attention. Even during live Zooms, she needed constant reminders to keep the camera on, sit up, pay attention, stop playing with the mute button, and participate. I found that if I didn't sit next to her, she would leave the table or go outside to play. Without question, she could not sit through a thirty-minute lesson, unless it was something she was interested in. At the time, I figured her less-than-enthusiastic engagement was due to being a first grader.

When I think back on 2020 and the ugly way it outed inequities in food, housing, and education for less-resourced families, I get sad. I think about learning loss for poor and neurodivergent children and the high rates of disparity between BIPOC and white households, rural communities versus a metropolis. The remnants of the COVID slide persist half a decade later because educational resources remain separate and unequal. I even opined about this in a short article, "Distance Learning Is Leading to 'Learning Loss' in Neurodiverse Kids," written for *Parents* magazine in 2021. In the piece, I wrote about the frustration neurodivergent students experienced trying to keep up with neurotypical peers and the depression that set in for those without access to Wi-Fi. From my own front seat, the struggle was real, and we had high-speed Internet. I felt sorry for Cherish, who really tried her best but 100 percent online learning plus ADHD did not complement her learning style. Like some parents who decided to unplug or unschool, we took the "L" for first grade, hung out within our cohort, and focused on not getting COVID.

Post-pandemic, more children and adults have been diagnosed with ADHD and ASD, largely due to disruptions in assessments, identification of neurodivergence, and delays in obtaining services. There are a couple of theories as to why the numbers have skyrocketed. Home learning, work from home, and endless togetherness during points of quarantine gave parents time to really see their children in action. For some, teaching their child algebra or how to read or write or use the toilet was painful. We learned that our kids don't always follow the rules, play fair, or complete assignments when asked. We also learned that they needed frequent breaks, ate too many snacks, and zoned out when the task at hand was boring. Parents made hilarious TikTok memes about scraping "Student of the Month" stickers off rear windshields or blowing a gasket because Caleb insisted that six was the result when the grocer added five apples to three pears to determine how much fruit he had in all. I cried a river and laughed out loud at these videos because I was failing as a first and seventh grade teacher/tutor/hazmat engineer. At the start of second grade, Cherish returned to school. The in-person setting was much better for her emotional health but the setbacks from the previous semester and loss of in-person therapy sessions yielded a child who was behind socially, emotionally, and academically.

With most of the technical distractions out of the way, parents, children, and young adults have resumed getting assessed. The young people are leaning into their mental health without shame. No longer a stigma, depression, anxiety, inattentiveness, and other hallmarks of neurodivergence are gaining more airtime. With help from 4X Grand Slam Singles Champion Naomi Osaka, who made an Instagram sharing her depression, millions of young people are having themselves checked out. Not to be outdone, NFL players and other celebrities are bravely sharing battles with anxiety, depression, dyslexia, and other neurologic differences.

I learned of a friend whose son, Drew, graduated high school during the pandemic and entered college online. Having been diagnosed with ADHD in middle school, he was able to get accommodations: extra test-taking time, a quiet space, and breaks backed into his daily schedule through high school. Drew's struggles with executive functioning and being organized spilled over into college. His freshman year was fraught with feeling different. He just wasn't catching on academically or socially and didn't know what to do. Drew could be in the midst of a crowd and simultaneously zoned out, because the stimulation was too much. He was able to perform this same mask as a child visiting Disneyland, billed as the Happiest Place on Earth. He went several times as a kid and always felt overwhelmed by all of the people, the bright lights, the music jumping out at him from the bushes, and the roar from the rides. No one knew of his agitation because he was able to go within to avoid a meltdown. At nineteen years old, online learning made him feel off, so he contacted the disabled student programs and services office and requested an assessment for autism spectrum disorder. His parents were shocked and proud. They were aware of his ADHD, had talked him through tantrums and enrolled him in schools with progressive curricula that supported his neurodivergence. Learning that Drew was also autistic filled in a lot of holes and was the start of a new treatment plan for this young adult who needed way more support than they ever knew.

More than the money and COVID pandemic were the emotional and cognitive costs of raising a neurodivergent child. Every day was different, and no amount of prayer could muzzle the omnipresent second guessing: *Am I doing the right thing? Did I hire the right tutor? Therapist? Sign him up for the right sport? How can I get him to eat? How many more years will we live like this?* I have no answers to those questions because I am living it. I do know that success is nonlinear. You probably missed that important point because that language was written in invisible ink in the treatment plan and parenting handbook.

I also know that parents and caregivers spend a lot of time in our heads. We fear oversharing will bore or run off our friends with neurotypical kids or kids with fewer issues. They try but don't truly understand what we're going through. We worry about being judged by everyone who thinks we *hired the wrong tutor, enrolled them in the wrong school, were wasting money on a therapist or neurofeedback or giving them medicine*. We worry about our kids constantly, wondering if they will ever catch up physically, emotionally, academically, and socially. At all times, we carry grief and hope in our hearts, believing if we won't give up on our sweet child, no one else should either.

I Don't Like That . . . Anymore

While it is a universal rite of parenting passage to buy a Costco-sized box of Goldfish because it's the only snack our child will eat, only to learn that she no longer eats Goldfish, the stakes are different for our kids. We get alarmed because she might go an entire day without eating or drinking water, which impacts her self-regulation and snowballs into a level-five tantrum, all because she is hungry. The food situation is intense and impacts every aspect of her life and the people around her.

There are many reasons why neurodivergent children find meals challenging. A child may have misophonia, which is the urge to throttle the person chewing, pen clicking, typing, tapping, or lip smacking next to you because the sound causes a visceral reaction.[2] Misophonia is Latin for "hatred of sound" and "can trigger a fight-or-flight response"[3] in people who experience it. Ask August how many times Cherish demanded he stop smacking when he wasn't, or the times she was near tears because he was swallowing too loudly. Dinner at the Austin household used to be crunk.

For those on the autism spectrum with sensory processing disorder, the sight, smell, texture, and taste of certain foods can create an aversion. Their palate is limited and strict adherence to mealtime schedules can make the difference between a peaceful mealtime experience and an epic tantrum or shut down. In "Autism and Food Aversions: 7 Ways to Help a Picky Eater,"[4] psychologist Emily Kuschner provides a list of ways parents can encourage their autistic children to add new food to their repertoire:

> **Rule out medical problems**: check your child's physical reaction to food. If they experience stomach upset and cannot express what is happening to their body after they eat, contact your pediatrician.
>
> **Stay calm**: you may have to introduce food more than one dozen times before your child decides she likes it. If that doesn't work, don't you get frustrated. Try something else.
>
> **Take steps toward tasting**: "give the food a kiss" or mix the new with the preferred food. Trying new food can be scary.

- **Tune into textures**: the feeling of the food in the mouth is the litmus test. If its raw form is rejected, blend, puree, fry, or bake it to see if that helps.
- **Play with new food**: model tasting and enjoying new food. Try cutting into different shapes or literally make a game of playing with the food to see if your child is willing to give it a try.
- **Offer choices and control**: within parameters you set, allow them to choose which foods they want to eat. Giving control over even a portion of the meal may encourage your child to eat a balanced meal with less of a fight.
- **Be careful with rewards**: the goal is twofold: eat and eat a balanced meal. Using treats to get them to eat vegetables will not teach them why a healthy meal is necessary for their growth and development.

Finding the Right Dose

For parents who opt for psychotropic medication, finding the right dose is a doozy. Psychiatrists or pediatricians typically start with the lowest dose—ten or twenty milligrams—and go up from there. It takes about two weeks for the medicine to work at an optimal level. All the while, caregivers, the school nurse, teachers, or psychologist are on the lookout for negative side effects: sleepiness, insomnia, withdrawn affect, depression, agitation, or suicidal ideation. Barring any of those symptoms, does the medication work? Is he able to focus? Is he less aggressive? If the answer is no, then the doctor will increase the dose, or if the answer is yes, but his appetite is suppressed, stomach is upset, headaches occur, or he can't sleep, the doctor will add or take away different types of medicine. If your child can't swallow pills or your insurance won't cover the price of liquid medication, caregivers have to spend their own money. Out-of-pocket costs can run up to $800 per month. Titrating medicine takes weeks with lots of parental oversight.

Not on the Same Page

Whether it's food or medication, the other common stressor for caregivers is when everyone in the house is not on the same page. Dominque, a mother of two neurodivergent children, felt that she always compromised, while her husband, Brady, did whatever he wanted. She felt guilty about her kid's picky eating habits and accommodated all food requests, did all of the shopping, cleaned her child's room, and intervened when it came to spending because their child had no sense of money management. Her husband saw things differently. Brady was less likely to weigh in and felt Dominque babied both kids. He was always pulling up the rear on issues regarding school and home and she was perpetually frustrated with him. Tension in their house ran high.

When parents and caregivers find themselves at odds, the household is just as dysregulated as the kids. In my case, I didn't have a partner to fight with but bumped up against inconsistent accommodations and teachers who were not trained to educate children with different learning styles.

Parents and caregivers are on overload being flexible, hypervigilant, and educating ourselves about our child's neurologic difference. We keep trying and failing, going to great lengths to meet the requirements of the treatment plan, even skipping vacations because our child with ASD requires a strict schedule and trusting someone else to do it is too great a risk. Many parents miss work, as they are asked to pick up their child who has had a meltdown, hit someone, or said something racist without understanding the impact of his words. Our kid's behavior is embarrassing at times, and we apologize for actions beyond their control. Whether we admit it or not, we go through states of mourning. It's not that we don't love our child or wish for a different kid, it's the circumstances that try our souls. We know our kid is doing her best, but the world doesn't always agree with our assessment. In fact, friends, partners, and educators think we're in denial. We are not. We are just hopeful for a better tomorrow, while simultaneously mourning the young person who may grow into an adult with high support needs. Our mourning may manifest as nervousness about our son with demand avoidance who incessantly masturbates as part of his rigid attachment to an activity that is soothing. Will he ever have a girlfriend or boyfriend? What will his trajectory be?

It's a question I ask myself often since nurture did not override nature the way it had with August, who was thriving. No matter the origin of Cherish's neurodivergence, the treatment plan was supposed to course correct. The memo I missed was that the treatment plan, much like her medication, was not magic. Cherish would have to have some skin in the game. She would have to use her tools, even when it was hard or didn't seem to make a difference. It was a tall order for a racing mind and getting out in front of meltdowns took a lot of effort.

By fourth grade, I learned to manage expectations around what a successful treatment plan looked like. Even after an assessment, diagnosis, team meetings, therapeutic specialists, and meds, there was no clock or yard stick with which to accurately measure success. I like to believe that I would have spent less energy trying to force Cherish, my pit bull in a skirt, to take control of her emotions. I would have stopped tying rewards to her earning all "ones" on a daily behavior chart. If I knew any better, I would have trashed the behavior charts, recognizing how it contributed to how negatively she felt about herself. I'm not knocking behavior charts. They do work, but only for a short while.

With the help of her therapist, I recalibrated and agreed that if we could get through dinner without a tantrum or excessive silliness, that was a win. If Cherish could transition through *most* of her school activities, that was a win. These small victories were powerful but would this be enough for the long term? I rested in the power of yet, believing that in time she would learn to self-regulate and stop avoidant behavior. More importantly, she would have a chance to learn. A bright girl, Cherish was suffering in all areas. Her self-esteem was in the toilet and she didn't want to go to school. I had a couple of meetings with the head of school about moving on after fifth grade. Her current school had a rigorous middle school that required a lot of independence and initiative of the children. The workload would increase significantly and Cherish would be expected to keep up. Even though the school had counselors and a special program for kids who needed support, if Cherish couldn't get through fifth grade, the suite of counseling services they offered would not be helpful. That was a sobering conversation that made me realize that we were all wanting Cherish to fit into a mold too small to contain her curiosity, creativity, strength, and sense of humor. That wasn't fair.

Finding the right treatment plan is booby trapped with trial and error. Although designed to be an individual plan, many of the suggestions were cookie cutter and didn't factor the spectrum aspect of neurologic differences and comorbid symptoms that exacerbate a diagnosis. This is the tool kit I was working with, not knowing Cherish had a learning disability, until midway through fifth grade. Aha, I could clearly see why we had so many starts and stops, changes in the medicinal dose, changes to the brand of medication, confusing setbacks, and momentary exhilarating wins. There was no way to call it.

Therapists, parents, caregivers, and educators have to work with more than the diagnosis, otherwise a losing game of Whack-A-Mole will ensue. We have to reframe the treatment plan as one of many strategies needed to support the functionality and success of our neurodivergent children. We should trade war stories, triumphs, and failures to remind us that we are doing our best.

As more kids and adults present with neurologic differences, the current talk around neurodivergence is becoming more progressive. Advocates, millennials, and Gen Zers are pushing back against old models of normalcy. They would probably laugh at Cherish's treatment plans, knowing that her trajectory is the best version of herself. These young people don't want to be normal. They want to be themselves, without being made to feel bad that they color outside the lines. They are taking agency over their mental health and questioning clinicians who create home and school treatment plans designed to teach them to conform to a system not designed with their strengths and weaknesses in mind.

These are the headwinds for children on the autism spectrum, whose treatment plans arrive in one form: applied behavior analysis (ABA). The tenets of the ABA: antecedent, behavior, and consequence are thought to explain why a behavior is happening and uses consequences to achieve a desired outcome. Developed by O. Ivar Lovass in the 1960s, ABA therapy was conceived as a behavior modification plan using positive reinforcement rather than punitive means to change behavior in kids with ASD. Over time, ABA expanded as a 1:1 therapeutic model where the therapist worked with a child in their home or at school, helped with sensory, psychotherapy, speech, and occupational therapy.[5] Of all the treatment plans, ABA sounded straightforward with measurable outcomes. Success was achieved by breaking tasks down and rewarding progress gained through repetition like enunciating clearly or sitting properly in a chair. Although Cherish was not autistic, ABA sounded good to me. Because Cherish was extrinsically motivated, she would totally respond to earning candy and praise from adults.

Well, Drew, the young adult who had himself assessed for autism, hated ABA. He expressed feeling like he was masking or suppressing his true self to fit into society's mode of how a normal young man acted. Drew and other critics comprise a vocal segment of adults who used ABA therapy as children or young adults. The one-size-fits-all approach "felt like we were being converted to normal, similar to conversion therapy used to make LGBTQ+ youth cisgender," he said. ABA therapy's emphasis on the elimination of stimming, flapping, and forcing eye contact that was not disruptive or harmful to the child was another point of contention. "It was a lot of repetitive lessons like maintaining eye contact. As long as I'm listening, who cares if I look at you? My needs didn't matter, as long as I pleased the therapist." Currently, #ABAIsAbuse is trending on social media. These young people report having PTSD from behavior charts, public humiliation, and low self-esteem from clinicians. They think ABA therapy is an antiquated mode of treatment.

Proponents of ABA therapy cite that every insurance carrier and Medicaid cover the cost at 100 percent. For desperate parents and caregivers at the start of implementing treatment plans for their neurodivergent kids, full coverage by insurance for any therapy is hard to pass up. Also, the repetition, delayed gratification, and reward tactics train children who are nonverbal, with high support needs, use words rather than melt down for hours because they are unable to communicate that they are pain. Some agencies use an inclusive play-based approach that takes into account the individual needs of children, which is more in line with a modern version of ABA therapy.

After studying both sides of ABA therapy, I don't think it would work for Cherish in the long run. She'd be motivated at the beginning, and as soon as she figured out the clinician was trying to get her to behave in a certain way, all bets would be off. Her aversion to being told what to do would kick in and the spirited girl I know and love would stop cooperating. Speaking with Drew, Melvin (dad), and Dominique (mom) was eye-opening. I had no idea there was a raging debate about ABA therapy or that it was the mainstay for autism treatments. I also have no firsthand experience with parenting a child on the autism spectrum and write with admiration for the new wave of neurodivergent advocates who are often neurodivergent. They are forcing everyone to reconsider the linear lens of the autism spectrum. The new symbol is an inclusive wheel or pie, with each symptom listed as a slice that can be cut into subcategories that cross comorbid conditions like ADHD, dyslexia or NVLD, anxiety, learning disabilities, and depression (Figure 5.1).

Although ABA therapy is the primary treatment plan for children on the autism spectrum, services from Regional Centers and mental health agencies provide free assessments, and counseling, genetic diagnosing, and case management are available. Youth with other developmental delays are eligible too, as long as the disability is considered substantial and meets the criteria listed in whichever state a family resides. Adults on the autism spectrum are also eligible for Regional Centers, which is great for young people who age out of the foster care system or K–12 educational and psychological supports. Like everything else, it is a daunting process that can take up to one year to get approved. Melvin described the journey of getting services for Drew as a test of endurance. "We were assigned an advocate who helped us with the application. We were denied initially, even though Drew had ADHD and was on the autism spectrum." For their appeal, Melvin and Dominique were given a list of independent facilitators and told to pick one, which the Regional Center paid for. They chose Alice, who knew the right buzz words to use during the upcoming appeal. Over the course of several days, she interviewed Drew and his parents for hours, to compile a profile of Drew's needs. In order to move his case forward, Drew had to be tested for autism because the Regional Center only used their own assessments. At this point, Drew was twenty-one years old and had been assessed for ADHD, OT, learning disability, anxiety, and depression, at least a half dozen times. He was recently assessed for autism, two years prior during his freshman year in college.

While it was free to apply for Regional Center services, if a person was denied they had to pay for the appeal. Luckily, Alice found a grant to cover the cost of the appeal. Weeks went by and Drew was finally approved. As an adult, his treatment plan differed from the

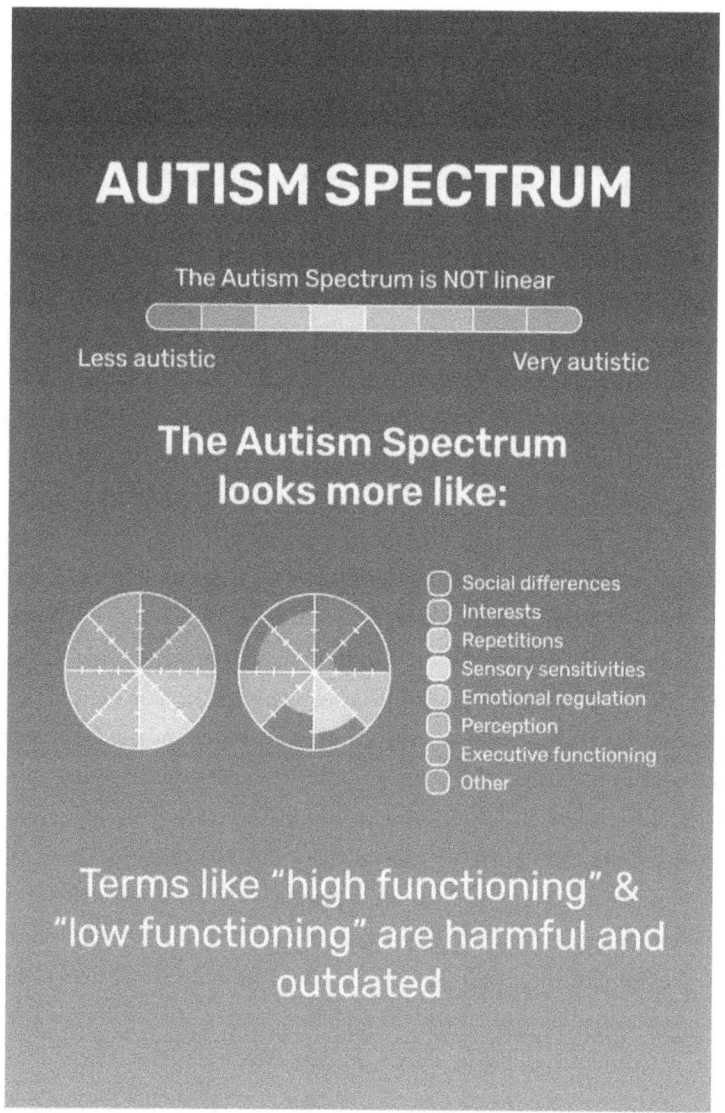

FIGURE 5.1 *The autism spectrum is more of a wheel with subcategories for specific symptoms. The size or color of each sector may be used to indicate the severity or importance of the symptom or characteristic and how they vary in severity or frequency. Source: getgoally.com.*

Table 5.1 Categories of the Autism Spectrum Wheel

Category	Description
Social Communication and Interaction	Includes symptoms such as difficulty initiating and maintaining conversations, a lack of interest in interacting with others, alongside difficulty understanding and applying nonverbal communication cues like eye contact, facial expressions, and body language.
Restricted and Repetitive Behaviors	This category includes symptoms like needing constant routines, displaying repetitive movements or behaviors, or showing intense interests in specific topics or objects.
Sensory Processing	This category includes symptoms like difficulty processing sensory inputs such as loud noises, bright lights, certain textures, difficulty regulating emotions, and challenges with self-regulation and self-care.
Cognitive and Learning Skills	This category in the autism wheel includes symptoms related to cognitive and learning abilities such as difficulty with problem-solving, memory, and attention, as well as challenges with learning new things.
Physical and Medical Needs	This category on the autism spectrum wheel includes symptoms related to physical and medical needs like challenges with self-care, sleep, and physical coordination, as well as any medical conditions or challenges related to autism.

one he had as a child. Drew had control over how best to support his neurodivergence.

The Regional Center established a Self-Determination Plan (SDP), where he picked a wide variety of activities to build life skills, improve social interactions, work on sensory issues, learn how to operate features on his smartphone, and encouraged to join a support group. Drew did not drive and received transportation vouchers for Uber and transit paid for by his state. He found a loophole to get activities like surfing, not a traditional therapeutic intervention, paid for.

As long as his or his parent's income would not pay for surfing to improve community integration or a life coach (same function as a therapist), or if the Regional Center did not offer these services, then the Regional Center would cover all costs. Here's the rub: the Regional Center used a vendor model, and some small businesses may not accept them. Or the vendor may not get paid for one month because Melvin had to request the invoice from the vendor, send it to the finance company that managed Drew's money in an account by the Regional Center, and wait for the Regional Center to pay the vendor. Easily a bureaucratic nightmare but worth it for parents and caregivers who cannot afford $300 per hour for specialists or services.

Reflection

Knowledge is power and the more information parents and caregivers have the more empowered they are to support their neurodivergent child at home and at school. Partners, parents, caregivers, and educators should have the same goal: quality, empathetic, inclusive, and age-appropriate care. Successful wraparound services from psychotherapists, pediatricians, case managers, and therapists ensure better outcomes for your child and her family. Ultimately, the treatment plan is where the rubber meets the road. Pace yourself because what works today may not work three months from now. In fact, the only way to determine if the treatment plan is working is trial and error.

Not that you asked, but here are my two cents:

Communicate, communicate, communicate.

Keep all care providers in the loop to avoid miscommunication.

Treatment plans are dynamic and should grow with your child.

Appeal a denial—do not let a "no" prevent your child from getting services.

Manage your expectations.

Be patient with your child and yourself.

There is no cure for neurodivergence.

Success is nonlinear.

6

Overcoming Stereotypes

This chapter reeks of stereotype, but it must be done.

If we are going to fully understand neurodivergence, let's move beyond stereotype and change our language. The best place to start is with the word *disorder*. Children and adults who are neurodivergent do not have a disorder—as in, their brains are not broken. Rather, they have a different lens through which they view the world. A neurotypical person may zone in on the face in front of them, taking note of expression, eye color, and tone, and are able to carry out directions immediately. A neurodivergent person may miss the face before her because the lush green trees in the distance are shimmering, the honking car is straining her ears, the boy crunching chips is making her see red, and now her tummy is rumbling because she realizes she has not eaten anything. She missed the initial conversation, and it may seem like she was ignoring you, being defiant when she did not respond, or doesn't care that you were speaking to her. Actually, when you called her name, all five of her senses responded and you need to repeat what you said. You might even have to come closer and say it a third time before your words fully register. Neurodivergence is a different way of processing information, not an indicator of intellect.

Now that we've stopped using the *d*-word, consider how age and gender continue to be cornerstones of a psychological diagnosis, even when we know that girls, Black, and Latine children experience delays or go underdiagnosed for longer periods of time. Why is the mental health of white boys prioritized over everyone else? Researchers at the Child Mind Institute report that "the framework for ASD evaluations relies heavily on research that's historically used white middle-class kids as their subjects, making it more difficult for clinicians to detect symptoms of autism in Black children."[1] Not all pediatricians are trained to identify autism spectrum disorder (ASD), attention-deficit/hyperactivity disorder (ADHD), dyslexia, or nonverbal learning disability (NVLD) and miss it. Some clinicians see developmental lags as short term, trusting that with time or PT, she will catch up. This was the approach our pediatrician used when she first met Cherish. Her advice worked out for us and Cherish eventually hit all of her developmental markers. I am mindful that that is not everyone's experience. Or they misdiagnose children, relying on persistently biased medical research that has limited information for how psychological issues present in marginalized groups. For those who are assigned female at birth, are poor, and members of the Black, Latine, LGBTQ+, and/or APIDA community, racism in healthcare detrimentally affects their outcomes, regardless of educational attainment or socioeconomic level. When it comes to mental health, it is disheartening that sexism and racism *still* infiltrate data needed to support all neurodivergent children.

For the purposes of this chapter, I'll focus on how stereotypes disadvantage children with ADHD, ASD, dyslexia, and those who identify as LGBTQ+.

ADHD

A well-meaning teacher told a dad that his son had severe ADHD. Come again? The father was unaware that ADHD comes in three flavors: inattentive, hyperactive/impulsive, or combined, not severe.

He did not know that the teacher was speaking out of turn. She did not know what she was talking about and made the father feel bad. Instinctively, he felt like his child was hopeless and would always have behavior issues because there didn't seem to be a comeback from *your child has severe ADHD.*

Educators reading this book, think before you speak. Consider the impact of your words, especially to a vulnerable, stressed-out parent of a neurodivergent child. While your intention is pure, your words have meaning and will seep into a parent's soul, take root, and spend days, weeks, months, and years germinating. Every now and then, a parent will flashback to an offhand remark you made or the time you spoke with authority you did not have. He will think long and hard about how you lost credibility with him. Soon, he will shake your words off, though they will rise to the surface every time he sees your face or hears your name. Forever, he will wonder how many other parents you made feel small with your unnecessary or incorrect statements. Parents have feelings, too.

On the ADHD spectrum, certain behaviors are persistently associated with cisgender stereotypes. A child who is bouncing off the walls—think: boy—will obviously get more attention. Not only is the child's gender under observation but so is his race. Therefore, teachers, school police, staff, and school psychologists, unaware of their own unconscious bias, will form an opinion and treat the child accordingly. If he is white, he will likely receive grace for unruly behavior in school and society because educators will be dismissive— he's just being a boy. Boys are active, rambunctious, risk-takers, and filled with energy. Mixed-race and adoptive parents need to keep an eye on this, because mistreatment by educators directly impacts how Black and Latine boys feel about their academic ability and their place in the educational system. Racism in education is widely documented, so I won't riff on that here, but will add that as I write these words, it is Election Day 2024. One of the candidates has been found guilty of thirty-two felonies and is still at the top of his party's ticket. If that's not white male privilege, I don't know what is.

The second reaction by educators to "boy" behavior is less nuanced. A punitive or authoritarian approach is often taken when a Black boy is unable to sit still, shout out the answers instead of raising his hand, or plays too rough. He is deemed uncooperative, out of control, aggressive, or disruptive. He will experience in-school suspension, be remanded to the counselor or principal's office for most of the school day, or face actual suspension for one to three days. Missing instruction and structure means learning loss, which will render him (further) behind in his studies and negatively impact his reentry to school. He may be teased or embarrassed and act out, thus repeating a vicious punitive cycle. This is often the scenario for Black boys in public and private schools, who are perceived as inherently bad, as opposed to playfully mischievous. The US Department of Education Office for Civil Rights posted a study in 2021 citing "recent national data for the United States show that Black boys account for 7.7 percent of total public school enrollment but receive 20.1 percent of in-school suspensions and 24.9 percent of out-of-school suspensions. In contrast, White boys account for 24.4 percent of public school enrollment and receive only 28.7 percent of in-school suspensions and 24.9 percent of out-of-school suspensions."[2]

This data mirrors a scenario with Dierdre, whose kindergartener kept getting in trouble. Christopher was the cutest little chocolate drop you've ever seen. He made fast friends and loved school. Shortly into the school year, Dierdre and her husband, Michael, began getting emails about his behavior. He didn't want to come in from recess, broke crayons, and didn't respond to redirection. Christopher had been sent to the assistant principal's office multiple times, had to sit during physical education (PE), lost choice time, and the teachers wanted a conference. This went on for months, including insinuations that there was trouble at home. Finally, Dierdre shared her concerns with a friend who suggested she have Christopher tested for ADHD.

His symptoms fit a possible diagnosis and would explain his inability to self-regulate. At first, Michael was opposed to the idea. He felt the teacher was singling their son out for age-appropriate six-year-old behavior. "It looks different when Christopher pushes a kid off the monkey bars," he told his wife. Dierdre agreed but pressed him on being open to determining if something else was afoot. They tried behavior modification techniques using a reward system. They changed his diet, thinking he needed more protein and fewer gummies, and limited the amount of technology he consumed. Weeks passed, and Christopher started to worry about getting in trouble at school. *He felt like he was being blamed for everything, even when it wasn't his fault. I felt so bad for my son.* Once again, Dierdre broached the subject of a neurologic assessment with her husband, reminding him that their older child had ADHD, making the likelihood of Christopher being neurodivergent high. Michael relented. Christopher was eventually diagnosed with ADHD and his symptoms placed him on the hyperactive/impulsive part of the spectrum. Relieved to know that their son wasn't "bad," like the teachers made them believe, they were able to make informed decisions about how to support their child.

Christopher falls into the more stereotypical category of children on the ADHD spectrum. But what about girls? Girls who are quiet, withdrawn, or prone to daydreaming may also be in trouble. While she poses no trouble to others, her inner struggles are missed by parents, caregivers, and educators. She may be an adult before she understands that her disorganization, inability to keep track of her lunch bag, and poor working memory were a result of inattentive type ADHD. According to the Centers for Disease Control and Prevention, "only 6% of girls ages 3 to 17 are diagnosed with ADHD, compared to 13% of boys in that age group.... Girls also are diagnosed an average of five years later in life than boys."[3]

While she waits to be diagnosed, she goes along with being labeled "space cadet" by friends and family and pretends that she doesn't mind that she's considered flaky or unreliable. Or she masks her neurologic difference with perfectionism. She stays up to all hours of the night completing homework, not because she loves school but because she has to reread the material over and over to understand and retain the material on the page. On the surface, she may appear accomplished and well adjusted but is actually great at compensating for her deficits. Masking will go on until puberty when her hormones destroy her carefully constructed house of cards, sending her into free fall. Suddenly, she can't keep up in school and is engaging in out-of-character risky behaviors. Or she'll survive to reach college, only to have picked up cutting, vaping, or other self-soothing techniques to get through the day. The point I'm making is, at some point, the wheels will fall off. The consequences are that

> [m]any women with ADHD can drown in internal and external shame and criticism, frustrated by their inability to be on time, control their emotions, or refrain from interrupting. It follows, then, that women with ADHD are at higher risk for anxiety and depression, self-harm, and eating disorders, research shows. One Canadian study found that one in four women with ADHD have attempted suicide.[4]

Similarly, the *Diagnostic and Statistical Manual of Mental Disorders*, fifth edition (*DSM-V*) defines ADHD as "a persistent form of inattention and/or hyperactivity impulsivity." The *DSM-V*, authored by the American Psychiatric Association, is filled with definitions and symptoms used by clinicians to diagnose and treat neurodivergence and other mental health issues. Although *DSM-V* is not widely used anymore, as the updated *DSM-VI* was published in June 2024, the belief that boys are hyperactive and girls are not remains a staple in mainstream consciousness, thereby delaying assessments and treatments for girls.

We cannot allow bias in research favoring earlier mental health assessments of boys at the expense of our daughters.

ASD

Across the board, girls are underdiagnosed for neurologic differences and their executive functioning ability is delayed. The pink or blue brain dichotomy with its rigid developmental and behavioral categories does not reflect the rich complexity of brains that processes information on a spectrum. In 2002, psychologist Simon Baron-Cohen proposed that "ASD can be seen as an extreme form of the male brain, which is better at systemising and understanding how things work than the female brain."[5] I don't even know what this means, but it sounds like an excuse to study boys over girls.

In the ASD community, mental health advocates have taken to TikTok and Instagram to dismantle myths, revising what the spectrum of autism actually looks like, and examining popular but outdated treatment plans. Starting with the reference to neurodivergence as a superpower, they are clapping back on the idea that all persons on the autism spectrum have an innate ability to leap over tall buildings or figure out the theory of relativity. This "Rain Man" stereotype is akin to the Model Minority and puts immense pressure on children to perform or emerge from their silence or whirling dervishes or inability to read social cues to do something incredible like using the laws of physics to decipher the theory of relativity. The superpower trope dismisses real symptoms, ignores the varied subcategories and comorbid conditions of those on the autism spectrum, and forces kids into two groups: savant or tragic. Per usual, society is focused on helping neurotypical people feel comfortable with and around neurodivergent people.

On the other hand, I understand the tendency to lean into a *super* version of supporting our kids. Fair enough, neurodivergence gives some children extraordinary focus to practice a skill for hours on end or notice details neurotypical kids may miss. However, this same intensity may be at the detriment of other tasks like eating or sleeping or cleaning up. As parents and caregivers, we hurt when our kids are teased or ostracized. We look for ways to affirm them, whether it's prowess on the field, insane test scores, or chess impresarios. We want them to have a healthy self-esteem and point to the accomplishments of Olympian Michael Phelps, who learned to work within his anxiety, depression, and ADHD to become the most decorated swimmer of all time. We sing along to Grammy winner Billie Eilish whose Tourette's cannot be heard in the sweet lyrics she sings. Even socialite and media personality Paris Hilton released "ADHD," a song celebrating her neurodivergence, in October 2024. She sings of her superpower being inside of her all along and accepting that ADHD is who she is. We tell ourselves and our children they too have a special ability. We do it to make sense of the world for them and us. The balance is to not get so wrapped up in attributing skills that only a fraction of the world's population possess that we delay having our child assessed and getting an effective treatment plan.

Young adults with ASD are learning to work within the confines of society and still be themselves. Their fierce determination against old models of therapy, stereotype, and language is moving the needle forward for the entire neurodivergent community and its allies. This is great news as the new descriptors are more inclusive and realistic.

Here is a cheat sheet to help you keep up with evolving language around ASD. Although relevant and meaningful today, some of the new terms may be passé by the publication of this book.

Asperger's. First called Asperger's syndrome then shortened to Asperger's in honor of the work of Dr. Hans Asperger who first observed the spectrum aspect of autism in children. The term eventually fell out of favor because Asperger, who worked with the Nazis during World War II, described some of the children on the autistic spectrum as "worthless," leading to them being euthanized for the sake of racial purity.[6] The Asperger's label was retired in 2013.

High-functioning autistic. The use of the word "functioning" suggests that support is not needed. Even a person who is independent in a couple of areas may struggle with social interactions or in other areas. The new reference is "Level 1 ASD" or "low support needs."

Low-functioning autistic. In this instance, "low" is considered an outdated term because it doesn't offer a holistic view of children with ASD. It lumps them into one group without accounting for areas of strength. Try "high support needs" instead.

Masking. A coping strategy used by people with ASD to appear neurotypical.

The reframing of autism spectrum disorder takes the stereotype and fetishizing out of the equation, allowing children to be seen and treated with dignity.

Dyslexia

I'll lead with the myth that dyslexia is not a disability. It actually is. Dyslexia is a language-based learning difference caused by a phonological processing issue in the brain. Stereotypes around dyslexia include the belief that a child who writes his letters backward or has bad handwriting has dyslexia; it is a vision problem that eyeglasses will fix; it's a form of laziness; dyslexia is easily caught by teachers trained in structured literacy; and my favorite, a child cannot be gifted and dyslexic. It is thought that boys are more likely to be dyslexic than girls. Going back to gendered neurological differences, the reason boys are diagnosed with dyslexia at higher rates than girls is a matter of behavior. In lower elementary school, a boy who is frustrated by an assignment may be loud and unruly or quietly hide behind his more outgoing classmates with the hope that the teacher has forgotten about him. That is a tried and tested strategy children use because teachers are frequently distracted by the other children and miss the shy boy in the back. Eventually, someone notices and has him assessed to determine what is causing the negative or overtly shy behavior and the poor grades. In the same scenario, a girl who is frustrated by an assignment may act in—struggle quietly and slip under the radar—because she is not being disruptive. Her dyslexia will go undiagnosed until she is older.[7]

As I mentioned at the beginning of this chapter, BIPOC children experience delays in assessments or are misdiagnosed because of racial bias in science and education. Dyslexia, like ADHD and ASD, presents on a spectrum, and early on kids learn to mask symptoms or act out in exasperation. The child's behavior or lack of development is often the driving motivator for parents to seek assessments, but a child's race can be a hindrance to care, because our society is still playing catch up at the intersection of race and mental health. We make assumptions about who gets to be neurodivergent, who is entitled to interventions, and fail to give Black and Latine males the benefit of the doubt. The consequences of illiteracy are dire, and this demographic is prone to drop out of middle and high school and have a history of behavior problems inside and outside academic environments, reduced employment opportunities, poverty, and criminal behavior.[8]

In a 2021 study of inmates in two maximum-security prisons in Louisiana, "almost half (47%) of the participants are classified as having dyslexia, 36% proficient, and 17% cognitive impairment."[9] These adults were diagnosed in prison and had experienced behavior challenges as youth and didn't finish high school, even when they were enrolled in special education and received accommodations.[10] These numbers cut across race and gender.

The other pervasive myth about dyslexia is that it will not occur if a developmental disability is present. We know that comorbid issues are the norm among neurodivergent children, and it is possible to have ASD and be dyslexic. In fact, according to a white paper about dyslexia prepared by the Consortium on Reaching Excellence in California (CORE), "about 12–24% of students classified as dyslexic also have ADHD/ADD. Interestingly, about 25–35% of students characterized with ADHD/ADD also have dyslexia."[11]

NVLD

While NVLD is not an official diagnosis, it is a real issue that mostly goes undetected. This lack of awareness spurred Laura Lemle into action. She founded the NVLD Project[12] when she noticed that neither special education nor mainstream environments were able to support her daughter. Lemle's nonprofit seeks to raise the profile of NVLD and have it recognized in the *Diagnostic and Statistical Manual of Mental Disorders*, fifth edition (*DSM V-TR*), used by psychiatrists and psychologists who diagnose neurodivergence and different learning styles.

Signs of NVLD include a child who read easily in first or second grade but may have trouble extrapolating the main idea of a passage in middle or high school. They may be unable to line up columns on a page, "run in the wrong direction during a soccer game. They may have trouble packing their backpacks, creating Lego structures, or trouble gauging when it is safe to cross the street."[13] Children across the neurodivergent spectrum may have NVLD but not know it because it mimics ASD, ADHD, and other barriers to learning. NVLD presents physically, psychosocially, and academically and may look like:

- physical awkwardness
- possess excellent memory
- missed social cues
- difficulty with word problems in math
- high verbal skills (think Chris Rock)
- messy handwriting
- concrete thinking
- problems with peer relationships

There are more symptoms, but the overlap with other diagnoses is clear and, currently, there is no designated accommodation because NVLD is not included in the *DSM*. If, however, the child has a different diagnosis, say ASD or dyslexia or ADHD, her accommodations can be expanded to include support for the NVLD symptoms. Parents are hoping that the new spotlight on NVLD will move the needle forward so that this rare learning difference gets the formal support it needs.

At the Intersection of Gender Identification and Neurodivergence

In our binary thinking, it is easier to consider things as either/or, because trying to grasp both/and concepts is too much to hold in our black-and-white-thinking brains. That's why people love discrete boxes. Having a neurodivergent child, however, will disabuse parents of relying on boxes to sort things out. Our kids have a neurologic difference or two-plus co-occurring issues: a learning disability or depression. Other times, it is the overlap of ADHD with dyslexia or NVLD. The list fluctuates as they reach puberty and college. With tools, they learn to self-regulate but being organized remains a challenge for years. Our kids have much to navigate, including gender identification beyond cisgender norms of male or female. "Neurodivergence is more common in the LGBTQ+ community than it is among cisgender, heterosexual people. Why is that? Researchers theorize that, as neurodivergent people are less likely to adapt to social norms, they are more likely to question and explore their gender and/or sexual identities."[14] Again, props to the millennials and Gen Zers who are coming of age at a time when owning their truest most authentic selves is a source of pride, not shame.

When it comes to mental health, the intersection of gender identification and neurodivergence isn't discussed enough. Some parents think their child who has ASD and uses pronouns "they/them" are going through a phase. Caregivers can be carelessly dismissive, because they are focused on the exigent mental health issue. Or having a gay child offends their religion, class status, or personal values. Parents don't know what to do with that information because gender identification and sexual orientation are not listed on the treatment plan that parents and educators rely on. This is a drawback of treatment plans that prioritize neurodivergence on a linear plane and ignores the strain of a child assigned female at birth (AFAB) but is actually a he. The stereotype that neurodivergence is more important than a child's simultaneous exploration of their gender identity creates internal stress and conflict, which will impact the family dynamic. For instance, a teen with ASD, who relies on a rigid schedule for self-regulation, is at odds with themselves for knowing their blue brain doesn't fit their pink body. This is a both/and scenario where rigidity meets fluidity. Given that scenario, "autistic people are more likely to be transgender,"[15] and a holistic support approach is best. Those with ADHD "may also be more common in transgender individuals compared to cisgender individuals,"[16] raising the need to understand the psychosocial and psychological needs of kids who are gender-diverse and neurodivergent.

Externally, some LGBTQ+ youth encounter rejection and violence from mainstream members of society who hate them because they do not understand them. This is called "minority stress," coined by Ilan H. Meyer, PhD,[17] Williams Distinguished Senior Scholar of Public Policy at the Williams Institute and Professor Emeritus of Sociomedical Sciences at Columbia University. Minority stress theory looks at the ways distinct social stressors related to prejudice and discrimination impact the physical health of LGBTQ+ people.[18] Even the adoption of pronouns—he/him/his, she/her/hers, they/them/theirs, zie/zir/zirs—can be a significant source of stress for those who feel marginalized when society writ large doesn't reflect these personal identifiers. This is a lot to navigate for a young person on top of being neurodivergent. Being gender-diverse and neurologically divergent is not curable but a child's path can be much smoother with love and acknowledgment from caregivers, educators, and clinicians.

Step-Down in Services

The last stereotype I will tackle for this chapter is equity and access. It is a myth and a disservice to believe that poor and/or underinsured children do not deserve quality mental health services. I watched it unfold in real time when I switched from paying for psychotherapeutic services to receiving them for free. My good friends at Amex allowed me to run up a significant bill, paying out-of-pocket for treatment modalities for Cherish. While I appreciated their generosity, I'll probably be paying them back until she starts college. I finally called UCLA Ties for Families. As an adoptive parent, I had access to free psychological, psychiatric, and medical services. Why didn't I contact them when Cherish was first diagnosed, you ask? Well, I forgot about the nine hours of training I completed way back in 2007 to become a Ties family. August hadn't needed any services until he was thirteen years old and feeling anxious about citywide curfews during the COVID-19 pandemic. Honestly, it didn't cross my mind until my Amex bill was through the roof. Then, when I remembered I had Ties certification, I didn't want to wait for free services, because Cherish needed help pronto. Having worked in the nonprofit space at a shelter for survivors of domestic violence, I knew what free meant. Free meant a wait list. The wait lists at the free clinic could be six months or more. And, after the pandemic, trying to get assigned a therapist was a two-year odyssey. Two years was a long time in the life of a neurodivergent child. Free also meant dealing with a gatekeeper who was tasked with setting up appointments and completing intake but who didn't fully understand the forms they were creating on my child's behalf. Free meant a clinician who may or may not be culturally competent or empathetic to the needs of Black children. Free meant an overworked, underpaid clinician who didn't have time to form a bond with our family. Having a safe, intimate relationship with a care provider was important, and I didn't want Cherish to be written off because she was Black and a former foster child.

Given how Cherish was struggling in kindergarten and first grade, time was of the essence. Her inability to self-regulate, escalating tantrums, and need to be redirected by not one but two teachers and an aide required an immediate intervention. When I finally made the call to Ties, the heavens opened. There was no wait. Cherish was assigned to a clinician who was a postdoctoral student in psychiatry. Her new therapist was also a medical doctor, so we were double lucky to have a doctor's doctor as her therapist. The weekly sessions were great, and my only complaint was that, each year, Cherish would receive a new therapist. UCLA Ties for Families was housed at my alma mater, the University of California, Los Angeles, offering training rotations for graduate and postgraduate students needing to complete hours for their advanced degrees in psychology and psychiatry. It's an amazing program, but the looming uncertainty of a new therapist was hard on Cherish. In the early days with the new clinician, she would not speak. Sometimes she would sleep or play with toys and ignore them completely. On occasion, I'd have to join the sessions to put everyone at ease. Once I learned that she could be assigned to one of the few full-time psychologists, I signed up. It took, you guessed it, two years, to finally have a permanent therapist. Cherish did not initially speak to Dr. Toni, which was annoying. I thought about the time and every step we had taken to get a permanent therapist, and she refused to engage. Thankfully, Dr. Toni was persistent. She eventually wore Cherish down and they developed a great rapport.

The other change to Cherish's mental health services was free OT. The first thing I noticed was the disparity between the length of the free sessions versus when I was a paying customer. Instead of one full hour with a debrief from the occupational therapist, Cherish spent twenty-five minutes in the small gym and was then sent on her way. Multiple weekly sessions were not an option, either. Free OT had fewer manipulatives—one giant ball, one swing, fewer blocks, fewer mats, and more people. In the ten-foot-by-twenty-foot room, there would be another child working with a different therapist. Each child was receiving a set of directions and expected to not be distracted by the other people in the room. For a child who was easily distracted, sharing close quarters during therapy was not optimum. We ran into the same situation with rotating clinicians, which was, once again, unsettling for Cherish. Every quarter, she received a progress report. Actually, it was a short checklist of the skills she was working on, where she started, and if she had satisfied the goal. I could forget about receiving a narrative and would have to make separate phone appointments if I wanted more information. At half the pace of paid OT, it didn't seem possible that Cherish would ever reach the benchmarks. Although we stuck it out for three years and signed up again after fifth grade, I am certain that she would have made more progress if OT lasted one hour per week with a dedicated therapist.

As an adoptive parent, I was grateful to receive free health insurance for both of my children, as there was no way I could have afforded $1,200 per month to carry both of them on my plan. That said, what became glaringly obvious was how services through Medi-Cal felt like a step-down in care. I'm not knocking physicians, dentists, psychologists, or other health professions who accept Medi-Cal. They are dedicated to the health of all children, and I am grateful. My gripe is that the California Department of Health Care Services (DHCS), which sets fee rates for Medi-Cal health insurance, doesn't think poor, underserved, foster, or adopted children deserve top-notch care.

Geographically, patients are automatically directed to under-resourced areas, as if adoption and foster care only happen in east or South Los Angeles. Other issues were ridiculous wait times to see a pediatrician or dentist that could last an hour. There were language barriers, and the race and culture of the clinicians did not always match the clientele. Essentially, access to care was available but equitable care was not. I love my state but "[w]e rank in the lowest 10% of states for providing critical early behavioral, social, and developmental screenings, and 48th in the nation in access to mental health services for children."[19] So embarrassing.

Children, whether or not their families have means, need access to quality mental health care. The current separate but unequal delivery of mental health services for some children, who are denied substantive services because they live in the wrong zip codes or their insurance won't cover it, is an injustice. As neurodivergence intersects with all races, religions, gender identifications, and socioeconomics, successful outcomes are achieved by early screening and appropriate treatment for all.

Reflection

Solely relying on age and gender are outdated modes of assessments and prove detrimental to girls as they grow through adolescence and adulthood. Caregivers should feel empowered to ask for screenings and not allow clinicians to take a wait-and-see approach with their daughter, because the shy, perfectly behaved student might actually be struggling mightily and need adult intervention to catch her before she falls. Similarly, Black children deserve the same grace white children receive when it comes to determining whether neurodivergence is the cause of unexpected behavior in school or at home. Racism is rampant in this space too, so caregivers of BIPOC children must keep their head on a swivel to call out mistreatment of their kids.

Minority stress is actually not minor. Environmental stressors for neurodivergent LGBTQ+ youth can exacerbate a child's behavior or cause them to mask symptoms for fear of harm or rejection from family and peers. Clinicians, educators, and parents must use affirming language and acceptance of how the child identifies on par with attention paid to their mental health diagnosis. Already marginalized, they should feel safe discussing whether their gender identity matches their assigned birth and be free to explore when it does not. Easier said than done, but leaning into our children's complex inner lives may save their lives.

Finally, language is important when discussing neurodivergence. Educating yourself and staying up on trends with ASD and other neurological differences will ensure that your child is receiving appropriate care and culturally respectful treatment from caregivers, educators, and clinicians. We are their first line of defense and must make it our business to dismantle stereotypes, gender bias, and racism when we see them.

Not that you asked, but here are my two cents:

Boys and girls experience mental illness at around the same rate.

Neurodivergent social media influencers are worth following.

Dyslexia is a disability.

Neurodivergent LGBTQ+ children have unique needs.

Have ears that hear what they have to say.

7

Comorbid Symptoms in Neurodivergence

Even when parents and caregivers suspect a difference in their child, we are surprised when the diagnosis has an *and* after it. ADHD *and* sensory processing disorder; dyslexia *and* ADHD inattentive type; ASD *and* dyslexia. These combinations make sense, as one or more symptoms from each neurologic difference triggered an assessment then a treatment plan. It is the added seasoning of depression, absence seizure, anxiety, sleep disorders, mood disorders, Tourette's syndrome, obsessive-compulsive disorders (OCD), oppositional defiance disorder (ODD), and so on that rock our world. The overlap of co-occurring symptoms is unique to each child, effectively expanding her specific neurological profile.

Our kids are under a tremendous amount of pressure to self-regulate, process speech and language, tolerate all textures, immediately respond to directions, control their bodies, filter external stimulation, read social cues, be a good friend, recognize faces, and read, write, and perform numeric equations by a certain age. This is a big ask for neurotypical children, let alone our unique kids. Acknowledging that comorbid challenges exist and intersect with all aspects of neurodivergence will make or break our kids, whose everyday functionality, academic success, and social and emotional relationships depend on all of these pieces being addressed when they arise.

For Cherish, managing her behavior was the top assignment. As long as she was turning cartwheels, eloping from class, or having epic tantrums, we would get nowhere. No learning could take place, and she was down on herself for disrupting the group. She also struggled with friendships, having bumped into fourth-grade mean girls who ran circles around her understanding of social cues. It was rough. She chewed on fingernails, cuticles, and toenails and needed to keep her hands busy. I'm not sure when the word *anxiety* was introduced into the mix, but it made sense. Cherish was anxious about going to school, anxious about who she would sit with at lunch, anxious about being able to understand directions, anxious that her teacher did not like her. The anxiety set fuel to her ADHD, making her easily aroused and hard to reason with, once she lost control of her emotions. The gloves would be off and everything was a ten on the social emotional scale of one to five. Or Cherish would be in tears. So sad. Wishing she was home. Wishing she didn't have ADHD. Wishing she was normal.

These feelings began to bubble up around age nine and set the tone for her academic and home environment for months. They forced many conversations with her therapist, teachers, and psychiatrist. Her meds were titrated up and then down, she had sessions with the school counselor, and her treatment plan was augmented to include anxiety, depression, sleeplessness, and mood changes. Up until this point, I was focused on executive functioning strategies with being organized, helping her to use her breath to self-regulate, and making sure her accommodations for more time on tests and chunked assignments were in place. I did not understand how her comorbid challenges were constantly upending any progress she made. I wasn't putting all of the pieces together though she was falling apart before my eyes. Her self-esteem was on a negative trajectory, group dynamics were stressful, and she was seen as and saw herself as *bad*, but all the while she wanted healthy relationships with peers and teachers. Cherish couldn't get there on her own and now I know why.

Parents and clinicians must resist the urge to focus on one neurologic difference, as neurodivergence does not happen in a vacuum. It's never just one thing. A child with dyslexia who has learned to work with her unique processing ability will not suddenly be able to sit still, if she has comorbid impulsive ADHD. It is easy to think otherwise because some clinicians zero in on the big print—ASD, dyslexia, and so forth—and craft a treatment plan accordingly. Everyone is working off a playbook that may casually reference anxiety or depression, but the emphasis is on the most common neurological difference. Educators and caregivers have an artificial sense of *I got this* and set about implementing accommodations, reward systems, or enrolling kids in extracurricular activities based on an incomplete diagnosis. When our kids don't positively respond to the shiny new treatment plan, their unexpected behavior leads to labeling: *apathetic, lazy, defiant,* and *aggressive.* Parents of Black and Latine children can count on seeing the latter two adjectives used to justify negative consequences about their child in school and the world at large. The child has done nothing wrong but be her best self. The problem is the emphasis on one neurological difference, which inadvertently ignores the comorbid issues that underscore the unexpected behavior. Frustrated and disappointed, kids are told:

You're not trying.
You're not using your tools.
You're seeking attention.
You're overreacting, again.

I can't tell you the number of times I've apologized to Cherish for making those statements.

Missed comorbid cues or dismissive advice that tantrums will stop leads to misdiagnosis or undertreatment. There is a common saying: you don't know what you don't know. Caregivers should take comfort in this aphorism and not kick ourselves for not recognizing symptoms that are now obvious. We didn't expect to have a neurodivergent child, were unprepared for what that meant, felt bad for our child and ourselves. In some instances, the caregivers are neurodivergent and perceived their child's behavior as normal. Some of us were in denial. Others believed that kids were just trying to get out of doing an assignment or chore. Usually, we didn't know which questions to ask and generally accepted the diagnosis given by the pediatrician or psychologist. Afterall, they are the experts. But even clinicians and counselors get it wrong, because co-occurring symptoms will not be denied. Your child will let you know how they *really* feel by externalizing behaviors (e.g., impulsivity, hyperactivity, aggression, conduct problems, and/or antisocial features) or through internalizing behaviors (e.g., withdrawal, dysphoria, and anxiety).[1]

Although kids outgrow some behaviors (lying, stealing), comorbidity affects all aspects of a person's life. In the short term, it might be easier to put out one fire at a time. The problem is that the fire never dies because the specific box your child has been placed in is too restrictive to contain the other deficits. These deficits "might impair various areas or domains of the individual's development and functioning and the person's overall quality of life since they negatively affect almost every aspect of their development and functionality on a personal, academic, social, and professional level."[2] It follows them into adulthood and manifests as antisocial and/or criminal behavior. Employment may be hard to sustain and self-medicating with cigarettes, vaping, marijuana, and other risky behaviors may overwhelm their ability to manage their neurodivergence. If kids transition to adolescence and adulthood without proper interventions, they will get stuck in a loop of discontent and be confused about why no one (even family members) wants to be bothered with them.

Anxiety and Depression

Given this chapter's focus on comorbid challenges for neurodivergent youth, it is useful to think about how anxiety and depression impact our Gen Z teens. According to the Pew Research Center, they are known as the most anxious generation with "70% of teenagers across genders, races and socioeconomic status report[ing] anxiety and depression as major problems among their peers."[3] Depending on their socioeconomic status, they worry about food insecurity, housing, academics, and the planet. Look no further than environmental activist Greta Thunberg, who coincidentally has ASD and has fearlessly lobbied political heads of states about the destruction caused by man-made climate change. She is not the only one worried about rising sea levels, clean air, or food insecurity. Gen Z laments a world that may not be safe for them or future generations, which adds to their anxiety.

Gen Z has contended with a myriad of issues pre- and post-COVID-19 pandemic and the racial reckoning of 2020. Born with a phone in their hand, they were raised on their parents' Facebook pages and segued into their own self-stardom with the invention of Instagram, Snapchat, YouTube, and other visual media. Communication is typically meted out over text or direct messages (DMs), removing the need to make eye contact, modulate tone, or learn how to shake hands. These outdated conventions of socializing have led to isolation, loneliness, and, ironically, an addiction to others, even strangers, via twenty-four-seven connectedness. Locked in a losing battle for perfection, likes, and "going viral" to achieve celebrity status, many young people get stuck in an algorithm that nourishes a negative self-image, fear of missing out (FOMO), and vulnerability to Internet predators. Despite concerns about social media, it isn't going anywhere. A 2023 Pew Research survey determined that girls, more so than boys, are likely to *constantly* use TikTok (22 percent versus

12 percent) and Snapchat (17 percent versus 12 percent),[4] while boys ranked higher with gaming, although YouTube dominates viewing by teens of all gender, races, and socioeconomic levels.

Social media has its upside, though. For LGBTQ+ teens and the neurodivergent seeking community, social media provides access and a lifeline for those who are marginalized. Connections are more easily made because the relationship is virtual and avoids in-person awkwardness and small talk. Children and teens can feel more accepted in these affinity spaces than in their families, communities, or school environments. Young people can use their voice to praise or condemn political policies, school practices like uniform requirements, hairstyles for textured hair, promote music, make-up, compare notes on therapies in real time, and show off their creativity. Anybody can start a business with free advertisement, and information can reach anywhere there is Wi-Fi. The caveat is that social media needs to be managed by parents and digital literacy should be taught early. Used responsibly, social media can be a fun outlet.

With so much life coming at them, anxiety is easy to miss. This is especially true for kids with a comorbid ADHD diagnosis and/or those who have lots of phobias. It may be irrational to an adult to be afraid of the dark at age eleven, but nyctophobia is a real condition for many adults, too. Phobias don't politely announce themselves. Kids may shake, tremble, get angry, scream, or take off running. If you mention the word *spider* to Cherish, she's out the door. It doesn't matter that the spider didn't do anything to her or is the size of her pinky fingernail. All she knows is that there is a spider in her bedroom, and she is not returning until it is gone.

Asking a tween or teen who is bouncing off the walls if he is anxious may or may not yield a truthful answer. They may not be able to process what you are asking because that is a big vague question. Try an open-ended question like, *What worries you?* to drill down on one or many issues the child is ruminating over. Your clinician can

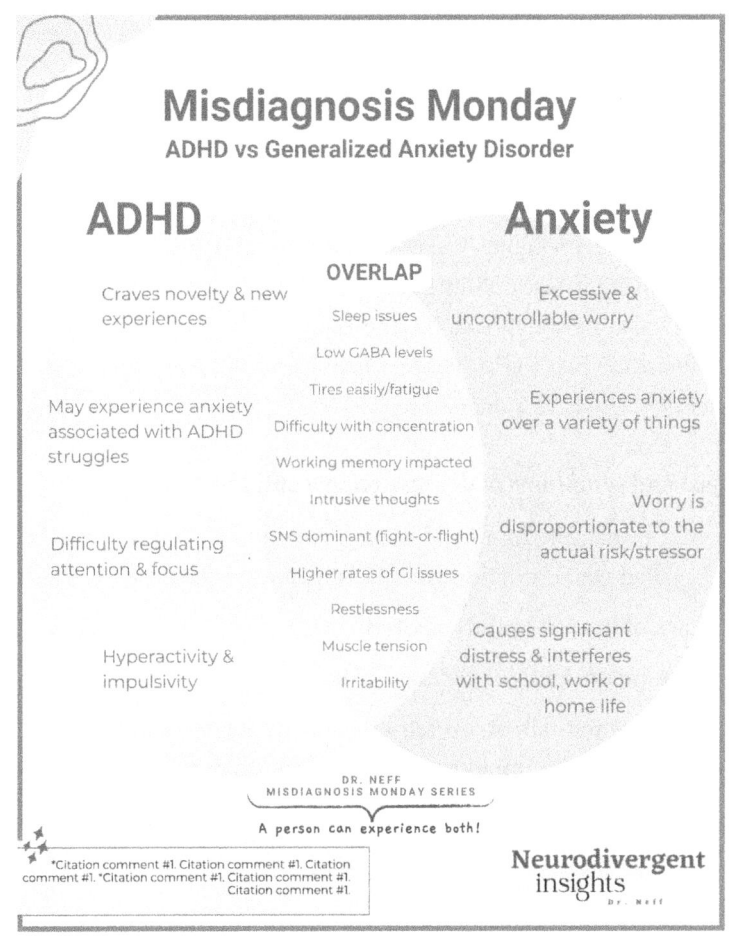

FIGURE 7.1 *ADHD vs. Generalized Anxiety Disorder. Similarities and differences of each diagnosis frequently lead to misdiagnosis though it is possible for a person to experience both.* Source: Dr. Neff, Neurodivergent Insights, neurodivergentinsights.com/misdiagnosis-monday/adhd-vs-autism

use the Screen for Child Anxiety Related Disorders (SCARED) rating scale to gauge anxiety, too. Ultimately, your child's actions will reveal the comorbid challenge they are experiencing at that particular time in their life.

Depression

When adults think of depression, we think of a person who is morose, withdrawn, unable to get out of bed, and has low energy. In children, depression looks different. Even those whose motor won't shut off can suffer from depression. It may manifest in poor grades or low self-esteem. Recent research estimates that 20 percent of children with ADHD also have depression.[5] The catch is that the symptoms have to persist for two weeks before a medical professional will consider labeling the behavior depressive.

Signs and symptoms of depression in a child include:[6]

> Mood changes. Your child might seem sadder or more irritable than usual, and they feel this way most of the time.
>
> Lack of interest in fun activities.
>
> Low energy levels or general tiredness.
>
> Negative self-talk or low self-esteem. You might hear your child say negative things about themselves. They may feel worthless.
>
> Eating more or less than usual.
>
> Trouble sleeping or sleeping too much.

Depression may not appear alone. When anxiety—racing heart, nervousness, and powerlessness—overlaps with depression,[7] a young person may experience excessive worry, agitation, and an inability to concentrate. These simultaneous symptoms make it possible to be both anxious and depressed.

Oppositional Defiant Disorder (ODD)

Among children with all three types of ADHD, ODD appears as frequently, if not more often, than anxiety. Within reason, defiance is a good thing and a natural characteristic of growing up. Kids should have agency to do things on their own, feel confident to take healthy risks, and grow through failures and successes on their own. They should feel empowered to defy peers who encourage bullying or drug abuse or stand up when an injustice occurs. When, however, defiance is a chronic pattern of refusal to follow rules or listen to authority coupled with big emotions, ODD might be the issue.

Absence Seizures (Non-Epileptic Spells)[8]

For kids with ASD, ADHD, and anxiety, "zoning out" or absence seizures are possible comorbid challenges for a portion of this population. The onset can occur during childhood, puberty, or adulthood and go undetected for years, due to repetitive actions and/or communication barriers some children on the autism spectrum exhibit. Sudden freezing, stiffening, or twitching can be disorienting for caregivers, teachers, and classmates. Although this type of seizure is without physical symptoms (eyes rolling back in the head), it will impact her ability to function, engage socially, and keep up academically. After the seizure, she may be dazed, confused, and nauseous. If a seizure occurs, your child needs medical attention ASAP and may need to take anti-epilepsy medication.

Obsessive-Compulsive Disorder (OCD)

OCD falls under anxiety disorders and is a combination of obsessive thoughts and compulsive behavior.[9] In adults and children, OCD shows up in unwanted thoughts accompanied by extreme rituals that interfere with daily activities. Fears and obsessions drive behaviors.

Therefore, a fear of germs leads to hand washing that can take an hour; superstitions around luck and safety require the individual to dress in the same sequence every single time; repeatedly checking to make sure the door is locked; counting and recounting excessively; perfectionism; heightened need for symmetry; obsession about harming others or things; and other symptoms that cause mental distress are red flags. Needless to say, OCD impacts functionality, quality of life, and social interactions. From a gender perspective, boys seem to exhibit OCD before puberty and girls during puberty and their twenties.

Interventions for Comorbid Symptoms

Once you learn about the additional comorbid symptoms your child has, you may wonder what to do. A psychologist may recommend cognitive behavioral therapy (CBT), which is useful in helping children replace negative thoughts with positive ones. The clinicians will teach self-monitoring so your child can be aware of when and what triggers the negatives feelings. When a child is at the onset of a panic attack or fully engulfed, whoever is closest can co-regulate with touch: gentle but firm pressure, soothing speech, and verbal acknowledgment of stress, inviting her to breathe deeply and slowly with you. There are a plethora of other strategies parents and kids can use for anxiety busting ranging from exposure therapy to breath work, to core body exercises and grounding techniques like the "333 rule"[10] (identify three things, identify three sounds, and move three parts of your body).

The other option is psychotropic medication. Your child may already be taking a multivitamin, a nonstimulant, or a stimulant medication depending on the type of ADHD she has or risperidone (Risperdal) and aripiprazole (Abilify) for ASD. The psychiatrist who works in tandem with your child's psychologist may add Adderall, Lexapro, or Prozac to your child's daily protocol. The psychiatrist should alert you and you should alert the school to serious side effects that could spark suicidal ideation, sleeplessness, agitation, rapid speech, depressed appetite, racing thoughts, and so on, which signal the wrong strength or an adverse reaction. Each medication has its pros and cons, and I would suggest reading the side effects carefully before giving it to your child. By all means, ask questions if you have them.

2e or Twice Exceptional

I'm including 2e kids here because their exceptional ability and disability create a conundrum for parents and educators. Future game changers in literature, music, engineering, medicine, and education, they are easily misunderstood because their abilities do not match their age or grade level. Highly gifted, they run the risk of slipping through the cracks because "[t]heir exceptional ability may dominate, hiding their disability; their disability may dominate, hiding their exceptional ability; each may mask the other so neither is recognized or addressed."[11] The opportunity for misdiagnosis is significantly increased because educators and clinicians are responding to a child's misbehavior rather than exploring the caregiver's description of their child as gifted with his hands but unable to self-regulate. Boys who are 2e are at higher risks for an inappropriate diagnosis because stereotypes around "boy" behavior are tied to specific neurologic differences or learning styles.

Self-described executive function expert nerd Seth Perler refers to these kids as *multi-exceptional* because their brains are a complex mix of neurodivergence and comorbid challenges with learning differences. He suggests, "you might have a 6th grader who reads at the 12th-grade level, has the fine-motor handwriting of a 1st grader, writes papers like a 3rd grader, understands math *concepts* at an 9th-grade level, *calculates* math facts at a 4th-grade level, can hold remarkably deep conversations with adults, and has temper tantrums like a 3-year-old."[12]

Residual COVID-19 Pandemic Issues

Don't underestimate the legacy of the COVID-19 pandemic. No doubt it was a frightening time that set neurotypical and neurodivergent adults and children behind socially, emotionally, and financially, in some instances. Physical and social isolation, lack of access to therapists, unequal educational delivery, disrupted Wi-Fi, health concerns, and the uncertainty of ever feeling safe again was felt all over the world. This may have been the formative years for your young child or the chaotic transition from tween to teen or the highly anticipated high school years for those set to launch into adulthood. Whatever the period in your family's life, the disruption's lingering stress of twin pandemics is still with us.

August was a brand-new teenager when his middle school closed. While he had the freedom to play outside with our neighbors and play video games with classmates with whom he could no longer engage in person, socially and emotionally something was missing. The citywide curfews, racial uprisings, and global protests scared him. He was thirteen years old and questioning his mortality. I had him assessed through UCLA Ties for Families right away. Because Cherish was in their system, I didn't have to start the long slog through intake paperwork again, although I did have a small mountain of forms to complete and so did August. After a few weeks, August's diagnosis was ready. He had anxiety and mild depression. His weekly therapy sessions with a Korean American therapist were fine. Sara was kind

FIGURE 7.2 *2e or Twice-Exceptional Student. Students who are gifted and talented but who also experience learning and behavior challenges. Source: This chart is reprinted with permission of Bridges 2e Center for Research and Professional Development.*[13]

and a good listener, though I'm not sure how much experience she had with Black boys who were worried about police killing Black people with impunity. At the time, Ties had no Black therapists, so my choices were: (a) allow August to suffer or (b) give him an outlet to share his feelings.

The sessions coincided with the start of eighth grade and though he worked through those feelings, I know those comorbid issues and social delays due to the pandemic linger just beneath the surface. I could tell by his hesitation with girls and uncertainty in finding his place in the hypermasculine all-boys high school he attended.

I noticed a reluctance to advocate for himself with teachers and overall avoidance of being the center of attention. Although August is naturally reserved, the COVID years have definitely left their mark. As he approached his late teens and the world re-opened, we worked together to regain the social and emotional development that was lost. Without question he, like so many in Gen Z, will be a late bloomer, because the pandemic skip spared no one.

Cherish was at the beginning of her educational, social, and emotional years when COVID-19 roared in. While her cohort returned to school, fully masked with a robust curriculum, I have often wondered if she would have benefited from a do-over. What if she had repeated first grade? What if every child had been given the gift of repeating where they left off in March 2020? I'm not delusional. Cherish would still be neurodivergent, but if she had been given more time to master the zones of regulation and received more realistic behavioral expectations from teachers and more compassion for her arrested development, would she have had greater skills to handle her future comorbid anxiety and depression? I'll never know.

Reflection

Comorbid symptoms will shape-shift as kids develop physically, socially, emotionally, and developmentally. For example, medication and a strict schedule may support ASD symptoms but not nail biting, which may escalate to other forms of self-harm like pinching, biting, or cutting. Advising your child to stop, chew a piece of gum, or carry something may stop the behavior in that moment but not address her anxiety. Or, if a neurodivergent child shows improvement in one area but not in another, caregivers should take their observations to their clinician and ask for a reevaluation of the original diagnosis. A new treatment plan reflecting the current needs of the child may be implemented; meds should start, stop, or change; and switching to a less stressful sport or academic environment may be needed to support the whole child. Flexibility and open and honest communication with clinicians and educators will help parents keep pace with the rapid emotional and physiological changes a child is experiencing. Until our kids learn to manage the intersection of neurodivergence and comorbid challenges for sustained functionality and independence, we're up.

Not that you asked, but here are my two cents:

- Expect comorbid challenges to present alongside neurodivergence.
- Comorbid challenges like anxiety and depression often overlap.
- Psychotropic medications may be useful for depression and anxiety.
  - Read the list of side effects carefully and discuss with a medical professional.
- Social media has pluses and minuses.
  - Parents should always know which platforms their child uses.
  - Parents and teens should partner over how and when to use social media.

8
It's a Family Affair

Living with a neurodivergent person is the ugly, messy portion of the program—and also the biggest opportunity for an outpouring of love for your child who has limited control over their behavior. It isn't their fault that their brain processes information differently. It's not the fault of parents or caregivers, either. Our kids are not trying to get on our nerves, be disobedient, or not trying their best. Like all children, they want to please but do not know how. Neurodivergence is a big pill to swallow and requires a commitment from every member of the family, including family pets.

Regardless of family configuration—LGBTQ+, cisgender, multigenerational, or single-parent household—families with two or more children are already surrounded by multiple personalities, needs, likes, and dislikes. There are sibling rivalries, favorites, jealousies, activities, and a lot of energy exerted by parents trying to manage it all. When one child's behavior is out of control or they're not thriving physically or emotionally, a wrinkle is added to the family dynamic. Even if families flounder at first, eventually everyone catches up.

Prior to a baby or child's arrival, caregivers baby proof everything. We anticipate an eye meeting the corner of the table, a head bumping a doorknob, pots and pans smashing little feet, and hot water scalding hands. We recognize the choking hazard presented by plastic eyes glued to the faces of stuffed animals, set limits on social media, and, as they gain independence, teach them about driving while distracted and scope out their peers for mean girls and ringleaders who drink or vape. We ensure the educational environment is supportive, filled with enrichment, and staffed by qualified educators. Unless prospective parents knowingly adopt a child with special needs, most caregivers plan a life for a neurotypical child, even when dyslexia, depression, and ADHD run in the family. We're hopeful that mental illness will skip a generation or not be present at all. Or, we have learned to navigate our own neurodivergent needs and have forgotten how hard we struggled as children; at least, until our bundle of joy arrives. Or we're unaware of our neurological difference, until our child's symptoms are stated aloud. Then, if we're paying attention, we recognize ourselves in our child.

A neurodivergent diagnosis upends denial and other carefully laid plans. It often catches everyone off guard, but we rally. Unconsciously, we restart the home-proofing process. This time, the adjustments are emotional, unless physical developmental enhancements are needed to support children on the autism spectrum. Tables may need to be raised or lowered, and furniture will be rearranged to accommodate wheelchairs or other adaptive equipment, and mood lighting will be introduced to reduce light sensitivity. Caregivers will consider incorporating tactile textures, removing tags in clothing, using compression tights, and giving bear hugs to help with regulation. At times, a child who is dysregulated benefits from deep pressure: a hug, squeeze, or the heft of a weighted blanket. For kids with sensory processing disorder (SPD), crunchy food supports their proprioceptive needs and helps them "accurately perceive body awareness, movement and body position."[1] Last, food on the same plate must not touch, lest the SPD monster arrive to cause one of three reactions: (1) over-response to it (e.g., screaming when their food touches) (2) under-response to it (e.g., has no reaction to food touching and just refuses to eat), or (3) sensory seeking/craving (e.g., wanting to put their hands in the food and play in it but not necessarily eat it).[2] There is no reasoning with a child whose central nervous system goes full throttle because the mac and cheese is touching the green beans.

Games, toys, Theraputty, kinetic sand, slime, noise-canceling headphones, trampolines, and other gadgets are ever at the ready. Gathering the physical accoutrements is easy, though caregivers may come out of pocket for the latest and greatest item on the mental health gadget market. The other expense is time—that is, the time spent researching how to create safe and functional spaces for neurodivergent kids. Time hoping that *this purchase* will ease tantrums, as demonstrated on Instagram. Time trying to get partners on board with the diagnosis or treatment plan. Time insisting that the school provide agreed-upon accommodations. Wishing for more time and understanding. Of all the things, emotional capital is the most expensive because it is hidden or only spoken of with our partners, child's therapist, or in a support group. We are reluctant to go public with the emotional price of neurodivergence. No one feels it more keenly than the immediate members of the household.

Siblings

Prior to receiving an official diagnosis, families have made adjustments. Caregivers and siblings have developed new skills to support medically fragile infants and toddlers. If the neurologic difference is ASD, dyslexia, or NVLD, which often presents in lower elementary, middle, or high school, a family has already adjusted to tantrums, poor academic performance, and watching their child withdraw from social groups. If any of these differences co-occur with ADHD and/or anxiety, everyone is on high alert for triggers of level five reactions for minor infractions. They are also on the receiving end of verbal assaults, theft due to impulsivity, lies about behavior, and lots of yelling and screaming. They are the proverbial squeaky wheel and suck all of the oxygen out of the room. This was a sore spot for August who was consistently asked to be empathetic and forgiving of Cherish, even when he was right and she was wrong.

It's not fair was a constant refrain in my house for a long time. Cherish would hide August's video games or take his Posca markers he purchased with his own money, without permission. She would scream or be overly silly during dinner to the point where I would allow him to eat in a different room until she calmed down. Tantrums could last for hours, taking my stress level up and eroding any sympathy he had for her. As I watched their relationship sour, I worried about the future. Would he have her over for holidays and birthdays? Cherish was oblivious that her behavior was opening a chasm between them. August would disappear into his room and lock the door. He wasn't interested in playing with her and she missed her big brother. My heart was heavy. August adored his little sister. In fact, when he was in kindergarten, he begged for a baby and now he resented her.

When I met August in 2007, he was a hefty, determined, inquisitive baby. As he stretched into a lanky little boy, he grew into a friendly child who was ahead of his peers academically. August hated being last and laughed with enthusiasm. Despite racial misconceptions about Black boys, he was on par with his classmates socially and emotionally. By contrast, Cherish was underweight when she arrived in our home on October 12, 2013. She lagged on traditional milestones like smiling, waving, and crawling. As for crawling, Princess Cherish was used to being carried and refused to exercise her arm and leg muscles. There was no way I was going to continue that behavior and promptly set her on the floor. Bright girl that she was, Cherish figured out that if she wanted to keep up with our Yorkies—LL Cool J and Sunday Morning—and her brother, she'd have to start moving.

The pediatrician instructed August and me to smile and wave to her, knowing that in time, Cherish would mimic our actions. In no time, she overcame those developmental delays. She also had a hearty appetite, which settled her acid reflux and allowed her to grow into a happy cherub. I was pleased with my new family and settled into raising two children, six years apart. August was a snaggletoothed first grader, thrilled with his new role as big brother. He loved on his baby sister without shame and bragged to friends at school that he had a baby at home. August fed Cherish, read to her, introduced her to Elmo and Thomas the Train, and tried to keep our dogs from kissing her on the mouth. Cherish's clothing and crib were in my room, and her toys were in the living room. There was no shortage of company as the kids' godfather, friends, and social workers were in and out weekly. We were living like New Yorkers with bikes, trikes, and kiddie miscellany taking over every corner of small apartment in Beverly Hills.

After we moved, the kids scootered up and down the gentle incline our house sat on. I loved watching Cherish, glittery sneakers on the wrong feet, helmet askew on her Afro puffs, trying to keep up with her brother and his friends. She would not be denied, and often I would be called to remove her from the middle of an impromptu baseball game on the front lawn. All of August's crew were boys and either had younger brothers or no siblings. Cherish became their de facto sister and the surrogate daughter of male friends who donated Y chromosomes to their wives in 2006.

She slept well and was routinely in the ninetieth percentile for height at physical exams. I thought of her as strong, feisty, and willful. I was proud to use those adjectives to describe my daughter and pictured her running a Fortune 500 company or ruling the world someday. Every now and then the social worker's words—*she'll have all the labels*—floated through my mind, but I dismissed them. There was no way this alert, sweet girl, who had suffered birth trauma, almost dying while being born for lack of oxygen, would be labeled anything other than a rock star. Cherish, who was expected to remain in the hospital for months, rallied within thirty days and was discharged into foster care, where we met her five months later. Cherish's will to overcome a drug-addicted mother, deceased father, disrupted placement, and the foster care system suggested a sparkling future. She had already beaten the odds.

As I prepared myself to parent a tenacious child no one expected to make it, I was clear that Cherish was not August. On the surface, they were night and day. Where Cherish was affectionate, demonstrative, and friendly, August was more like me, approachable but reserved. August had been an only child for six years and was adept at entertaining himself with his science books, trains, and baseball. Cherish needed more personal interaction. Her love languages were touch and quality time. The kids shared a love of art, swimming, eating, and video games. Where August was a rule follower, Cherish operated within her own set of parameters, choosing to kiss and hug her way out of trouble. Cute and cuddly, she tended to get away with murder wherever she went. Eventually, that got old. August was no longer impressed with his sister's antics and Cherish was unable to regulate her emotions or her body. Trying to explain that hitting and name-calling was not the best way to get positive attention from him was useless. Socially and emotionally, she just didn't get it.

August was pretty patient, but when he'd had enough of being told *I hate you!*. Whoa Nelly! While he was not violent with Cherish, he was angry and hurt. Her words stung. She had done all of the things and managed to turn it around to make him the bad guy. Although I asked him to ignore the taunts and negative behavior—after all, he was the older brother, the more mature sibling, the one with a neurotypical brain, the one who manifested her into our lives—he couldn't always do it.

You always take her side.

I had to sit with that. I had to check in with myself and think about why Cherish always got a pass and he did not. The obvious answer was her neurodivergence. I also felt sorry for her. She had struggles in school and with friends that he would never have. Cherish would always have to work harder to maintain relationships, focus, complete tasks, and self-regulate. August did not have these issues, and I wanted him to empathize with her reality. Unwittingly, he was turning into a "glass child" because my focus was on responding to emails from teachers, ferrying her between OT and therapy, titrating her meds so she could regulate, and asking him to understand. A "glass child" is not a medical term, but it sums up the feelings of many neurotypical siblings as described by Alicia Arena, founder/CEO of Sanera, The People Development Co., at a 2010 TEDx Talk in San Antonio, Texas. She said, "[w]e are called glass children, because our parents are so consumed with the needs of our brothers and sisters that when they look at us, they look right through us as though we're made of glass."[3]

There was no one thing that happened but I realized that if I continued to allow Cherish to dominate our home, I would lose both of them. I wasn't interested in raising children who, after becoming adults, wouldn't visit because one child felt protected and the other did not. August and I had been the dynamic duo for nearly seven years before Cherish arrived. She enhanced us, made us so much better, and I needed to keep our family together, loving, and committed no matter what. I enlisted her therapist who suggested family counseling. The COVID-19 pandemic was in full swing, so we had a telehealth appointment. I was present for the first part of the call and then gave the therapists and kids their privacy. I also made a point to openly support August when he felt wronged. I wanted Cherish to understand (as best she could) that she was one part of our trifecta of love, not its entirety.

Just as I had been open with him about his adoption, I revealed Cherish's diagnosis to him. A seventh grader, August learned about her triggers: hunger, fatigue, overstimulation, close quarters in the back seat of the car, and so on, and engaged his help in recognizing when a tantrum was afoot. I empowered him to set firm boundaries to protect his space and use his words when her dysregulation was spilling over unto him. I stressed that Cherish's ADHD and SPD was a family affair. As the kids have gotten older, they have had other sessions with Cherish's therapist. I will keep this option for them for as long as they need it.

The balancing act for all parents of *when to weigh in* or *when to let them figure things out* is heightened for kids in neurodivergent homes. I decided to strike a counterintuitive stance. Cherish's love language was quality time, so we arranged August to give Cherish thirty minutes of his time once per week. They would play a board game, listen to music, watch YouTube or TikTok videos, or play video games. Also, August was forbidden from making her the butt of jokes in front of company. I would not allow him to humiliate her. She loved this special time with him, and it cut down on the negative ways she sought his attention. Cherish and I would play cards or sit in my bed and watch a movie. She loved to snuggle and though the hot flashes liked to kill me, I snuggled back. These worked for us for a good while and then we were back to the drawing board.

Lest you think August has been an angel, I want to make it clear that he antagonizes and teases her. Sometimes, he goes too far and has to apologize. All in all, they have a typical sibling relationship. August has learned not to take her insults personally, ignore unwanted behavior, and redirect her antics. They still spend time together but Cherish has slowly but surely developed her own interests and doesn't always want to be bothered with him. It's not perfect, but transparency smoothed many expected and unexpected landmines in the Austin household.

August was kind enough to indulge me by answering a couple of questions for my book.

August Austin
Age Seventeen

Mom: What's it like growing up with a neurodivergent sibling?
August: I've had to grow up faster.
M: In what way?

A: I am more empathetic because she is neurodiverse, but I still antagonize her. But when it's serious, I leave her alone. She has always been strong, and I have to be aware of the fact that she is different.

M: Do you feel more mature than your peers?

A: Sometimes. I mean, it was either gonna be my friends or family who would force me to mature faster. It happened to be my sister.

M: Do you think your friends understand your sister or what you go through?

A: No one really asks. It's the same with us being adopted. I don't think they care.

M: How would you define your relationship?

A: Typical.

And that, folks, is all I got from my teenager.

As the only adult in the house, I have more control over settling disputes than conflicts that arise between adult partners. I also set the tone in my house and accept that Cherish's neurodivergence is part of her identity but does not rule our family. Although it may seem necessary to allocate all financial and emotional resources to the neurologically different child, the emotional needs of siblings should not be minimized. Nor should siblings be parentified and expected to raise their neurodivergent siblings alongside caregivers. They are not capable of this heavy lift and may suffer from diminished self-esteem or develop drug addictions, poor relationships with others, and resent their sibling when they become adults. Neurotypical siblings often carry conflicting feelings of guilt and survivor's remorse. Here is a breakdown of some of the feelings siblings experience as the "glass child":[4]

Fear—Did I cause this? Can/will this also happen to me?

Resentment—time taken away from them and extra attention placed on their sibling.

- **Pressured/perfectionism/high standards**—too many demands placed on them, feeling they can't make a mistake; they must do things perfect to "not rock the boat."
- **Silenced/feeling forgotten**—let them have a voice, they want to be seen and heard.
- **Fiercely independent**—they don't ask for help when they need it and feel more responsibility at a younger age.

Anyone who was deemed the "good" child, while their sibling was demonized, knows exactly how glass children feel. I was determined to not let that happen to August.

Adult Partnerships

I have friends with partners who (still) struggle with consenting to an assessment, giving psychotropic medication to their children, respecting routine, or even being willing to reinforce treatment plans. It's usually my mom friends who complain, though not always. They say their spouse doesn't agree with the diagnosis; is more punitive or less punitive; believes in natural consequences and won't intercede when it is obvious their child is suffering; is lax about giving their child meds on time; leans on them for direction; and then resents them for being controlling. Like glass children, the other spouse feels that the needs of the neurodivergent child supersede everyone else's and shuts down. Now, all of the responsibility sits on one partner's shoulders. This bad energy is even worse for split households. I suggest scheduling an appointment with your child's therapist or obtaining a separate psychologist to help parse through emotions that can easily overwhelm couples. If couple's therapy is too expensive or not covered by insurance, there are podcasts and YouTube videos like Dayna Abraham's *Calm the Chaos*, "How to

Parent Neurodivergent Kids When Your Partner Isn't on Board" that may be useful.

The consequences of not getting on the same page is akin to Cassandra affective deprivation disorder (CADD) or Cassandra syndrome,[5] where one partner is neurotypical and the other may or may not be formally diagnosed with neurodivergence but exhibit the hallmarks of such. I am using this nonmedical term, coined by counselor and author Maxine Aston, to describe a neurotypical person married to a person with ASD, as an umbrella experience between a neurotypical and neurodivergent couple. Whether it's the neurotypical partner who doesn't feel heard or the neurodivergent partner who feels misunderstood, devalued, or ignored, something has to give. Neurodivergence runs in families and crosscurrents of resentment, confusion, loneliness, and frustration felt by glass children also show up in adult relationships. Try not to blow up your relationship, because you're better together and so is everyone in the home.

Reflections

Parents of neurodivergent children are physically, emotionally, and mentally overstretched. We are consumed with all aspects of a diagnosis, trying our best not to crack under the weight of assessments, treatment plans, and therapists, and worry about how our children are faring out in the world away from us. But in our zeal to make things make sense for one child, we take the other one for granted. We make a lot of assumptions about how empathetic our neurotypical children should be and forget that they are grieving too. As caregivers, we should set aside time just for them; declare, *I see you*, to the one who appears "fine"; and regularly ask, *Are you okay?* so they know there is enough love for everyone in their family.

Not that you asked, but here are my two cents:

Neurodivergence is a family affair.

Check in . . . often . . . with neurotypical siblings—offer them a safe space to vent.

Don't dismiss the neurotypical child's experience with their neurodivergent sibling.

Family therapy—an impartial third party can cut through the noise to support families navigating neurodivergence.

Sibling therapy—provide a safe space for kids to learn how to communicate and support each other.

Couple's therapy—get help achieving common ground for the good of the household.

9

Growing with Your Child

In chapter 2, I talked about parenting styles. I even owned up to my helicopter-snowplow tendencies born out of necessity. Black parents and caregivers openly stress about our kids' physical, social, and emotional well-being in white spaces. We know about the role unconscious bias plays when punishments are meted out and grades are assigned. Our racial awareness keeps us on our toes because existing in predominantly white neighborhoods, sports teams, therapeutic communities, and academic environments has lifelong consequences. If that isn't enough, neurodivergence and its comorbid cousins add to our child's interesting and stressful day-to-day lived experience.

As the mom of a neurodivergent Black girl, my hypervigilance is insane. Cherish needs it. Needs me to advocate for her to receive appropriate services that support her ADHD and sensory processing disorder (SPD). Early on, I carved out a space for her in our family to honor and celebrate her differences and made no apologies for the way she processes information. I didn't wake up so fabulous; I had to grow into this level of advocacy so that she knows that she is worth every email and team meeting.

Cherish is worth all the energy, money, and time I have invested in embracing her neurodivergence. I remain a stalwart fan of her gifts, even when she doesn't see them or when those around her discount her abilities because they cannot see past her behavior. Things were different with my son, who was helping me get my steps in as a lighthouse parent. When he entered high school, I began to ease up, trusting August and the strength of our relationship. His burgeoning manhood blew my mind and suggested that it was almost time to hand him the reins. August's flight from the nest will change our dynamic and that's a good thing. Cherish, on the other hand, is already showing signs that having all of Mom's attention is no longer fun.

I'm not a baby.
I can do it myself.
You don't have to keep reminding me.
Ugh.

And so it began with my sweet daughter, who is flexing her independence more frequently and making it clear that I get on her nerves. That is quite the coincidence, because she gets on mine, too. She experiences my snowplow parenting style as overbearing and has language to let me know that she can log in to Zoom for her weekly therapy session on her own, get dressed for school without reminders that time is not our friend, and organize her desk without support. What I know is that Zoom sessions are tricky, because the likelihood of logging into Roblox or playing with the special effects giving herself bright red lips or a silly face is high. Or Cherish's channeling of mid-1990s Prince to remain on mute and type out responses, rather than speak with her therapist. I used to lurk in the hallway, making sure Cherish was sitting up and engaging. While I would not listen to their conversation, I was at the ready to unmute Cherish or unmute the video when she was not cooperating. Over time, I let her psychologist handle what I perceived as Cherish's inattention. My intervention was creating tension during a window that was supposed to bring her calm. I also learned that while I considered her behavior disrespectful, her therapist was less concerned with how it looked and more interested in Cherish's participation, however little. They would learn to communicate with each other and did not need my help.

I was forced to grow with Cherish but did not recognize it in the way I did with August. His pushback was much quieter than his sister's loud fuming, slamming of doors, or complete shutdowns. She was entering puberty and taking us down. Even our dogs learned to skedaddle when Cherish was cranky. We weren't communicating well, and I thought if this was ten, we wouldn't make it to fourteen. We needed to get past the angst and understand each other's motives for either being too helpful (me) or wanting some independence (her). Fate intervened when my work schedule changed and she got some of the flexibility she desired. Cherish's new school was fifteen miles north of our home, so she rode the school bus for more than an hour in each direction every day. She relished this freedom, and I received the gift of time. While we're still negotiating other things—when she can wear press-on nails, crop tops, and makeup (lordy) outside the house—her pushback is helping both of us. The truth is, neurodivergent or not, my baby is growing up.

As parents with an augmented toolkit—different learning styles, diagnosis, treatment plans, comorbid challenges, social emotional learning, new vocabulary, and faux pharmacological expertise in stimulant and non-stimulant medication—we are still unprepared for the pushback. Our children who have depended on us to guide the ship of their neurodivergence, responding to every new wrinkle with patience and empathy. We find ourselves outdone when they suddenly refuse to take their meds or stop going to therapy or mask their difference so as not to be different around their peers. This new awareness of difference seems to happen around fourth or fifth grade for neurotypical kids and even earlier for ours, who've had either pull-out or push-in services, a shadow, or need to take medicine during the school day. Kids who are on the neurodivergent spectrum are used to being in the margins and now want in. They want to be part of the main clique. They do not want to be called weird or dumb or SPED (shorthand insult for special ed) by friends and may reject their existing treatment plan and/or start to act out. Grades may plummet, attitudes may turn sour, and comorbid challenges with anxiety and depression may increase or decrease in intensity, making the rejection sting.

All the while, life is life-ing, and physical and emotional maturation lend itself to curiosity around gender identity and racial identity for mixed-race youth, seeking place in multigenerational family configurations, transracial adoptive families, kids with LGBTQ+ adoptive or biological parents. So much is at stake during the young teen through early adult years for neurodivergent children. Kids who did not feel heard or seen have resorted to extreme measures to relieve the stress and confusion. They want to know how to make their neurodivergence work for them but do the opposite of finding an answer because their executive functioning skills have yet to fully develop. Not ready to turn them loose and unsure of how to handle their resistance of our influence, parents are in an impossible situation. To help this quandary we find ourselves in, I interviewed a school counselor and a therapist who have worked with families and children of all ages, racial and neurodivergent status, and family dynamics to get their perspectives on how neurodivergent teens actually feel and what they need from their caregivers.

I met Latoya Boston, LMFT, and founder of Real Moms Live: Child and Family Counseling in Los Angeles, California, before the COVID-19 pandemic. Latoya was referred to me by a mother of three, whose son was described as bright but socially awkward. Today, we would correctly identify him as having low support needs and anxiety. Seeing Latoya and members of her staff was a positive experience for Cherish and for me. Culturally, I didn't feel a need to explain my pedigree, nor was I treated as an outlier for adopting two kids on my own. I could say *I don't know what to do* without feeling judged because I was a single Black mother. I didn't realize it then, but having a Black therapist was rare. After Cherish's time at Real Moms Live, it would be four years before she was assigned a therapist who looked like her.

Among the many offerings were small group seminars. Working with kids her age would be beneficial for Cherish's social and emotional development. The sessions were helpful. Over the years, Latoya and I have kept in touch. I asked her several questions about how parents of neurodivergent kids can grow with their kids.

Latoya Boston, LMFT

Specializes in working with children, adolescents, and their families
Number of years in practice: twenty-four
Business: Real Moms Live

What have you learned about parents of neurodivergent kids?
The biggest shock to parents is that their kids are not who they thought they were going to be. Parenting a neurotypical child who is independent is a cakewalk. For neurologically diverse kids, parents have to always create structure and routines to help them become independent. They require a lot more support and parents are not ready. Some parents are angry, frustrated and do not understand what's happening with their child because they are comparing their childhood or other kids to their own. That's not fair. Over 70 percent of neurologically diverse kids are negative labeled because parents don't understand, or kids are under- or misdiagnosed. Once they are labeled "bad," the kids don't get the support they need. On the other hand, there are lots of proactive parents who know that something is not right with their child and seek opportunities to discover what's going on. This is tied to the education and awareness level

of parents, but anyone can get up to speed if they are open to their child's diagnosis.

What do you wish parents knew about their neurodivergent child who has suddenly grown defiant?

When your child triggers you, look within to see what that's about. Nine times out of ten, it's about you and the fears you have about your kid. Be patient, because things will work out. Some of the things we saw growing up won't happen to your kids, and the majority of things can be repaired (respect can be rectified). This requires a joint effort, though. Parents can't expect kids to fix a situation or blame them for being "bad." From a kid's point of view, she thinks, *I'm not the problem. They're disrespectful to me so I am disrespectful to them.* Change your language so your child knows that getting along is a joint process. Try "I'm investing in you." "We're doing this together." "Let's create a family unity plan" so they know that they are part of the puzzle that makes your family work.

What do we do when we have put so many stopgaps in place and now our child is rejecting it?

Acknowledge they need those services because it is part of their well-being. Tell them that the treatment plans and therapy will help when they get older, and you are not around to remind them to take their medicine or use their tools. Ask your child to accept the opportunity . . . give it a try. Or, come up with a remix. It's okay to follow your kid's lead. This helps them get in touch with their resistance, which is easier to get them to reframe treatment. On their own terms, they may stay the course. Give them agency and (small) independence over themselves so they feel part of the decision.

What advice do you have for adoptive parents?

Adopted children need more than unconditional love. Be cognizant that there is a stigma for children when their adoptive parents do not look like them. Create a community that is culturally diverse to learn everything to make sure that child is aware of their origins and how people in that culture behave. There is so much diversity among Black and Latin communities. Adopted kids have to know that their culture is not a monolith.

What advice do you have for parents whose child has declared himself part of the LGBTQ+ community?

Acceptance is key. Accept their choice. Allow them the chance to become educated and explore their identity from different perspectives. By their mid-twenties, they will have worked out their gender identity. When they're teens, confusion or alternate gender identity expression is a way for kids to push back. They are looking for love and acceptance and may adopt identities without any sexual experience. Just know that kids are waiting later in adolescence and into their early twenties to have sex. They may spend years confused about who they like or who they are, because they are going off what they've seen on social media and find out later that those scenarios don't always work or apply to them. Social media is powerful, and parents can combat digital influence through acceptance.

Next, I interviewed another friend, Phyllis Fagell, who is a licensed clinical counselor in the Washington, DC, area. Like Latoya, she has reams of experience supporting children and parents.

Phyllis Fagell, LCPC

Author of *Middle School Superpowers: Raising Resilient Tweens in Turbulent Times* and *Middle School Matters: The 10 Key Skills Kids Need to Thrive in Middle School and Beyond—and How Parents Can Help*

How many years have you been a counselor?

Just under twenty years.

What do you wish parents knew about their neurodivergent child?

I wish parents understood that when kids understand how they learn and what they need to be successful, they have more self-compassion, are better able to self-advocate, and are more successful. It is affirming and helpful. Kids are relieved to know they have a diagnosis. Also, solid info should be communicated with the school, and everyone needs to be on the same page. You'll get better results and better reactions, especially if there are unwanted behaviors. Educators will approach the kids differently when they have all the facts.

What have you learned about neurodivergent kids in middle school?

They reject because they are eleven years old. They are developmentally separating from parents, exercising their independence, and not doing what others are doing or what they are being told to do. They are not rebelling against the diagnosis; they just don't want to be "different" or feel bad and unwanted. If the child had celiac disease or diabetes, parents would elicit a similar reaction. My advice is to make sure you are not ascribing the wrong meaning to their action, because kids tell themselves a different story. They may not have self-understanding, so be mindful of the developmental phase they're in as a young adolescent.

Do you think neurodivergence is a superpower?

Parents think they are protecting kids by using euphemisms to describe their difference. Kids respond best to authenticity. For every perceived weakness, there are a couple of embedded strengths. For example, a child with ADHD brings dynamism or is the first to take risks, which makes other children comfortable with taking (healthy) risks too. A child with language issues is less likely to get frustrated as he gets older because he worked on it longer. His persistence paid off.

How can parents grow with their kids?

Adjust: Parents need to find a source of support other than their child to process with. Adults should talk issues over with other adults. Don't make your issue your child's and don't withhold that type of support from yourself. It takes time to process and adjust to a diagnosis, fear of the future, ups and downs. Be patient with yourself even if you are not fully adjusted to your family's new reality. There will be times when it's really hard and other times when it's easier. Parents should have a sense of agency: hire the right person or join a social/support group; focus on what you can do. You can't change the reality, but you can make things a little better.

Support: Do your best to meet them where they are; co-regulate with them and help them stay calm. Fake it until you make it sometimes but make no ad hominem attacks. In other words, call out the behavior, not the person. Keep the focus on teaching and relating, not berating, your child. Enjoy them. Do fun, light things. Everything doesn't have to be so serious. Keep in mind, every challenge isn't related to their learning challenge or diagnosis; they are doing what they are supposed to be doing as an adolescent.

Warning Signs

If your child is suicidal, call or text 988—Suicide and Crisis Lifeline

I spent an entire book suggesting that parents be open out their child's diagnosis, struggles with not knowing what to do, and an admission that failure is most definitely an option. As we speak freely with our children about their neurodivergence, comorbid challenges, gender identity, and side effects of psychotropic medication, we need to talk about suicide. We cannot assume that our child hasn't or wouldn't think about it or even attempt suicide and part of growing with our child is being able to have mature conversations about serious matters. No one wants this to happen to their loved one and it is important to know that "suicide is the second leading cause of death for people ages 10 to 34 in the US."[1]

Parents, caregivers, educators, and our children need to know the risk factors: feeling like a burden, bullying, cyberbullying, undiagnosed neurodivergence, social marginalization, depression, undiagnosed depression, ruminating on negative thoughts, isolation, hopelessness, and access to guns or pills to complete the act. Depression shows up differently in children of different cultures, races, and ethnicities making it harder to recognize it in Black boys, who are overdiagnosed for ADHD. The focus is on high irritation, anger, or aggressive behaviors "when in fact, these could be manifestations of an underlying depression."[2] Sadly, suicide ideation can start younger than eight years old for children with ASD, researchers at the Kennedy Krieger Institute in Baltimore, Maryland, discovered.[3] This alarming study has pushed these researchers to suggest that pediatricians should include risk screenings alongside regular health check-ups. In 2022, the American Academy of Pediatrics recommended that universal screenings[4] that include assessment for depression, suicide, and other mental health concerns start at twelve years old. Given the evidence of suicidal ideation in young children, this seems late.

Due to stigma and mistreatment, LGBTQ+ and questioning young people are at significantly increased risk for suicide, also. Many young people in this demographic experience bullying, rejection by family, and ostracism leading to elevated rates of depression. Equally distressing are higher numbers for Black transgender and nonbinary youth "with 58% seriously considering suicide and 1 in 4 (25%) attempting suicide in the past year," according to the Trevor Project. Indigenous youth, who are two-spirit/LGBTQ+ reported "almost a quarter of suicide attempts in the past year, compared to 14% among the overall sample of LGBTQ+ young people."[5] The takeaway is that systemic racism in medicine, mistrust of the medical system, trauma, and persistent oppression contribute to disparities in suicide rates of BIPOC youth.

Between fifteen to twenty-four years of age, Black girls and Asian Pacific Islander Desi, American (APIDA) youth are also showing increased rates of suicide, with "59% among Black female youth in this age group (from 2.7 to 4.3 per 100,000 individuals) and 42% among Asian or Pacific Islander female youth in this age group (from 3.6 to 5.1 per 100 000 individuals)."[6]

Beyond obvious risk factors, it is still undetermined why the numbers are steadily increasing, but this is a public health crisis.

Suicide impacts the entire family, school community, sports team, and every place your child has touched. Those left behind suffer from grief, guilt, and unbearable sadness. Suicide prevention is key to keeping our kids mentally, emotionally, and physically safe. There are protective measures we can put into place: culturally competent clinicians, establish a feeling of belonging in families and communities. We can also practice the 3 Cs[7] of suicide prevention, as described by suicide prevention expert Dr. John Draper:

Connection: implies that the person in crisis is made to feel understood and not isolated.

Collaboration: involves working collaboratively with the individual to investigate and identify potential solutions.

Choice: involves empowering the individual by involving them in the decision-making process for their care and recovery.

Reflection

Pushback from children is to be expected. As Phyllis shared, "not every challenge is related to their learning challenge or diagnosis." Sometimes kids are just being kids, going through their developmental paces. It's hard to remember that in the moment, because parents are either stuck in the past or focused on the future. Including them in their treatment, sharing their diagnosis, and talking with them about their medication and its purpose and side effects may make them less likely to rebel against the existing scaffolds. We need to be in the moment, growing with them as they grow. As they master milestones, we master them too. Our growth may require us to sit on our hands and not help with baking or choosing their outfit. Unless they are endangering themselves or others, we have to slowly man down and allow our neurodivergent children to blossom into their best selves.

Not that you asked, but here are my two cents:

Allow neurodivergent youth a voice in their treatment.

Practice acceptance to connect.

Stay connected through puberty and beyond.

Youth who question their gender identity need time to explore who they are.

Suicide rates for Black youth are on the rise.

10

Educational Trauma and Triumph

It's the day of the test. Students' iPads are out, and they are logging into the spelling app.

> Teacher: You have ten minutes.
> Nikki: What are we doing?
> T: We're taking a vocabulary test today.
> N: *Struggles silently. She doesn't remember the lesson and is afraid to ask, so she says nothing.*
> T: We went over the words yesterday. Did you forget?
> N: *A million thoughts race through her head. Should she ask to go to the bathroom? (Elope.) Her stomach is hurting, should she ask to go to the nurse? (Avoid.) This is a good time to organize her desk, so she pulls everything out and items spill to the floor.*
> T: Put those things away so you can take your test.
> N: *Instead of answering, she starts to put everything away. In her mind, she is working as fast as she can.*
> T: *Feeling ignored*—You're being disruptive."

You see where this is going. By now, the room is silent, or kids start to snicker, which only infuriates and embarrasses Nikki, who is trying to clean up so she can take the test she forgot she was taking today. As other students do as they are told and quickly finish, Nikki feels even smaller. Humiliated by the teacher and sensing twenty pairs of eyes on her, Nikki puts her head down on her desk and cries. She might break a pencil, leave the classroom, or yell that she hates everyone on her way out. Then, the teacher emails Nikki's parents and gives her a "0" for the assignment. Because the teacher is focused on behavior, the parent may also reprimand Nikki for being disruptive. Nikki's self-talk:

Everyone else knows more than me.
I'm stupid.
I always do the wrong thing.

What a painful experience for a neurodivergent child and yet this scenario is played out in public, private, and parochial schools every day. Kids like Nikki are made to feel ashamed of their learning differences and how their brains process information. What did this do to Nikki's self-esteem? How did it impact her academic curiosity? Given the teacher's declaration that she was being "disruptive," what do her peers think of her? Nikki was effectively othered by the adult in charge, creating an internal (inattentive ADHD) or external (impulsive or combined ADHD) snowball effect that will stay with her the rest of the day, week, or semester. She might take her humiliation out on her classmates, harm herself, or completely shut down. No matter what path she takes to protect herself, Nikki will not know how to climb out of this boat without support.

I offer the above example as an entry point to talk about neurodivergent affirming care. The term applies to all children on the spectrum and the expectation is that caregivers, educators, clinicians, and parents honor, respect, and recognize the whole child with a focus on "strengths and identifying accommodations for individuals to flourish, moving away from concentrating on deficits."[1] By creating an inclusive environment for all learners, educators ensure that different learning styles are welcomed and children feel like they belong in that space. There are a couple of ways to achieve this, starting with:

Call a thing a thing. If a child has ASD, say that. Don't dance around it and refer to him as "quirky" or "different." Though seemingly harmless, those adjectives suggest something is wrong with that child.

Make accommodations available for all kids. Even neurotypical kids need a break. Give all children a chance to be their best selves by honoring breaks or talk-to-text or fidgets to keep anxious hands busy.

There are mental health agencies and schools that already take this approach though being neurodivergent-affirming happens more intentionally at schools with special education programs. From the Windward School in New York to the Auburn School and Commonwealth Academy in the District of Columbia metropolitan area, to Westmark School, Rolling Hills Preparatory School's Renaissance Program, and Park Century in California, exclusive private schools have the resources to provide specialized education to neurodivergent children with language-based differences. For parents with modest budgets, nonpublic schools (NPS)—free private schools that contract with local school districts—offer similar services. I will explore ways parents can apply for an NPS later in this chapter. Both types of schools have a neurodivergent-affirming approach woven into the philosophy, teaching methodology, and inclusive nature of the school. Of course, public schools have special education services, too, and there is ongoing debate as to whether public schools are better equipped to serve neurodivergent students.

I decided to ask an expert and interviewed Claudia Koocheck, Head of School at Westmark School in Encino, California, which opened in 1983 for children with dyslexia, dyscalculia, dysgraphia, and other diagnosed language-based learning differences. Because comorbid challenges accompany neurodivergence, many of the students have ADHD and some are on the autism spectrum. It is a college preparatory first-through-twelfth-grade school, sending youth far and wide into the college stratosphere. They know the on-ramp from educational trauma to independent, confident young people who have learned to work within strengths is long, and they put a lot of resources into achieving successful outcomes for their students. Having met Claudia during the COVID-19 pandemic, I thought then and believe now that working with neurodivergent children is her ministry. She was born for this work and her approach to educating students, teachers, and parents about neurodivergence is worthy of national duplication.

Claudia Koocheck

Head of School, Westmark School

Tell me what inspired you to work in the special education space.

When I was seventeen years old, I watched the Special Olympics Telethon. Immediately, I saw myself helping children with different handicaps. That show opened a window into my future and I never looked back. My dad, however, was grooming me to take over the family business, and was disappointed in my choice. After college, I became a teacher and worked with children with visual impairments. Having a perspective as a person who was not blind, I had to be resourceful and creative to help them experience the world with the same passion I had. I learned Braille and how to be very descriptive with my language. Their disability helped me refine my skills and see the world of special ed as a gift.

Can anybody teach special ed?

It requires very committed people who will inspire and bring light into children's and parents' lives. Parents don't know how the child will blossom and grow. They need someone like a gardener, who is always watering the garden. You're not sure when the next bloom will come but you keep watering. You have to be ready.

What insight do you bring to what parents and caregivers of neurodivergent children need/experience?

When I came to the United States from El Salvador, I lived with a family for ten years. They had children who were neurotypical and neurologically diverse, so I was an eyewitness to the struggles. Most teachers only see what happens in the classroom. I got to see when dinner got hijacked by one child who was dysregulated and the pressure it put on the neurotypical child. This experience led to my passion and devotion to supporting teachers to support students and their parents. We need to help future teachers, who are in college right now, learn more about the neuroscience of different learning styles, and its impact on students' social and emotional ability to grow as balanced human beings.

What are two things that teachers can do to support neurodivergent children of all ages?

Teachers need the right language to reach neurologically diverse kids. For example, the way a teacher corrects a student with say short-term memory issues should be open and nonjudgmental. Don't make assumptions that they will remember just because you taught it yesterday. Our kids with short-term memory—they will forget. So instead of saying, "We learned it yesterday, did you forget?" You could say, "Yes we learned this yesterday and we are going to talk about it again." This makes the child who forgot the previous lesson open to learning and provides a refresher for everyone else.

Be predictable. Predictability keeps worry at bay and eases performance anxiety. A child who never knows when they will be called out to read aloud or if the teacher will make a comment about what they're doing will always be trying to get ahead, spending emotional capital to protect themselves and their self-esteem. Their amygdala is firing (flight, fight, freeze) and they can't focus.

What are parents up against educationally?

Parents were told to trust the education system, trust teachers because there was not enough information out there to support children who needed special education. Parents believed their kids were gonna outgrow certain behaviors and told, "Don't baby them," or, "They are fine." Teachers said, "They did it yesterday but not today. They are manipulating you."

Parents fell into this trap, thinking, *I was like that; look at me now.* But children aren't always able to clearly express *I feel left out; I can't catch up; I can't make friends.* Do parents really want their kids to go through what they went through?

A child's profile has highs and lows, and the system is not always right. Neurodiversity is a journey that requires a pivot. The brain will grow and evolve, and we have to change, too. It's up to educators to get up to speed on neurodiversity and learning disabilities and proactively support students. Parents have to be preventative so children can believe in themselves and have agency over their learning. The older they get the harder it is to close that gap. If you see symptoms, don't say *it's going away.* Parents must treat the child's differences like a medical condition—it's neuroscience. Difficulty with reading is a metacognitive profile that requires intervention.

How can educators reconsider their approach to teaching?

Continuity is everything. You could spend fifty hours on special education methodology and pedagogy but if you're not ready to let go of old practices, nothing will work. The educator needs to be open, willing, and ready to change his practices to new learning styles. Our ways are based on our learning strengths, and we need to be aware of how we teach. If we like to lecture, we need to add kinesthetic activities and visuals for children who can't sit still or need to see the information being presented. It is the teacher's responsibility to design a lesson for all learners. When I was a teacher, I posted the class picture on the wall in my home. I would look at their faces to connect with them as I was planning. I knew that I needed to do one activity one way for kid A and adjust the same lesson for kid B. You have to remember their needs. It all starts with the educator as learner.

How are parents feeling?

Many parents of neurologically divergent children have post-traumatic stress disorder (PTSD). They are in survival mode. Our kids need more help and more resources, and siblings are forced to grow up faster and become more independent earlier. Vacations are skipped or tutoring is not available for one child because the sibling who needs support is taking all of the family's money and time. Adoptive parents need to recognize how the adoption journey worked for them, especially if there are other kids at home. Parents need to develop empathy for their neurotypical kid, as they manage the demands of supporting their neurodiverse child.

What do parents need?

Family is first, so don't compare your situation to someone else's. Keep the partnership tight. Have date nights, go to dinner, and do things away from your children. You are stronger together.

What does educational trauma look like?

Adverse childhood experiences or trauma happens before kids are eighteen years old. It could be violence, abuse, neglect, witnessing violence or aggression in the home environment or in the world that they are exposed to. There could be mental health issues, too. Kids are sensitive to their environments. So those who are not in the right learning environment have trauma from not wanting to fail, shamed, or teased because they're the only one who can't do things.

What is the best learning environment for neurodivergent kids?

Educators create a safe environment that celebrates their strengths. Children must be seen, heard, and recognized for who they are. I like Universal Design for Learning because the focus is on inclusion, equity, and access to ensure that the environment supports every learner, regardless of diagnosis or perceived ability. Even schools that offer a suite of services: counseling, push-in or pull-out services, or accommodations, etcetera, won't get you to what our kids need, if it's not the right environment. The intentions are there but that's not enough.

I had never heard of Universal Design for Learning (UDL) and looked it up. According to the UDL website, the following guidelines "inform the design of learning environments to support learner agency that is":[2]

- **Purposeful**—internalized self-efficacy, acting in ways that are personally and socially meaningful.
- **Reflective**—self-awareness and metacognition to identify internal motivations and external influences that support learning and make adjustments when necessary.
- **Resourceful**—understanding and applying assets, strengths, resources, and linguistic and cultural capital.
- **Authentic**—increasing comprehension and deepening understanding in ways that are genuine.
- **Strategic**—setting goals and monitoring learning with intentionality and planfulness.
- **Action-oriented**—self-directed and collective action in pursuit of learning goals.

My takeaway is that the best educational environment is one that continues to evolve. Emphasis is placed on a child's strengths from a multidimensional approach rather than insisting that they fit into a normative educational structure. This strategy encourages children to take agency over how they learn. Using an example from Claudia's time working with blind students: *Blind people know when you're walking down the hallway. They recognize your gait, hold your arm, feel your clothes and fabric. They learn to apply all senses in one lesson when they can't see a thing.*

Having learned about neurodivergent-affirming care and UDL, let's revisit the scenario from the start of this chapter.

It's the day of the test. Students' iPads are out, and they are logging in to the spelling app.

> Teacher: You have ten minutes.
> Nikki: What are we doing?
> T: We're taking a vocabulary test, but before we start, let's review.
> Other students: *Groan.* We did this yesterday.
> T: And we're going to do it again.
> N: *Relaxes. She doesn't remember yesterday's lesson and needs the refresher.*

Instead of scheming her way out of taking the vocabulary test, Nikki leans in. As the teacher goes over the words, Nikki starts to feel capable. She knows more than she realizes and earns a high grade. This small tweak not only supported Nikki's short-term memory and gave the other children additional practice time but the teacher created an inclusive environment where Nikki felt like she belonged. That was a win for everyone.

No One *Wants* to Change Schools

When in the thick of raising a neurodivergent child, it is easy to feel alone, especially when our children struggle at school. Whether it is the neighborhood school or the elite private school across town, it is disheartening when the placement doesn't work out.

For children, changing school means being the new kid, possibly losing touch with old friends and adjusting to a new culture and structure. No matter how terrible their current educational experience might be, our sensitive learners feel unmoored because the unknown is very scary. For parents, the decision to make a change is necessary but not easy. Most of us think that once our children start school, we won't have to think about transitions until sixth or eighth grade. This was the natural trajectory for ourselves and other kids in the family. We had planned for those transitions and are shocked when that date arrives before we are ready. In hindsight, I bet parents in this situation would admit that their child had given every signal in the world that they were in the wrong place. In our defense, parents and educators are often committed to making the accommodations: more test-taking time, more breaks, chunking assignments, quiet spaces, more play work, and so on. In Nikki's situation, nothing worked and when it finally all went to hell and Nikki announced:

I'm stupid.
I don't have any friends.
I hate myself.
I wish I was dead.

Her parents made a move. Saddled with guilt and their own educational trauma, they worked hard to overcome feeling angry, resentful, or disappointed with teachers or the school, all the while trying to find a new school. Forced to accept that *that* school and that *those* teachers were unable to support Nikki, her parents realized that they were not the only game in town. There were tons of schools that would be a better fit for Nikki.

Generally speaking, changing schools requires even more emotional labor for parents still coming to grips with the fact that a traditional path is not optimal for their child's different learning style. Possibly still grieving that their child's educational and social trajectory will look different, they take a breath and get to work. Parents research schools, visit campuses, and interview administrators about their teaching philosophy. For some families, this will be their first IEP and the caregivers' first notion that free nonpublic schools (NPS) exist. They may hire educational consultants or even homeschool their child, if the change occurs mid-year. After being transparent about diagnosis, treatment plans, what worked, what didn't, why a change was necessary, disclosing their child's triggers, and state of mind, parents need to know if the new school is inclusive, sees neurodivergence as a strength and has teachers trained or certified in special education. Knowing how comorbid challenges impact ADHD, dyslexia, ASD, and NVLD, we ask about small class sizes, if the middle and high school students rotate classrooms, if there is a counselor skilled to work with neurodivergent children on staff, and what type of accommodations are used to catch kids up who have fallen below grade level in reading, writing, and math.

Nonpublic Schools

To access an NPS for the purpose of obtaining a free appropriate public education (FAPE) or seeking reimbursement from the local school district to pay for private school, there are requirements parents must meet. First, your child needs an assessment from the school district (if you have one from a private psychotherapist, they will take it under advisement, as they conduct their own assessment); a diagnosis; treatment plan; physical; eye exam and anything else that goes into crafting the IEP. As long as your child qualifies for an IEP, the assistant principal or special education coordinator or the school psychologist will recommend public schools in your area as a possible placement. If the public school's special education class or special day class (SDC) is at capacity or the student was enrolled and it didn't work out, caregivers must notify the person who assembled their child's IEP.

Effectively declining the public school placement is step number two. Whoever is in charge of the IEP will forward this information to the district's special education department, who will then email parents a list of NPS to start step number three. Before applying to any school on the list, the family sets up an appointment. You will be asked if you have a letter from the district giving you access to the NPS, and the expectation is that you will bring your child with you on the day of the tour and apply for enrollment at its conclusion. The NPS has the option to accept or decline your application.

All NPS's are neurodivergent affirming and typically go up to twelfth grade. Heads of schools, teachers, deans, and other specialists who work in these schools have experience with neurodivergent students, those with physical handicaps, high and low support needs, and those with an emotional impairment (the term "emotionally disturbed" is headed to retirement). All of the children have comorbid challenges, making the energy predictably unpredictable. Some kids will find this environment stressful, and others will not. Parents must be clued in on their child's comorbid and sensory issues when selecting this type of school. Class sizes are very small, boy heavy, and typically there is one teacher plus an aide, who may or may not have certification in special education. Often subject matters are clustered: a middle school reading class will have sixth, seventh, and eighth graders in the same class. This gives the older students with phonological or auditory processing deficits a chance to catch up. The curriculum follows that of the local public school district, who takes direction from the state department of education, and of course, ultimate oversight is the US Department of Education. While the websites of the NPS are amazing and describe ideal educational environments for kids like ours, a simple perusal of Yelp, Niche, or GreatSchools will reveal their rankings, test scores, and personal testimonials written by parents. Prospective caregivers can also request to speak with current parents to get a sense of what happens when the teachers, counselors, and aides are not looking.

By now, you have probably figured out that I am writing from experience. Cherish switched schools during the middle of her fifth-grade year. Those weeks of waiting to hear from the special education office, touring NPS, waiting to be accepted or rejected, all the while knowing her new private school was the best educational environment for Cherish, were some kind of stressful. I was grateful that she landed on her feet, but the bureaucratic path to get FAPE felt like it would never end. There has to be a way to streamline the process.

Let's quickly rewind to 2012. August attended Westside Neighborhood School (WNS) from kindergarten to eighth grade and I had hoped that would be Cherish's path too. Progressive with a strong community, we had wonderful memories and amazing experiences during our family's twelve years there. The teachers were loving and kind and the head of school was smart, intentional, and willing to grow with the times. He was passionate about the racial and socioeconomic diversity of the faculty, staff, and student body. I knew my children were safe at WNS and felt that the administrators were a top-notch group of men and women. It was there I learned about social emotional learning, having a growth mindset, and the importance of failure. August loved WNS and so did Cherish though it didn't show up in an expected way. And, even with support from counselors and teachers, she was not thriving. Cherish was hurt, misunderstood, and feeling like a failure. She acted on those feelings too. I homeschooled her for the last two months of the fall semester and set about learning my rights as a parent and her rights as a special education student.

My initial plan was to get a raise. Cherish was going to go to public school and I'd get a break on paying tuition. The elementary school listed on her IEP had a great reputation. The special day class had twelve students, and those students would stay together for core subjects— reading and math—and be mainstreamed for science and physical education (PE). That sounded great, until I visited. Multiple grade levels in one class with five adults in one classroom was going to set Cherish's sensory and spatial processing sensitivities on edge. As I was mentally scratching the claustrophobic classroom off my list, the assistant principal informed me that the class was at capacity.

Meanwhile, Dr. Robeson, Cherish's psychiatrist, made a suggestion that mirrored advice I received from Allison, a former WNS mom. Allison said that if I wanted to keep Cherish in private school, our local school district might pay for it. Say less. Allison warned that there were no guarantees, and I'd have to take my paces through the NPS process. If I still didn't find a good educational fit, I'd have to hire a lawyer. Serendipitously, Dr. Robeson recommended Vanaman German, LLP, which was the same law firm my friend told me about. Vanaman German, LLP, specialized in helping children and families with disabilities "receive appropriate educational programs and other benefits to which they were entitled."[3] Who knew such a branch of law existed?

The other ace up my sleeve was Sonya. She alerted me to a grave major error made by the psychologist who wrote Cherish's psychoeducational evaluation. Earlier in this book, I describe how treatment plans are created and that information about learning disabilities and neurodivergences are derived from an assessment. Cherish was reassessed in early fifth grade, because her kindergarten assessment was too old. While some aspects of her profile remained unchanged—ADHD and SPD—Cherish now had identified comorbid challenges with anxiety and a learning disability.

When the public school I visited didn't work out and the NPS's proved not to be the best environment for Cherish, I dove back into private education. I narrowed the choice down to two schools. One was a traditional private school with two programs for neurodivergent students who would be educated alongside their mainstreamed peers, and the other school was strictly for students with language-based differences. Both had excellent reputations with college preparatory curriculums, honors, and advanced placement (AP) courses, music, art, counselors, sensory classrooms, small class sizes, and were fifteen miles from our home though only one had a school bus from our area. Both specialized in teaching neurodivergent children where they were to help them find their strengths as learners and members of the community. I was excited that Cherish would be part of a community of neurodivergent learners with similar diagnoses and comorbid challenges just like hers. At either school, she'd find an educational home, make new friends, and have teachers who understood and celebrated her. Cherish went on shadow days and loved both. After weeks of tears, I was thrilled to see her smiling again.

Apples to apples, either choice would work for Cherish and our family. I based my final decision on practical concerns and mother's intuition. Cherish needed a physically small school with an intimate class size. Anything over ten students would send her fight, flight, or freeze into motion. I needed financial aid, the availability of a school bus, and uniforms. Cherish didn't need the daily drama of what to wear or what other people were wearing. There was just one catch. In order for Cherish to attend, she had to have a specific language-based learning disability. While it was implied that she had one, it wasn't clear what it was. On Cherish's IEP, other health impairment (OHI) was listed, but this catchall term, which included ADHD, was too vague. Luckily, Sonya caught the missed learning disability, which was listed but the box was unchecked. Sonya told me that psychoeducational evaluations were created from a template, and whoever completed it had not proofread it before copies were sent to me or the school district. Holy moly! I couldn't believe it. Her error almost cost Cherish a spot at the new school.

After sending a detailed email highlighting the errors and requesting a revised assessment, the psychologist responded. She "acknowledged" receipt of my email. She said she knew that I must have been stressed and agreed to fix her mistakes. No apology. Just an "acknowledgment." Taking the win, the new assessment specifically stated that Cherish "does evidence psychological processing deficits, in sensory-motor processing and phonological processing, which may adversely impact educational access and performance at this time." With a sigh of relief, I submitted this document to the director of admissions and Cherish became the sixteenth member of her new class.

In the end, everything worked in our favor but the stress we endured was incredible. The PTSD Claudia spoke of is real and I had help. I think of the thousands of parents who don't have a friend who is capable of reading an IEP or psychoeducational report or can't afford a lawyer to enforce the state's mandate to appropriately educate all children in their district.

Parents Have Rights

Parents and caregivers don't always know where to turn, so I am including information about parents' and children's educational rights as a starting point *before and if* a change in the educational environment becomes necessary.

National

Public schools, private schools, or agencies that receive federal funding are governed by the US Department of Education's Family and Educational Rights and Privacy Act or FERPA. Under FERPA, parents have the right to access their child's records, "the right to seek to have the records amended, and the right to have some control over the disclosure of personally identifiable information from the education records."[4] When a student turns eighteen years old, these rights transfer to the student, which is why colleges cannot release details about their child's mental health or grades to the parent. Colleges and universities, like the California State

University system, have a form that gives young adults the option to consent to sharing information about them with parents. The form is specific about who can receive information, and parents gearing up to send their child off to college should read the document carefully.

Additionally, the Department of Education oversees the Office of Special Education Programs, which provides money to states and school districts for infants, toddlers, children, and youth with disabilities ages birth through twenty-one.[5]

State

I live in California, which is ranked twenty-third in education by *U.S. News & World Report* and fortieth in public education by WalletHub, which uses metrics that included quality and safety.[6] We're so ahead of the curve on immigration, LGBTQ+ rights, access to abortion, and carbon emissions but can't seem to get our public education system together. Growing up, I loved my public educational experience and wish my kids could have followed in my footsteps, but conflicting priorities of such a large, unwieldy school district weren't conducive to the educational trajectory I had in mind. I was also in a position to send them to schools that offered science, music, art, technology, and project-based learning and believed this to be the best environment for their interests and strengths.

If you are considering switching schools or need more information regarding parent and student rights, I have included a link[7] in the endnotes. Essentially, parents have a significant amount of rights that include classroom visits, parent–teacher conferences, school choice, early intervention services, and notices written in the parent's native language. Parents do not have to consent to an assessment of their child and can seek legal remedies against a school district, if necessary. All in all, parents and caregivers should make themselves familiar with special education rights in their states.

Local

On the local level, go to your school district's website to find guidelines for special education. There may be information about free assessments for neurodivergence, workshops on IEPs, disputes, nonpublic schools, and links to specific departments within special education to get the ball rolling. Regardless of where you live, there is overlap between federal, state, and local rights for parents and children, putting us in the driver's seat when requesting accommodations or a school transfer. As we know, identifying neurodivergence early is key to a child's well-being, functionality, and academic success.

Reflection

Environments that are neurodivergent affirming are the best fit for neurodivergent youth. Their approach is supportive, and they are knowledgeable about the spectrum aspect of learning differences and comorbid challenges with ASD, ADHD, NVLD, and dyslexia. They do not expect children with the same diagnosis to behave similarly and treat each child with the dignity and respect they deserve. If our children feel good about themselves, parents usually do too. We are easy to please and seek ways to mitigate our PTSD and get out of survival mode so we can help our kids thrive.

Just as our kids need us to advocate for them, parents need an ally to navigate IEPs, psychoeducational evaluations, and other legal documents that control the fate of our child's education. If you have dealt with people at the district level who did not know the law, gave wrong information, or sent you on a fool's errand in search of services your child was already entitled to, you already know the importance of advocacy. If you can afford it, hire an educational consultant or attorney who specializes in disability rights or comb your network for friends and acquaintances who work in public education. Another great resource are principals, school psychologists, and counselors who can decipher acronyms, translate the lingo, and might even know the point person in the special education department in the local district office. Know that your child may need multiple advocates to get her what she needs.

Finally, a comment Claudia made as we were wrapping up her interview stuck with me. I asked her what she learned about neurodivergence. She said, "Education is a social justice issue. The ability to learn how to read and write is a human right not a privilege." I agree.

Not that you asked, but here are my two cents:

Seek neurodivergent-affirming care in all areas of your child's life, otherwise the track team or school environment will be a disappointing experience.

Change schools when or if the current school can no longer support your child.

Find a parent advocate.

Know your rights.

11

Dream a New Dream

Congratulations on getting through what must have felt like a Mount Everest of information. There is so much more research and scholarship on neurodivergence, comorbid challenges, and learning differences on the horizon. The hope is that the information reaches policymakers, health insurance companies, legislators, and those who make decisions on behalf of our amazing children. The need for more funding, education for educators, and the expansion of culturally competent special education at all levels of education is great. As Claudia stated, education is a human right, and all children should have access to quality neurodiversity-affirming environments, wherever they go.

While we wait for the government to catch up, it is time to dream a new dream. The new dream has the same cast of characters but a better understanding of who the wonderful, amazing young person standing in front of you is and can be. Our children have brought a lot of fears to the surface, and we've had to face those fears. The mirror they hold is telling us to deal with our stuff so we can help them.

Everyone's parenting experience is different, and regardless of whether you are raising a neurotypical or neurodivergent child, things don't always go according to plan. Even the most rigid parent comes to accept that being flexible (or inflexible) will make or break the entire family. At the end of the day, neurodivergence is a family affair.

Everyone is impacted, and it is never too early to let neurotypical siblings and other family members know what's going on with your child. They, too, have to mourn their dreams of what grandparenting was going to be, so the entire family can be the support your child needs. The Africans were right: it takes a village to raise a child, and we cannot do it on our own.

As a purveyor of words, I think a lot about the word *pivot*. Parents are the original kings and queens of the proverbial pivot. We change plans on a dime, reorganize carefully constructed lives that do not serve our child's needs, change jobs, and homeschool, even when there is no time or money to bolster the pivot. On a regular basis, we move heaven and earth to ensure our neurodivergent kids have been properly assessed, engaged in the latest mental health trend to lessen the symptoms of their diagnosis, hired and fired therapists, changed schools, and fought school systems, all so our child can be in neurodiverse-affirming educational environments. Our emotional IQ is off the charts, as the diagnosis that changes everything forced us to learn a new language. We are bilingual advocates in *DSM*-speak and can effectively communicate with clinicians, pediatricians, psychiatrists, and pharmacists. Our need to know everything about our child's comorbid neurodiversity is unrelenting. It has to be.

In all of this, we mourn openly or secretly about the child we did not get, the parenting experience we were robbed of, and can't wrap our minds around how out of control our lives are at times. If you are a boomer or Gen Xer who was not allowed to suck all of the air out of the room because you were frustrated, you know where I'm going with this. Notes home from the teacher, failing grades, back talk, and meltdowns past the age three were not tolerated. Some of our folks were reactionary and punitive. They were simultaneously loving and believed in natural consequences. Millennial parents were more like the softer side of Sears. More tolerant and overindulgent, they expected a level playing field. There would be no *Lord of the Flies* mentality because everyone who participated earned a ribbon, and every child was amazing and fantastic for just being. Of course, I am painting in broad strokes, because many Black parents subscribe to the idea that we must be twice as good to get half of what they (white people) have. Immigrant and other families of color live by a similar ethos. We do this out of memory, forgetting that the pressure we put on our BIPOC and first-generation children to succeed can severely compromise their mental health. All in all, our parents ingrained in us that hard work would pay great dividends.

We listened to them and did all the things: college, career, partnership, experienced the world, and made plans to raise a family. When it was our turn to become parents, we deigned to practice an updated version of how we were raised, never once expecting the loop the universe threw our way. *We . . .* would be blessed with a special child who would make us not only rethink our parenting style but reimagine who we are in relation to our child. But it doesn't stop us from asking, *Why? Why me? Why us?*

Parents are desperate to know if they did something wrong and the answer is no. According to Dr. Baudino, "there are a lot of unknowns." In her practice, she focuses on predictability in parenting, "if we recognize patterns that were already there in the womb or the birth story or from toddler to teen years, we will see a correlation. 'Why' equates to accusing and blaming, but once you see the pattern and know that if you do this it will make the situation better or dissipate, parenting can be joyful and humorous." She adds,

> After receiving the first diagnosis, parents wonder if their child will be okay. I help them see that their kids had to adapt to survive. They have a new tool kit and the behavior served them at one time but not now. It is a genuine fear of parents that their kid's behavior won't change. I want to shift this thinking.[1]

The ability to shift perspective is at the heart of this book. Parents of neurodivergent children have had to cultivate this skill. This is our ask of educators. Shift your perspective to see through our kids' eyes and believe us when we tell you that their world does not follow in a linear fashion. Their growth and success moves like a crab: sideways, forward, backward, and then forward again. We are on their schedule and no parenting style or trend will eclipse this.

We have a lot of information and so little control over our child's evolution. Yes, we can put up guard rails and enforce treatment plans, but there are no guarantees that when we put in "X" we will get "Y." We wish friends, coworkers, and family members could understand this. Try as they might, though, they don't fully get it and that's okay. Part of dreaming a new dream is accepting that we may need a new tribe of like-minded parent friends with whom to commiserate, bounce off ideas, and heal. For if we have learned nothing else, it is this: the brain always wins.

Much of *She's Just Spirited* revolves around school because our kids spend the majority of time there. Therefore, what we know about our child, we learn from teachers, counselors, administrators, and clinicians who share their observations, which shape our understanding of who our child is. With a few exceptions, the fullness of the picture doesn't reveal itself until the situation is dire or has gotten out of control. On the hot seat, so many things race through a parent's mind: Is my child being stereotyped because she is Black, transracially adopted, LGBTQ+, and/or neurodivergent? Am I wrong for asking for accommodations? Has my child been labeled as bad? Will we have to leave the school? Like the educator, we are spitballing, trying to determine the source of the meltdown or lack of performance.

Children know and feel when educators have thrown up their hands. It always amazes me how adults get in their feelings about something a neurodivergent child said or did. They are the professionals that we have entrusted our kids with, and some teachers are unable to separate the behavior from the child. One remedy for this is culturally competent special education training. We know teachers are human, with triggers and feelings, who are also equipped with tools to shake off oppositional behavior. Our children cannot. They will misinterpret the teacher's exhaustion, frustration, or inadequacy as something they did wrong. They will internalize these feelings to such a degree that school is no longer a fun or emotionally safe space for them, then the learning stops.

Intent on avoiding our kids shutting down, we change. We morph into advocates who don't have all the answers but know that requesting accommodations, for example, is not the same as asking for special treatment. We find our voice and insist that our lens of our child's motivations and strengths are just as valid as theirs. We ask educators who are unfamiliar with supporting neurodivergent children to listen to us. We ask them to acknowledge our expertise about our child's unique needs in order to form a reciprocal relationship. We ask for their humility in admitting that they don't know everything and ask them to commit to investigating techniques to support our kid's neurodivergence and learning differences. An educator's role is vital for their functionality and independence. Let's continue to work together.

Finally, I'll end this book on a win. Like many of you, I have wildly successful friends from all walks of life. Many are in the medical profession, some are lawyers, entrepreneurs, social workers, C-suite powerhouses, and dedicated educators. When Cherish came along, we were all enchanted with her. Adopting another child, a baby girl this time, earned me high praise and put me even further behind in my mom pack. In a few years, they would start planning retirement and adults-only trips, while I'd still be on carpool and field trip chaperone duty. Oh well, I'd be the old mom all over again, if it meant I got to have Cherish.

With two kids, my world shifted, and I lost and gained new friends along the way. Taylor is one of these folks. We were good friends in college, and for about a decade after, but lost touch. When she became a mom, August and I babysat her son while she and her husband worked. They were growing their family and needed support. A micro-preemie and surviving twin, Dylan had tubes in his ears, asthma, and so many ailments. Dylan's birth trauma led to ADHD and learning challenges when he got older. Remembering this, I shared Cherish's diagnosis with Taylor. I was griping about how she kept hoarding food. I would find wrappers, napkins, and half-eaten crackers in drawers and on the side of her bed. No matter how many times I explained the risk for ants or how the food would make our dogs, who were on a special diet, sick, she couldn't seem to stop. Plus, she lied about how the food got there. It was like my admonishments exacerbated the sneaking and lying. This had been going on for some time. The therapist suggested I create a grab bag of snacks that Cherish could access anytime she wanted. She was helping me train Cherish that she always had more than enough food and there was more, so there was no need to hoard. The therapist warned that it would take weeks for Cherish to adopt this new behavior. Well, we tried it. Honestly, that technique only worked when the items in the bag were nonpreferred. As long as Ritz crackers, chips, or cookies were in the house, Cherish was willing to risk it all for white carbs, sugar, and salt.

Taylor laughed. Dylan was now an adult, and she shared that she too had ADHD and was dyslexic. I couldn't believe it. We'd known each other thirty years and I never knew of her neurodivergence or dyslexia. Not only that, Taylor had a bachelor's degree in English. She also earned a master's in public health, attended medical school, and spent a few semesters in professional psychology school. She ultimately earned a degree as a physician's assistant. My mind was blown. How was she able to achieve so much, given a learning difference and inattentive-type ADHD? Taylor said that her mom had her assessed as a child and then decided she didn't need therapy. Again, this was the 1980s, and parents in general, but especially Black parents, were not trying to hear that their child needed therapy.

Taylor advised me to chill. She explained that Cherish was stuck in a loop and it would pass. She recalled her own loop with calling the Psychic Friends Network every day after school for weeks and payments to speak to Miss Cleo would appear on the phone bill.

Taylor was fascinated by the commercials, which led to an obsession with calling the hotline. *I couldn't help it. My mom and dad would be so mad at me*, she recalled. These are the days when being a latchkey kid was the norm, so she had plenty of time to use the phone connected to the wall before her parents came home from work. Taylor was running up the phone bill, and no matter the size of the punishment, she kept calling. Then one day, the bubble burst. *I just stopped calling. I guess I was over it.* And just like that, I had a new tool, and Cherish got a reprieve. The hoarding still happens, but I have learned to not make a big deal about it. I'll point to the offending wrapper and leave her room. Cherish apologizes for being impulsive and I remind her to use her tools—breathe, take a sip of water, or eat a full meal to avoid hunger later. She's trying.

Taylor adjusted her parenting style to match Dylan's development, allowing him to flourish into a kind, well-adjusted young man. At a young age, he found his passion in dance, though his father pushed sports. Although he played soccer for a time, Taylor recognized Dylan's strength of movement, and the peace that passes all understanding spread across his face. She saw how at one he was with the music . . . how he bathed from the light within and watched him transform into a beautiful work of art. Taylor nurtured his strength as a Black male ballet and hip-hop dancer, all the while weathering academic struggles, family criticisms, social misfires, and the fact that he may never finish college.

Dylan's gift of dance has taken him all over the world as a performer and instructor. This is his calling, and he got there with the support of parents who embraced his neurodivergence and the diagnosis that changes everything.

RESOURCES AND RECOMMENDED READING

Chapter 1

Reber, Deborah. *Differently Wired: Raising an Exceptional Child in a Conventional World*. Workman Publishing Company, June 2018
www.tiltparenting.com
The OT Butterfly podcast: www.otbutterfly.com
ADDitude Magazine: www.ADDitudemagazine.com
Morris, Q., *Pushout: The Criminalization of Black Girls in Schools*, New York: The New Press 2016.
Siegel, Daniel J., and Bryson, Tina Payne, *The Whole-Brain Child: 12 Revolutionary Strategies to Nurture Your Child's Developing Mind*

Chapter 2

Dr. Lori Baudino: drloribaudino.com
The NVLD Project: nvld.org
Gulley, Marquesha, Bolden, Jeremiah, and Bolden, Joshua, *Black Boy Brown Boy: ADHD & Me*, independently published, February 2021.
Lamay, Brian, *Parenting Kids and Teens with ADHD: Practical Tools and Effective Strategies to Support Your Child's Educational Advocacy, Emotional Well-Being, and Social Development*, independently published, July 2024.
Autism Speaks: www.autismspeaks.org
Autism Parenting Magazine: www.autismparentingmagazine.com
Hunt, Lynda Mullaly, *Fish in a Tree*, Nancy Paulsen Books; reprint edition March 2017

Chapter 3

Prepare for your IEP: www.undivided.io/resources

Shore, Milton F., Brice J. Patrick, and Love, Barbara G., *When Your Child Needs Testing: What Parents, Teachers, and Other Helpers Need to Know About Psychological Testing*, New York: The Crossroad Publishing, 1992.

Understanding and preparing your child for psychoeducational testing: www.greatschools.org

Chapter 4

Find a specialized therapist:

www.betterhelp.com

www.psychologytoday.com

www.goodtherapy.org

Nash, Ellen, *Dyslexia Outside the Box: Equipping Dyslexic Kids to Not Just Survive but Thrive*, Transformation Books, May 2017.
Therapy for Black girls: www.therapyforblackgirls.com
National Alliance on Mental Illness (NAMI): www.nami.org
National Directory of Black Psychiatrists of America: Black Mental Health Alliance: www.blackmentalhealth.com/black-psychiatrists
Black and Dyslexic with Winifred Winston (podcast)
Science of Reading: The Podcast

Chapter 5

Apps that support dyslexia:

Dyslexia Quest: www.nessy.com

ClaroPDF.com

Eggy Phonics.com: www.readingeggs.com

HairyPhonics.com: www.nessy.com

Snaptype.com: www.snaptypeapp.com

Bit board spelling bee: www.bitsboard.com

Ginger Software Dyslexia: www.gingersoftware.com

Orton-Gillingham: www.orton-gillingham.com

BrainChild, *Orton Gillingham Tools for Kids with Dyslexia: 100 Activities to Help Children with Dyslexia Differentiate and Correctly Use "B," "D," "P," and "Q" letters. 6–8 Years*, independently published, August 2021.

ChildNexus Podcast: Diverse Thinking Different Learning with Dr. Karen Wilson

Malik-Hasbrook, Joy, *A Kids Book About Nervous System Regulation*, Kids Book About, Inc., March 2023.

Hurley, Katie, *The Stress-Buster Workbook for Kids: 75 Evidence-Based Strategies to Help Kids Regulate Their Emotions, Build Coping Skills, and Tap into Positive Thinking*, PESI Publishing, Inc.; Workbook edition, November 2021.

Jones, Audrey R., and Jones Larry A., *Falling Through the Ceiling: Our ADHD Family Memoir*, Smart Management Inc. 2018.

Chapter 6

Stixrud, William, and Johnson, Ned, *What Do You Say? How to Talk with Kids to Build Motivation, Stress Tolerance, and a Happy Home*, Penguin Life, 2022.

Lewis, Katherine Reynolds, *The Good News About Bad Behavior: Why Kids Are Less Disciplined Than Ever—And What to Do About It*, PublicAffairs, 2019.

Trans Lash: Resources For Trans People on the Spectrum: https://tranlash.org

Autistic Women and Non-Binary Network: www.awnnetwork.org

Queer ADHD: www.queeradhd.com

Mendes, Eva, and Maroney, Meredith R., *Gender Identity, Sexuality, and Autism: Voices from Across the Spectrum*, Jessica Kingsley Publishers, January 2019.

The National Queer and Trans Therapist of Color Network: www.nqttcn.com

International Dyslexia Association: www.dyslexiaida.org

Chapter 7

Autism Speaks: www.autismspeaks.org

Lahey, Jessica, *The Addiction Inoculation: Raising Healthy Kids in a Culture of Dependence*, Harper 2021.

International OCD Foundation: www.ocfoundation.org

Anxiety and Depression Association of America: www.adaa.org

Chapter 8

Center for Parent and Teen Communication: www.parentandteen.com

Understood: understood.org

Martin, Areva, *The Everyday Advocate: Standing Up for Your Child with Autism or Other Special Needs*. Berkley; Reprint edition April 2011.

Peete, Holly Robinson, Peete, R. J., and Peete, Elizabeth, *Same but Different: Teen Life on the Autism Express Paperback*, Scholastic Press, reprint edition, February 2018.

Calm the Chaos podcast
The Neurodiverse Love podcast
Arad, Pnina, *When Your Man Is on the Spectrum: To Know, Understand & Transform Your Relationship*, independently published September 2020.

Chapter 9

Fagell, Phyllis L., *Middle School Matters: The 10 Key Skills Kids Need to Thrive in Middle School and Beyond—and How Parents Can Help*, Da Capo Lifelong Books, August 2019.

Silver, Rick, Puglisi, Mary Jo, Fenix, Alyssa, *Neurospicy: A Parent Empowerment Guide: Life Hacks for Families with Neurodivergent Young Adults Reaching for Launch*, independently published, November 2023.

Borba, Michelle, *UnSelfie: Why Empathetic Kids Succeed in Our All-About-Me World*, Touchstone; reprint edition May 2017.

Heitner, Devorah, *Screenwise*, Routledge; second edition, October 2023.

Kennedy Krieger Institute: www.kennedykrieger.org

The Congressional Black Caucus Emergency Task Force on Black Youth Suicide and Mental Health: www.watsoncoleman.house.gov

National Organization for People of Color Against Suicide (NOPCAS): www.nopcas.org

The Society for the Prevention of Teen Suicide: www.sptsusa.org

Suicide Prevention Resource Center (SPRC): www.sprc.org

The Trevor Project Lifeline: thetrevorproject.org

Chapter 10

Divergent Conversations podcast
xMinds: "Understanding Neurodiversity-Affirming Care" YouTube www.youtube.com/watch?v=DFxroDlbV5w

Chapter 11

Baudino, Lori, and Singer, Rachel, *Moving Moments in Childhood (DMT with Infants, Children, Teens and Families)*, Routledge, 2024

Lythcott-Haims, Julie, *How to Raise an Adult*, Holt Paperbacks, reprint edition August 2016.

Edit Your Life with Christine Koh, Podcast.

Monke, Audrey, *Happy Campers: 9 Summer Camp Secrets for Raising Kids Who Become Thriving Adults*, Center Street, May 2019

Book List for Children and Teens

Ages Three to Seven

My Body Sends a Signal: Helping Kids Recognize Emotions and Express Feelings (Resilient Kids) by Natalie Maguire

Listening to My Body: A Guide to Helping Kids Understand the Connection Between Their Sensations (What the Heck Are Those?) and Feelings so That They Can Get Better at Figuring out What They Need Gabi Garcia, Ying Hui Tan, Illustrator

The Color Monster: A Story About Emotions Hardcover Book by Anna llenas

Brilliant Bea: A Story for Kids with Dyslexia and Learning Differences by Shaina Rudolph

Masterpiece: An Inclusive Kids Book Celebrating a Child on the Autism Spectrum (The Incredible Kids) by Alexandra Hoffman

My Brother Charlie by Holly Robinson Peete and Ryan Elizabeth

Ages Nine to Twelve

Autism and Me: An Empowering with 35 Exercises, Quizzes, and Activities! Autism Book for Kids by Katie Cook MED BCBA

D.A.R.E. Detectives: The Mystery on Lovett Lane (Dyslexia Font) (Dyslexia Reading Books for Kids) by Robin Gillingham

The Out of My Mind Trilogy (Boxed Set): *Out of My Mind; Out of My Heart; Out of My Dreams (The Out of My Mind Series)* by Sharon M. Draper

A Tween Girl's Guide to Feelings and Emotions: Mastering Self-Love and Building Self-Esteem. The Essential Emotional Wellness Handbook (Tween Guides to Growing Up) Part of: *Tween Guides to Growing Up* (six books) by Abby Swift

The Civil War of Amos Abernathy by Michael Leali

COBS 1: The Spider Trilogy (Dyslexia friendly reading books for kids, book 1) by C. M. Neary

Young Adult

Taking Care of Myself 2: for Teenagers and Young Adults with ASD by Mary Wrobel

The Power of Now: A Guide to Spiritual Enlightenment by Eckhart Tolle

Quiet: The Power of Introverts in a World That Can't Stop Talking by Susan Cain, Kathe Mazur, et al.
Queer Up: An Uplifting Guide to LGBTQ+ Love, Life and Mental by Alexis Caught
Obsessed: A Memoir of My Life with OCD by Allison Britz
Lavender Clouds: Comics about Neurodivergence and Mental Health by Bex Ollerton

Streaming

Love on the Spectrum
Raising Dion
Wednesday
Everything Everywhere All at Once
Like Stars on Earth
Deaf U
Percy Jackson and the Lightning Thief
Extraordinary Attorney Woo
Carl the Collector
The X-Men series

Schools That Support Different Learning Styles

When it comes to finding a neurodivergent-affirming educational environment, start with your local public school. If you are interested in learning about a NPS, review chapter 9 on how to access nonpublic schools. Private schools are governed by the National Association of Independent Schools (NAIS) and may have a list of schools that cater to neurodivergent students and those with learning disabilities parents can peruse. Parochial and religious schools offer STEP programs and honor a child's IEP to craft accommodations. Ultimately, in my experience, the best way to find a school is word of mouth.

EDUCATORS' READER GUIDE AND DISCUSSION

I've come up with a few discussion questions and topics to spark conversation between educators. I hope these questions add context for when parents are in survival mode and need you to have a sense of what is going on with them and their child.

Introduction
- Do you think parenting styles help or hinder families with neurodivergent children?

Chapter 1
- When you notice that a child behaves differently from other children, what is your first thought? It's important for educators to realize that unconscious and implicit bias and stereotype happen within seconds and will guide whatever decision you make next.
- How can educators reclaim labels so they are not weaponized against neurodivergent students?
- How can educators support adoptive parent(s) who are raising a neurodivergent child of a different race or gender identity?

Chapter 2

- Among educators, ADHD seems to be the go-to, especially when it comes to students of color. Why do these stereotypes persist in educational environments?

- When a child presents with learning differences, how do parents take the news? What supports are in place for parents and caregivers and their child?

- What stereotypes did you have about neurodivergence that changed once you realized that "15–20%"[1] of the world's population processes information differently?

Chapter 3

- How can educators, counselors, and administrators allay parent's fears around having their child assessed?

- Would it be beneficial to identify a staff member to explain what and how a psychoeducational assessment works during faculty professional development meetings? Parents have real concerns that administrators or counselors who aren't in the classroom have the information but the teacher is never fully informed about their child's needs.

- Thinking about Blake from chapter 2, how can teachers ensure an assessment is fair and racially unbiased?

- How do assessments impact outcomes for neurodivergent youth?

- What would streamlining the assessment process look like?

Chapter 4

- Now that you know that a neurodivergent diagnosis rocks a family's foundation, in what ways can educators be empathetic to parents who are struggling with the news?

- This next question is controversial. Should educators suggest therapy and/or psychotropic medication to parents and caregivers? Or is this a personal matter?

Chapter 5

- Whether or not a child has a unique skill, is there someone you highlight when explaining how some people use their neurodivergence as a strength?
- Have you observed the legacy of the pandemic skip on students? Do you have a suggestion on how to deal with its impact?
- In finding a treatment plan or accommodations that work, schools hire specialists and invite experts to professional development meetings. Should parents also be invited to discuss whether the specialist's information, though valuable, is practical or just theoretical? After all, what sounds good on paper does not always translate in the real world.

Chapter 6

- Give examples of how cultural competency is a core value of working with neurodivergent students.
- Does your school offer neurodivergent simulations? These programs allow educators and parents an opportunity to experience dyslexia, learning differences, and the like. The simulations also promote empathy and understanding, and spark ideas for creative solutions for educators who may need fresh ideas.
- Recount a time when you missed the cultural nuance of a child's behavior and reacted negatively.

- Who is responsible for the emotional and academic protection of neurodivergent Black and Latine children in predominantly white educational environments?

- In what ways has progressive language that describes neurodivergence in positive terms made a difference for students you work with? For example, using *difference* instead of *disorder*.

Chapter 7

- Educators of kindergartners often take a "wait and see" approach to young children who are struggling with self-regulation, language, or development. Is this a good strategy for all children or should observations be individualized?

- Which apps have you used to support student's neurodivergence in your classroom?

- What are your thoughts on people who think parents are overparenting and therefore the source of anxiety and depression in their children?

Chapter 8

- Neurodivergence is private and public. Should parents share their child's diagnosis with their class?

Chapter 9

- Does your educational environment provide information about gender identity and neurodivergence to students and families?

- In mean girl situations, how can educators break this behavior, which can have severe consequences for kids struggling with anxiety and depression?

Chapter 10

- How can educators balance the emotional and academic needs of neurodivergent and neurotypical students in the same class?
- Parents don't always know which way to turn. Who can direct them to the appropriate contact within the special education department of your school or school district?
- How does sharing information and resources with parents of neurodivergent children improve everyone's, including neurotypical students', educational experience?
- Typically, there are not enough Black, Latine, and APIDA teachers to go around. What strategies does your school or district employ to recruit and hire more teachers of color, especially in special education?

Chapter 11

- How can educators help parents lean into their child's strengths for better functionality and independence?
- For veteran and new teachers, how has working with neurodivergent students improved your teaching skills or made you a better counselor or administrator?

PARENTS' READER GUIDE AND DISCUSSION

There is no way to take in everything you just read in one reading. You may refer to chapters based upon need or curiosity. Depending on the age, diagnosis, and comorbid issues your child is experiencing, you will need different interventions at different times. I've come up with a few discussion questions and topics to spark conversation between parents. Whether you belong to a support group or are just parents meeting over coffee, I hope these talking points are useful.

Introduction
What is your parenting style? Is it helicopter, snowplow, gentle, lighthouse, or a hybrid?

Chapter 1
When did you notice your child was different?

How can parents reclaim labels so they are not weaponized against their neurodivergent child?

How can (an) adoptive parent(s) prepare to raise a neurodivergent child, especially if she is of a different race or gender identity?

Chapter 2
What were some of the behavior patterns your child exhibited that tipped your hand that she might be neurodivergent?

Did you recognize your child's learning differences in yourself or your partner?

What stereotypes did you have about neurodivergence that changed once you realized that your child processed information differently?

Chapter 3

Was there any fear around having your child assessed?

What did you hope to learn from your child's assessment?

Thinking about Blake from chapter 2, how can parents ensure an assessment is fair and racially unbiased?

How do assessments impact outcomes for neurodivergent youth?

What would you change about the process?

Chapter 4

How did you process the diagnosis?

Was this a turning point for your family? Why or why not?

What did you learn about your child that you did not know prior to the diagnosis?

Which mode of therapy did you start with and why?

If there were objections to psychotropic medications, did you reach a compromise with your partner? If so, how?

Chapter 5

How many different types of therapy did you try? What worked?

Whether or not your child has a unique skill, is there someone you highlight when explaining how some people use their neurodivergence as a strength?

Parents of neurotypical children don't know the half of what parents of neurodivergent children go through. What is one thing you wish your friends/family knew about your day-to-day lived experience?

In what ways has the pandemic skip impacted your child?

Chapter 6

Who did you choose to be part of your child's treatment team?

Were expectations around the first or second treatment plan realistic?

Recount a time when you had to manage your expectations around your child's ability to self-regulate.

In what ways has progressive language that describes neurodivergence in positive terms made a difference for your child? For example, using difference instead of disorder.

Chapter 7

Should clinicians continue to take a "wait and see" approach or assess for everything during the first assessment?

Which apps have you used to support your child's neurodivergence?

What are your thoughts on people who think parents are overparenting and therefore the source of anxiety and depression in their children?

Chapter 8

What is the advantage of telling younger siblings about their sister or brother's neurodivergence?

Knowing what you know now, how would you handle the discussion about your child's differences with family and friends?

If your partner feels that all of your bandwidth is going to your neurodivergent child, how can you maintain the partnership when you are doing the heavy lifting?

Chapter 9

At what age did your child begin to push back against her treatment plan? How did you handle this?

Where does your child get information about gender identity and neurodivergence?

What was your idea of family counseling before reading this chapter? Once you read it, did your opinion change?

How will you address the needs of other family members?

Chapter 10

How did you prepare your child's team to support her learning style?

What is the value of having a contact with someone in the special education department of your school or school district?

How does sharing information and resources with fellow parents of neurodivergent children improve everyone's, including neurotypical students', educational experience?

Chapter 11

How has having a neurodivergent child made you a better human being?

ACKNOWLEDGMENTS

The parenting space remains a tight-knit club. Most of the faces do not look like mine nor do the perspectives include my experience as a Black mother raising Black children. In the neurodivergent space, the numbers are even smaller. While our families experience ADHD, ASD, dyslexia, NVLD, anxiety, depression, OCD, suicide, and gender diversity in comparable numbers, our narratives do not make mainstream publishing lists. For this reason, I am grateful to my indomitable agent, Kate McKean, for doggedly shopping my book proposal until she got a "yes"; and to my editor, Christen Karniski, who agreed that there is room in this genre for Black parent writers.

Thank you to Debbie Reber and Phyllis Fagell for walking me through a really early outline. They provided essential guidance on how to compose a user-friendly book on a really tough and personal subject. For the last four years, I've had the pleasure of hanging with an insightfully generous and smart group of writers, a.k.a. the Parenting Squad. Without them and an invitation from Kakki Lewis-Reynolds to join Parenting in Place 2020, I don't think I could have written this book.

As usual, my besties showed up by reading samples, giving me words of encouragement, and sending hilarious TikToks and Instagram posts to keep me going. The Internet will not be defeated. In no particular order, many thanks to: Dr. Lisa Kirtman, Lori Williams, Dr. Marguerite Archie-Hudson, First Tuesdays Book Club, Dr. Alita Anderson, Kim A., the Williams Family, Sherri McCovey, Charlie Brookins, the Village, Bosco Senior Parents, Troop 7765, the Westmark School team, and Jamey Hatley, who heard the panic in my voice when I hit the wall. Big hugs to Kim Bryant, who started this journey with me when our kiddos were in first grade, and to Monica Young, who is helping me plot my next chapter.

I spent the most amazing twelve years at Westside Neighborhood School—what a wonderful launchpad for August and Cherish. When it was time to move on, both had a seamless transition, and Cherish's new educational environment resurrected a smile and love for learning that was buried beneath her diagnosis. Thank you for seeing her many strengths and encouraging her to thrive.

Thanks again to Dr. Lori Baudino, Latoya Boston, Claudia Koocheck, Sherrelle Kirkland-Andrews, Miriam Ha, Johannes Austin, Veronica Penn-Turner, and Phyllis Fagell for indulging my request for interviews. Your perspectives are invaluable, and it is my hope that parents and educators who read this book reconsider their words and actions when supporting a neurodivergent young person.

Though my grandparents have gone to glory, they are never far away. I think of them often and thank them constantly for everything. And for the rest of my family: Carolyn, Seibu, Greg, Kisha, Janeé, the next generation, the newest member, and those out of state, thanks for your continued support.

Finally, a sweet note of gratitude for my kids, who chose me and let me love them.

NOTES

Introduction

1. US Department of Justice, Bureau of Justice Statistics, Survey of Prison Inmates, March 21, 2016, *Disabilities Reported by Prisoners*, https://bjs.ojp.gov/content/pub/pdf/drpspi16st.pdf.

Chapter 1

1. "Foster Care Facts," Children's Law Center of California, n.d. https://www.clccal.org/resources/foster-care facts/.

2. "What to Expect: Newborn Screening Tests and More After Delivery," Henry Mayo Newhall Hospital, 2021, https://www.henrymayo.com/news-publications/news/2021/what-to-expect-newborn-screening-tests-and-more-after-delivery/#:~:text=Your%20doctor%20will%20do%20Apgar,Metabolic%20screening.

3. Ying Ying Choo, Pratibha Agarwal, Choon How How, and Sita Padmini Yeleswarapu, "Developmental Delay: Identification and Management at Primary Care Level" *Singapore Medical Journal* 60, no. 3 (2019): 119–23.

4. "Kaiser Permanente Study Finds Children Exposed to Complications Before or During Birth at Higher Risk of Developing Autism Spectrum Disorder," Kaiser Permanente, Department of Research and Evaluation, Southern California, n.d., https://www.kp-scalresearch.org/kaiser-permanente-study-finds-children-exposed-to-complications-before-or-during-birth-at-higher-risk-of-developing-autism-spectrum-disorder/.

5. Darios Getahun, George G. Rhoads, Kitaw Demissie, Shou-En Lu, Virginia P. Quinn, Michael J. Fassett, Deborah A. Wing, and Steven J. Jacobsen, "In Utero Exposure to Ischemic-Hypoxic Conditions and Attention-Deficit/Hyperactivity Disorder," *Pediatrics* 131, no. 1 (2013): e53–e61. https://doi.org/10.1542/peds.2012-1298.

6. Margaret Michaels and Qi "Susie" Duong, "Neurodivergent Individuals Can Make Significant Contributions at Work When They Feel Included,"

Institute of Management Accountants, April 2, 2024, http://www.imanet.org/blog/2024/04/neurodivergent-individuals-can-make-significant-contributions-at-work-when-they-feel-included.

7 "Foster Care," California Department of Children and Family Services (CDSS), 2024, www.cdss.ca.gov/inforesources/foster-care#:~:text=Thousands%20of%20children%20in%20California's,for%20weeks%3B%20some%20for%20years.

8 George F. Still. "Some Abnormal Psychical Conditions in Children: The Goulstonian Lectures," *The Lancet*, April 12, 19, and 26, 1902. https://wellcomecollection.org/works/ydzjmfqe/items?canvas=5.

9 "Definition Consensus Project," International Dyslexia Association, n.d., www.dyslexiaida.org/definition-consensus-project/.

10 "Dyslexia FAQ," Yale Center for Dyslexia and Creativity, 2022, www.dyslexia.yale.edu/dyslexia/dyslexia-faq/.

11 "Dyslexia FAQ."

12 Sally Shaywitz, *Overcoming Dyslexia*, second edition (New York: Vintage, 2022), 122.

13 Ashley Bell, "Is Autism Genetic?" UCLA David Geffen School of Medicine, April 10, 2024, www.medschool.ucla.edu/news-article/is-autism-genetic.

14 "Nonverbal Learning Disorder," Ignite Healthwise Staff, University of Michigan Health, Michigan Medicine, July 31, 2024. www.uofmhealth.org/health-library/te7868.

15 Monique Q. Morris, *Pushout: The Criminalization of Black Girls in Schools*, (New York: The New Press 2016).

16 Morris, *Pushout*, 11.

17 Kelly Henderson, "Finding the Sweet Spot: Foster Care, Disability and Special Education." *Fostering Families Today*, July 7, 2021. https://formedfamiliesforward.org/wp-content/uploads/2022/03/Finding-the-Sweet-Spot_-Foster-Care-Disability-and-Special-Education-%E2%80%93-Fostering-Families-Today.pdf.

18 Jenny Clark Brack, *Learn to Move, Move to Learn: Sensorimotor Early Childhood Activity Themes* (Newark, DE: Autism Asperger Publishing Company, 2004).

19 Brack, *Learn to Move, Move to Learn*, 1–8.

Chapter 2

1. Dr. Lori Baudino, personal website, https://www.drloribaudino.com/.

2. "What Is ADHD?" *Attention-Deficit/Hyperactivity Disorder: What You Need to Know*, National Institute of Mental Health (US Department of Health and Human Services, 2024), https://www.nimh.nih.gov/health/publications/attention-deficit-hyperactivity-disorder-what-you-need-to-know.

3. "What Is ADHD?"

4. Faith Wilkins, *Why Do Black Children with Autism Get Diagnosed Late?* Child Mind Institute, April 10, 2024, https://childmind.org/article/why-do-black-children-with-autism-get-diagnosed-late/#:~:text=According%20to%20one%20of%20the,autism%20during%20their%20medical%20education.

5. Wilkins, *Why Do Black Children with Autism Get Diagnosed Late?*

6. "FASD Facts," Fetal Alcohol Spectrum Consultation, Education, and Training Services, https://fascets.org/fasd-facts/.

7. Catherine Griffiths ©2020 by FASD CYMRU.

8. "What Is the Neurobehavioral Model?" Fetal Alcohol Spectrum Consultation, Education and Training Services, https://fascets.org/.

9. Cynthia M. Zettler-Greeley, "Understanding Dyslexia," Nemours Teen Health, May 2022, https://kidshealth.org/en/teens/dyslexia.html#:~:text=You%20probably%20will%20read%20slowly,remembering%20what%20you've%20read.

10. "Specific Learning Disabilities," Learning Differences Aotearoa Trust, Dyslexia Support South, 2024, https://www.dyslexiasupportsouth.org.nz/school-toolkit/specific-learning-difficulties-and-processing-disorders/#:~:text=These%20include%20dyslexia%2C%20dyscalculia%2C%20dysgraphia,common%20ones%20we%20come%20across.

11. Alexa Tomassi, "New Study Highlights Potential Missed Diagnoses of Dyslexia in African American Students," Yale School of Medicine, February 8, 2024. https://medicine.yale.edu/news-article/new-study-highlights-potential-missed-diagnoses-of-dyslexia-in-african-american-students/.

12. "What Is Nonverbal Learning Disorder?" NVLD Project, n.d., https://nvld.org/non-verbal-learning-disability/#:~:text=People%20with%20Non%2DVerbal%20Learning,social%20barriers%20throughout%20their%20lives.

Chapter 3

1. Richard W. Woodcock, *Woodcock Reading and Mastery Tests*, revised edition (Circle Pines, MN: American Guidance Service, 1998).

2. Gary S. Wilkinson and Gary J. Robertson, *Wide Range Achievement Test*, fifth edition (Bloomington, MN: Pearson Assessments, 2017).

3. "Tests for Dyslexia and Learning Disabilities," University of Michigan, n.d., https://dyslexiahelp.umich.edu/dyslexics/learn-about-dyslexia/dyslexia-testing/tests.

4. Sally Shaywitz, "Shaywitz DyslexiaScreen," Yale Center for Dyslexia and Creativity, n.d., https://dyslexia.yale.edu/resources/educators/instruction/shaywitz-dyslexiascreen/.

5. John N. Buck, "The H-T-P Technique, a Qualitative and Quantitative Scoring Manual," *Journal of Clinical Psychology* 4, no. 4 (1948): 317.

6. "Common Neurological Tests," New York University Langone Health, New York University, n.d., https://nyulangone.org/care-services/neurosurgery/common-neurological tests#:~:text=Neurological%20Examination,orientation%2C%20mood%2C%20and%20cognition.

7. "Common Neurological Tests."

8. Individuals with Disabilities Education Act, 20 U.S.C. § 1400 (2004).

9. "Function," section of "Individualized Education Plan," Virginia Department of Education, 2022, https://www.doe.virginia.gov/programs-services/special-education/iep-instruction/individualized-education-program-iep#:~:text=An%20IEP%20is%20comprised%20of,the%20child%20can%20meet%20the.

10. Section 504 of the Rehabilitation Act.

11. Bettina Weil, "IEP and 504 Plans: Differences and Similarities," *Niche*, April 23, 2021, https://weilcollegeadvising.com/iep-and-504-plans-differences-and-similarities/

12. Carolyn Jones, "Parents' Guide to 504 Plans and IEPs: What They Are and How They're Different," EdSource, March 29, 2022. https://edsource.org/2022/parents-guide-to-504-plans-and-ieps-what-they-are-and-how-theyre-different/669493#:~:text=A%20504%20plan%20is%20geared,have%20one%20or%20the%20other.

Chapter 4

1 "House-Tree-Person (H-T-P)," in *Encyclopedia of Child Behavior and Development*, edited by Sam Goldstein and Jack A. Naglieri (Boston: Springer, 2011), https://doi.org/10.1007/978-0-387-79061-9_4801.

2 Crystal Short, Kathy DeOrnellas, and Robert Walrath, "Draw-A-Person Test," in *Encyclopedia of Child Behavior and Development*, edited by Sam Goldstein and Jack A. Naglieri (Boston: Springer, 2011), https://doi.org/10.1007/978-0-387-79061-9_894.

3 Florence L. Goodenough, *Measurement of Intelligence by Drawings* (New York: Harcourt, Brace, and World, 1926).

4 Grace Counseling, "Are There Different Types of Play Therapy?" https://www.grace-counseling.com/rehab-blog/are-there-different-types-of-play-therapy/.

5 Zahra Hassani, Fatemeh Hosseinpour, Mina Sadat Mirshoja, and Abolfazi Boozhabadi, "Effectiveness of Cognitive-Behavioral Play Therapy on Improving Anxiety and Aggression Disorders in a Child with ADHD: A Case Study," *Case Reports in Clinical Practice* 6, no. 3 (2021): 116–19.

6 "Functional Family Therapy (FFT)," DC Department of Human Services, accessed November 21, 2022, https://dhs.dc.gov/page/functional-family-therapy-fft.

7 Katie Hurley, "Group Therapy for Kids: What It Is, How They Can Benefit, and When Not to Send Your Child to Group Therapy," Health Central, updated October 7, 2022, https://www.healthcentral.com/mental-health/group-therapy-children.

8 "What Is Neurofeedback Therapy Used For?" Drake Institute of Neurophysical Medicine, n.d., https://www.drakeinstitute.com/what-is-neurofeedback-therapy-used-for#:~:text=Neurofeedback%20helps%20patients%20self%2Dregulate,associated%20with%20ADD%20and%20ADHD.

9 Pagona Kytzidis, "In Loco Parentis: The Role Schools Must Play to Provide Mental Health Resources," *Columbia Undergraduate Law Review*, August 30, 2017, https://blogs.cuit.columbia.edu/culr/2017/08/30/in-loco-parentis-the-role-schools-must-play-to-provide-mental-health-resources/.

10 United States Supreme Court, John and Jane Parents 1 v. Montgomery Board of Education, No. 23-601, https://www.supremecourt.gov/DocketPDF/23/23-601/294860/20240104101635975_23-601%20Amicus

%20Brief%20of%20Professors%20S.%20Ernie%20Walton%20and%20Eric%20A.%20DeGroff.pdf.

11 V. Freibergs and V. I. Douglas, "Concept Learning in Hyperactive and Normal Children," *Journal of Abnormal Psychology* 74, no. 3 (1969): 388–95.

12 Benjamin L. Cook, Nicholas J. Carson, E. Nilay Kafali, Anne Valentine, Juan David Rueda, Sarah Coe-Odess, and Susan Busch, "Examining Psychotropic Medication Use Among Youth in the US by Race/Ethnicity and Psychological Impairment," *General Hospital Psychiatry* 45 (2017): 32–9, doi: 10.1016/j.genhosppsych.2016.12.004.

Chapter 5

1 Created by Leah Kuypers, *The Zones of Regulation Digital Curriculum*, created by Leah Kuypers (2011; second edition 2024), https://zonesofregulation.com/.

2 James Cartreine, "Misophonia: When Sounds Really Do Make You 'Crazy,'" *Harvard Health Blog*, June 24, 2019, https://www.health.harvard.edu/blog/misophonia-sounds-really-make-crazy-2017042111534.

3 Sara Berg, "What Doctors Wish Patients Knew About Misophonia," American Medical Association, April 5, 2024, https://www.ama-assn.org/delivering-care/public-health/what-doctors-wish-patients-knew-about-misophonia.

4 Emily Kuschner, "Autism and Food Aversions: 7 Ways to Help a Picky Eater," Autism Speaks, n.d., https://www.autismspeaks.org/expert-opinion/autism-and-food-aversions#:~:text=If%20you%20have%20a%20picky,)%20and%20meal%2Drelated%20tantrums.

5 "ABA Therapy History: Who Invented ABA Therapy?" Golden Steps ABA, September 4, 2024, https://www.goldenstepsaba.com/resources/aba-therapy-history#contemporary-aba-therapy.

Chapter 6

1 "Advocacy, Education, Support," Autism in Black, https://www.autisminblack.org, accessed November 4, 2024.

2   "2017–18 State and National Tables," Civil Rights Data Collection Office for Civil Rights, US Department of Education, 2021, https://civilrightsdata.ed.gov/estimations/2017-2018, last updated March 4, 2025.

3   Melissa L. Danielson, Angelika H. Claussen, Rebecca H. Bitsko, Samuel M. Katz, Kimberly Newsome, Stephen J. Blumberg, Michael D. Kogan, and Reem Ghandour, "ADHD Prevalence Among US Children and Adolescents in 2022: Diagnosis, Severity, Co-Occurring Disorders, and Treatment," *Journal of Clinical Child & Adolescent Psychology* 53, no. 3 (2024): 343–60.

4   Anna Medaris, "Brain Breakthroughs, How High Energy, Hyperfocus, and Little Tolerance for the Mundane—Hallmark Symptoms of ADHD—Affect Sports Performance," *Women's Health*, November 4, 2024, https://apple.news/AB6NSFtFrQC2iqsF7_3fL-w.

5   Santriani Bohari Jaon, "Beyond 'Pink Brain, Blue Brain': Gender Differences in Neurodiversity and Their Consequences," *The Karyawan*, January 18, 2023, https://karyawan.sg/beyond-pink-brain-blue-brain-gender-differences-in-neurodiversity-their-consequences/.

6   Herwig Czech, "Asperger, National Socialism, and 'Race Hygiene' in Nazi-Era Vienna," *Molecular Autism* 9 (2018): article 29, https://doi.org/10.1186/s13229-018-0208-6.

7   "Dyslexia Myths and Facts," *My Dyslexia Help*, n.d., University of Michigan, https://dyslexiahelp.umich.edu/dyslexics/learn-about-dyslexia/what-is-dyslexia/dyslexia-myths-and-facts.

8   National Association for the Advancement of Colored People (NAACP), *Dyslexia Resolution*, 2014, https://naacp.org/resources/dyslexia.

9   Laura Cassidy, Kayla Reggio, Bennett A. Shaywitz, John M. Holahan, and Sally E. Shaywitz, "Dyslexia in Incarcerated Men and Women: A New Perspective on Reading Disability in the Prison Population," *Journal of Correctional Education* 72, no. 2 (2021): 61–81.

10 Cassidy, Reggio, Shaywitz, Holahan, Shaywitz, "Dyslexia in Incarcerated Men and Women."

11 Jack M. Fletcher and Jeremy Miciak, "Comprehensive Cognitive Assessments Are Not Necessary for the Identification and Treatment of Learning Disabilities," *Archives of Clinical Neuropsychology* 32, no. 1 (2017): 2–7.

12 Laura Lemle, the NVLD Project, https://nvld.org/.

13 Brooke Shultz, "Nonverbal Learning Disorder, Explained," *Education Week*, August 27, 2024, https://www.edweek.org/teaching-learning/nonverbal-learning-disorder-explained/2024/08.

14 *Neurodiversity and Gender-Diverse Youth: An Affirming Approach to Care 2020*, National LGBT Health Institute, August 2020, https://www.lgbtqia healtheducation.org/wp-content/uploads/2020/08/Neurodiversity-and-Gender-Diverse-Youth_An-Affirming-Approach-to-Care_2020.pdf.

15 Anna I. R. van der Miesen, Hannah Hurley, Anneloes M. Bal, and Annelou L. C. deVries, "Prevalence of the Wish to Be of the Opposite Gender in Adolescents and Adults with Autism Spectrum Disorder," *Archives of Sexual Behavior* 47 (2018): 2307–17, https://doi.org/10.1007/s10508-018-1218-3.

16 Emily Thrower, Ingrid Bretherton, Ken C. Pang, Jeffrey D. Zajac, and Ada S. Cheung, "Prevalence of Autism Spectrum Disorder and Attention-Deficit Hyperactivity Disorder Amongst Individuals with Gender Dysphoria: A Systematic Review," *Journal of Autism and Developmental Disorders* 50, no. 3 (2020): 695–706

17 "Ilan H. Meyer, Distinguished Senior Scholar of Public Policy," UCLA School of Law, the Williams Institute, n.d., https://williamsinstitute.law.ucla.edu/experts/ilan-h-meyer/.

18 I. H. Meyer, "Minority Stress and Mental Health in Gay Men," *Journal of Health and Social Behav*ior 36, no. 1 (1995): 38–56.

19 California Children's Trust, "Children in Medi-Cal Are Being Left Behind," Equity Through Engagement, 2019, https://cachildrenstrust.org/our-work/equity-through-engagement/#:~:text=Children%20in%20Medi%2DCal%20Are,and%20their%20families%20are%20served.

Chapter 7

1 Nicole T. Buchanan and Lauren O. Wiklund, "Intersectionality Research in Psychological Science: Resisting the Tendency to Disconnect, Dilute, and Depoliticize," *Research on Child Adolescent Psychopathology* 49, no. 1 (2021): 25–31, doi: 10.1007/s10802-020-00748-y.

2 Brenda Salley, Joy Gabrielli, Catherine M. Smith, and Matthew Braun, "Do Communication and Social Interaction Skills Differ Across Youth Diagnosed with Autism Spectrum Disorder, Attention-Deficit/Hyperactivity Disorder, or Dual Diagnosis?" *Research in Autism Spectrum Disorders* 20 (2015): 58–66, doi: 10.1016/j.rasd.2015.08.006.

3   Juliana Menasce Horowitz and Nikki Graf, "Most US Teens See Anxiety and Depression as a Major Problem Among Their Peers," Pew Research Center, February 20, 2019, https://www.pewresearch.org/social-trends/2019/02/20/most-u-s-teens-see-anxiety-and-depression-as-a-major-problem-among-their-peers/.

4   Monica Anderson, Michelle Faverio, and Jeffrey Gottfried, "Teens, Social Media and Technology," Pew Research Center, December 11, 2023, https://www.pewresearch.org/internet/2023/12/11/teens-social-media-and-technology-2023/.

5   Melissa L. Danielson, Rebecca H. Bitsko, Reem M. Ghandour, Joseph R. Holbrook, Michael D. Kogan, and Stephen J. Blumberg, "Prevalence of Parent-Reported ADHD Diagnosis and Associated Treatment Among US Children and Adolescents," *Journal of Clinical Child & Adolescent Psychology* 47, no. 2 (2016): 199–212, doi: 10.1080/15374416.2017.1417860, https://www.ncbi.nlm.nih.gov/pmc/articles/PMC5834391/pdf/nihms937906.pdf.

6   "Depression in Children," Cleveland Clinic, medically reviewed November 9, 2023, https://my.clevelandclinic.org/health/diseases/14938-depression-in-children#:~:text=What%20are%20the%20symptoms%20of,sleeping%20or%20sleeping%20too%20much.

7   Hans-Jürgen Möller, Borwin Bandelow, Hans-Peter Volz, Utako Birgit Barnikol, Erich Seifritz, and Siegfried Kasper, "The Relevance of 'Mixed Anxiety and Depression' as a Diagnostic Category in Clinical Practice," *European Archives of Psychiatry and Clinical Neuroscience* 266, no. 8 (2016): 725–36.

8   Tasleema Khan, "Epilepsy and Autism: Is There a Relationship?" Epilepsy Foundation, University of South Florida, Tampa, March 21, 2017, https://www.epilepsy.com/stories/epilepsy-and-autism-there-relationship.

9   American Academy of Child and Adolescent Psychiatry, "Practice Parameters for the Assessment and Treatment of Children and Adolescents with Obsessive-Compulsive Disorder," *Journal of the American Academy of Child and Adolescent Psychiatry* 51, no. 1 (2012): 98–113.

10 Caitlin Harper, "What Is the 333 Rule for Anxiety?" *My Wellbeing*, n.d., https://mywellbeing.com/therapy-101/what-is-the-333-rule-for-anxiety#:~:text=It's%20an%20easy%20technique%20to,move%20three%20different%20body%20parts.

11 Lois Baldwin, Susan Baum, Daphne Pereles, and Claire Hughes, "Twice-Exceptional Learners: The Journey Toward a Shared Vision," *Gifted Child Today* 38, no. 4 (2015): 206–14. doi: 10.1177/1076217515597277.

12 Seth Perler, "Executive Function Is the Key," *Is My Child Twice Exceptional or 2e? [The Ultimate Guide]*, n.d., https://sethperler.com/child-2e-twice-exceptional-ultimate-guide/.

13 S. M. Baum and R. M. Schader. *Viewer's Guide for 2e2: Teaching the Twice Exceptional Documentary*, movie by Thomas Ropelewski (Studio City, CA: Bridges 2e Center for Research and Professional Development [2ecenter.org], 2018).

Chapter 8

1 "12 Ways to Help your Child who is Sensitive to Textures (tags, socks, sand)," North Shore Pediatric Therapy, February 1, 2024, https://www.nspt4kids.com/specialties-and-services/occupational-therapy/12-ways-to-help-your-child-who-is-sensitive-to-textures-tags-socks-sand#:~:text=Add%20cooking%20oil%20and%20boiling,Fun%20activities%20to%20try.

2 Dawn Winkelmann, "Sensory-Based Feeding Issues: Food Can't Touch," ezpz blog, n.d., https://ezpzfun.com/blogs/feeding-challenges/sensorybased-feeding-issues-my-child-cant-have-food-touch?srsltid=AfmBOopU14y5-SPPw_3R-C2fDCxuwYFIvIbSVNvkndm4i0HCvG34AO6x.

3 Alicia Maples, "Recognizing Glass Children: What It Means to Be a Sibling of a Child with Special Needs," TEDx San Antonio, YouTube video, 2010, https://tedxsanantonio.com/2010-speakers/alicia-arenas/.

4 "Understanding Glass Child Syndrome," SSM Health Cardinal Glennon Children's Hospital blog, October 2023, https://www.ssmhealth.com/newsroom/blogs/ssm-health-matters/october-2023/understanding-glass-child-syndrome#:~:text=Glass%20child%20syndrome%20isn't,with%20chronic%20illnesses%20or%20disabilities.

5 "Everything You Need to Know About Cassandra Syndrome as a Neurodivergent Couple," Hart Centre website, n.d., https://www.thehartcentre.com.au/everything-you-need-to-know-about-cassandra-syndrome-as-a-neurodivergent-couple/.

Chapter 9

1 "Children with Autism Twice as Likely to Report Suicidal Thoughts, According to New Research from Kennedy Krieger," Kennedy Krieger Institute, Baltimore Maryland, October 21, 2022. https://www

.kennedykrieger.org/stories/news-and-updates/research-news-releases/children-autism-twice-likely-report-suicidal-thoughts-according-new-research-kennedy-krieger.

2   Working Group Members and APA Staff, *Health Disparities in Racial/Ethnic and Sexual Minority Boys and Men*, American Psychological Association, APA Working Group on Health Disparities in Boys and Men, 2018, http://www.apa.org/pi/health-disparities/resources/race-sexuality-men.aspx.

3   "New Research Shows Alarming Number of Suicidal Thoughts Among Young Children with Autism Spectrum Disorder," Kennedy Krieger Institute, Baltimore, MD, April 4, 2024, https://www.kennedykrieger.org/stories/news-and-updates/research-news-releases/new-research-shows-alarming-number-suicidal-thoughts-among-young-children-autism-spectrum-disorder.

4   "Screening for Suicide Risk in Clinical Practice," American Academy of Pediatrics, last updated February 22, 2023, https://www.aap.org/en/patient-care/blueprint-for-youth-suicide-prevention/strategies-for-clinical-settings-for-youth-suicide-prevention/screening-for-suicide-risk-in-clinical-practice/.

5   The Trevor Project, "Facts About Suicide Among LGBTQ+ Young People," LGBTQ+ Mental Health Resources, December 15, 2021, last updated January 2024, https://www.thetrevorproject.org/resources/article/facts-about-lgbtq-youth-suicide/.

6   Rajeev Ramchand, Joshua A. Gordon, and Jane L. Pearson, "Trends in Suicide Rates by Race and Ethnicity in the United States," *JAMA Network Open* 4, no. 5 (2021): e2111563. doi:10.1001/jamanetworkopen.2021.11563

7   "Suicide Crisis Response: Connection, Collaboration and Choice," Relevance, September 15, 2023, last updated January 8, 2025, https://relevancerecovery.com/blog/the-significance-of-suicide-prevention-awareness-saving-lives/#:~:text=Suicide%20Crisis%20Response%3A%20Connection%2C%20Collaboration,feel%20understood%20and%20not%20isolated.

Chapter 10

1   Laurie Stevens, "QUESTION: What Does It Mean to Be 'Neurodivergent-Affirming'?" Help Group, n.d., https://www.thehelpgroup.org/question-what-does-it-mean-to-be-neurodivergent-affirming/#:~:text=In%20essence%2C%20being%20neurodivergent%2Daffirming,about%20our%20schools%20and%20programs%3F.

2 "The UDL Guidelines," *Universal Design for Learning Guidelines version 3.0*, Center for Applied Special Technology (CAST) 2024, https://udlguidelines.cast.org.

3 Vanaman German LLP, https://vanamangerman.com/.

4 US Department of Education, *Protecting Student's Privacy*, Family Educational Rights and Privacy Act (FERPA), n.d., https://studentprivacy.ed.gov/ferpa.

5 US Department of Education, "About," Office of Special Education Programs, n.d., https://www.ed.gov/about/ed-offices/osers/osep#About-OSEP.

6 "Public School Rankings by State 2024," *Word Population Review*, WalletHub, 2024, https://worldpopulationreview.com/state-rankings/public-school-rankings-by-state.

7 Jeff Hoch and Carol Kocivar, "What Are the Rights of Parents?" *Ed 100*, https://ed100.org/blog/parent-rights.

Chapter 11

1 Lori Baudino, "Dr. Lori Baudino," personal website, n.d., https://www.drloribaudino.com/.

Educators' Reader Guide and Discussion

1 Nancy Doyle, "Neurodiversity at Work: A Biopsychosocial Model and the Impact on Working Adults," *British Medical Bulletin* 135, no. 1 (2020): 108–25, doi: 10.1093/bmb/ldaa021.

BIBLIOGRAPHY

American Academy of Child and Adolescent Psychiatry. "Practice Parameters for the Assessment and Treatment of Children and Adolescents with Obsessive-Compulsive Disorder." *Journal of the American Academy of Child and Adolescent Psychiatry* 51, no. 1 (2012): 98–113.

American Academy of Pediatrics. "Screening for Suicide Risk in Clinical Practice." Last updated February 22, 2023. https://www.aap.org/en/patient-care/blueprint-for-youth-suicide-prevention/strategies-for-clinical-settings-for-youth-suicide-prevention/screening-for-suicide-risk-in-clinical-practice/.

American Psychological Association, APA Working Group on Health Disparities in Boys and Men. "Health Disparities in Racial/Ethnic and Sexual Minority Boys and Men. 2018. http://www.apa.org/pi/health-disparities/resources/race-sexuality-men.aspx.

Anderson, Monica, Michelle Faverio, and Jeffrey Gottfried. "Teens, Social Media and Technology." Pew Research Center, December 11, 2023. https://www.pewresearch.org/internet/2023/12/11/teens-social-media-and-technology-2023/.

Autism in Black. "Advocacy, Education, Support." Accessed November 4, 2024. https://www.autisminblack.org.

Baldwin, Lois, Susan Baum, Daphne Pereles, and Claire Hughes. "Twice-Exceptional Learners: The Journey Toward a Shared Vision." *Gifted Child Today* 38, no. 4 (2015): 206–14. doi: 10.1177/1076217515597277.

Baudino, Lori. "Dr. Lori Baudino." Personal website. n.d. https://www.drloribaudino.com/.

Baum, S. M., and R. M. Schader. *Viewer's Guide for 2e2: Teaching the Twice Exceptional Documentary*. Movie by Thomas Ropelewski. Studio City, CA: Bridges 2e Center for Research and Professional Development (2ecenter.org), 2018.

Bell, Ashley, "Is Autism Genetic?" UCLA David Geffen School of Medicine, April 10, 2024. www.medschool.ucla.edu/news-article/is-autism-genetic.

Berg, Sarah. "What Doctors Wish Patients Knew About Misophonia." American Medical Association, April 5, 2024. https://www.ama-assn.org/delivering-care/public-health/what-doctors-wish-patients-knew-about-misophonia.

Brack, Jenny Clark. *Learn to Move, Move to Learn: Sensorimotor Early Childhood Activity Themes*. Newark, DE: Autism Asperger Publishing Company, 2004.

Buchanan Nicole T., and Lauren O. Wiklund. "Intersectionality Research in Psychological Science: Resisting the Tendency to Disconnect, Dilute, and Depoliticize." *Research on Child Adolescent Psychopathology* 49, no. 1 (2021): 25–31. doi: 10.1007/s10802-020-00748-y.

Buck, John N. "The H-T-P Technique, a Qualitative and Quantitative Scoring Manual." *Journal of Clinical Psychology* 4, no. 4 (1948): 317.

California Children's Trust. "Children in Medi-Cal Are Being Left Behind." 2019. https://cachildrenstrust.org/our-work/equity-through-engagement/#:~:text=Children%20in%20Medi%2DCal%20Are%20Being%20Left%20Behind&text=Medi%2DCal%20insures%20more%20than,entitled%20to%20in%20the%20program.

California Department of Children and Family Services (CDCC). "Foster Care." 2024. www.cdss.ca.gov/inforesources/foster-care#:~:text=Thousands%20of%20children%20in%20California's,for%20weeks%3B%20some%20for%20years.

Cartreine, James. "Misophonia: When Sounds Really Do Make You 'Crazy.'" *Harvard Health Blog*, June 24, 2019. https://www.health.harvard.edu/blog/misophonia-sounds-really-make-crazy-2017042111534.

Cassidy, Laura, Kayla Reggio, Bennett A. Shaywitz, John M. Holahan, and Sally E. Shaywitz. "Dyslexia in Incarcerated Men and Women: A New Perspective on Reading Disability in the Prison Population," *Journal of Correctional Education* 72, no. 2 (2021): 61–81.

Center for Applied Special Technology (CAST). "The UDL Guidelines." *Universal Design for Learning Guidelines version 3.0.* 2024. https://udlguidelines.cast.org.

Children's Law Center of California, "Foster Care Facts." n.d. https://www.clccal.org/resources/foster-care facts/.

Choo, Ying Ying, Pratibha Agarwal, Choon How, and Sita Padmini Yeleswarapu. "Developmental Delay: Identification and Management at Primary Care Level." *Singapore Medical Journal* 60, no. 3 (2019): 119–23.

Cleveland Clinic. "Depression in Children." Medically reviewed November 9, 2023. https://my.clevelandclinic.org/health/diseases/14938-depression-in-children#:~:text=What%20are%20the%20symptoms%20of,sleeping%20or%20sleeping%20too%20much.

Cook, Benjamin L., Nicholas J. Carson, E. Nilay Kafali, Anne Valentine, Juan David Rueda, Sarah Coe-Odess, and Susan Busch. "Examining Psychotropic Medication Use Among Youth in the US by Race/Ethnicity and Psychological Impairment." *General Hospital Psychiatry* 45 (2017): 32–9. doi: 10.1016/j.genhosppsych.2016.12.004.

Czech, Herwig. "Asperger, National Socialism, and 'Race Hygiene' in Nazi-Era Vienna." *Molecular Autism* 9 (2018): article 29. https://doi.org/10.1186/s13229-018-0208-6.

Danielson, Melissa L., Angelika H. Claussen, Rebecca H. Bitsko, Samuel M. Katz, Kimberly Newsome, Stephen J. Blumberg, Michael D. Kogan, and Reem Ghandour. "ADHD Prevalence Among US Children and Adolescents in 2022: Diagnosis, Severity, Co-Occurring Disorders, and Treatment," *Journal of Clinical Child & Adolescent Psychology* 53, no. 3 (2024): 343–60.

Danielson, Melissa L., Rebecca H. Bitsko, Reem M. Ghandour, Joseph R. Holbrook, Michael D. Kogan, and Stephen J. Blumberg, "Prevalence of Parent-Reported ADHD Diagnosis and Associated Treatment Among US Children and Adolescents," *Journal of Clinical Child & Adolescent Psychology* 47, no. 2 (2016): 199–212, doi: 10.1080/15374416.2017.1417860, https://www.ncbi.nlm.nih.gov/pmc/articles/PMC5834391/pdf/nihms937906.pdf.

DC Department of Human Services. "Functional Family Therapy (FFT)." Accessed November 21, 2024. https://dhs.dc.gov/page/functional-family-therapy-fft.

Doyle, Nancy. "Neurodiversity at Work: A Biopsychosocial Model and the Impact on Working Adults." *British Medical Bulletin* 135, no. 1 (2020): 108–25., doi: 10.1093/bmb/ldaa021.

Drake Institute of Neurophysical Medicine. "What Is Neurofeedback Therapy Used For?" n.d. https://www.drakeinstitute.com/what-is-neurofeedback-therapy-used-for#:~:text=Neurofeedback%20helps%20patients%20self%2Dregulate,associated%20with%20ADD%20and%20ADHD.

Fetal Alcohol Spectrum Consultation, Education, and Training Services. "FASD Facts." n.d. https://fascets.org/fasd-facts/.

Fletcher, Jack M., and Jeremy Miciak. "Comprehensive Cognitive Assessments Are Not Necessary for the Identification and Treatment of Learning Disabilities," *Archives of Clinical Neuropsychology* 32, no. 1 (2017): 2–7.

Freibergs, V., and V. I. Douglas, "Concept Learning in Hyperactive and Normal Children," *Journal of Abnormal Psychology* 74, no. 3 (1969): 388–95.

German, Vanaman, LLP. Personal website. n.d. https://vanamangerman.com/.

Getahun, Darios, George G. Rhoads, Kitaw Demissie, Shou-En Lu, Virginia P. Quinn, Michael J. Fassett, Deborah A. Wing, and Steven J. Jacobsen. "In Utero Exposure to Ischemic-Hypoxic Conditions and Attention-Deficit/Hyperactivity Disorder." *Pediatrics* 131, no. 1 (2013): e53–e61. https://doi.org/10.1542/peds.2012-1298.

Golden Steps ABA. "ABA Therapy History: Who Invented ABA Therapy?" September 4, 2024. https://www.goldenstepsaba.com/resources/aba-therapy-history#contemporary-aba-therapy.

Goldstein, Sam, and Jack A. Naglieri. "House-Tree-Person (H-T-P)." In *Encyclopedia of Child Behavior and Development*. Edited by Sam Goldstein and Jack A. Naglieri. Boston: Springer, 2011. https://doi.org/10.1007/978-0-387-79061-9_4801.

Goodenough, Florence L. *Measurement of Intelligence by Drawings*. New York: Harcourt, Brace, and World, 1926.

Grace Counseling. "Are There Different Types of Play Therapy?" n.d. https://www.grace-counseling.com/rehab-blog/are-there-different-types-of-play-therapy/.

Griffiths, Catherine. *FASD*, CYMRU, 2020.

Harper, Caitlin. "What Is the 333 Rule for Anxiety?" *My Wellbeing*, n.d. https://mywellbeing.com/therapy-101/what-is-the-333-rule-for-anxiety#:~:text=It's%20an%20easy%20technique%20to,move%20three%20different%20body%20parts.

The Hart Centre. "Everything You Need to Know About Cassandra Syndrome as a Neurodivergent Couple." n.d. https://www.thehartcentre.com.au/everything-you-need-to-know-about-cassandra-syndrome-as-a-neurodivergent-couple/.

Hassani, Zahra, Fatemeh Hosseinpour, Mina Sadat Mirshoja, and Abolfazi Boozhabadi. "Effectiveness of Cognitive-Behavioral Play Therapy on Improving Anxiety and Aggression Disorders in a Child with ADHD: A Case Study." *Case Reports in Clinical Practice* 6, no. 3 (2021): 116–19.

Kelly Henderson, "Finding the Sweet Spot: Foster Care, Disability and Special Education." *Fostering Families Today*, July 7, 2021. https://formedfamiliesforward.org/wp-content/uploads/2022/03/Finding-the-Sweet-Spot_-Foster-Care-Disability-and-Special-Education-%E2%80%93-Fostering-Families-Today.pdf

Henry Mayo Newhall Hospital. "What to Expect: Newborn Screening Tests and More After Delivery." 2021. https://www.henrymayo.com/news-publications/news/2021/what-to-expect-newborn-screening-tests-and-more-after-delivery/#:~:text=Your%20doctor%20will%20do%20Apgar,Metabolic%20screening.

Hoch, Jeff, and Carol Kocivar, "What Are the Rights of Parents?" *Ed 100*. https://ed100.org/blog/parent-rights.

Horowitz, Juliana Menasce, and Nikki Graf. "Most US Teens See Anxiety and Depression as a Major Problem Among Their Peers." Pew Research Center, February 20, 2019. https://www.pewresearch.org/social-trends/2019/02/20/most-u-s-teens-see-anxiety-and-depression-as-a-major-problem-among-their-peers/.

Hurley, Katie. "Group Therapy for Kids: What It Is, How They Can Benefit, and When Not to Send Your Child to Group Therapy." Health Central. Updated October 7, 2022. https://www.healthcentral.com/mental-health/group-therapy-children.

Ignite Healthwise Staff. "Nonverbal Learning Disorder," University of Michigan Health, Michigan Medicine, July 31, 2024. www.uofmhealth.org/health-library/te7868.

Individuals with Disabilities Education Act, 20 U.S.C. § 1400 (2004).
International Dyslexia Association. "Definition Consensus Project." n.d. www.dyslexiaida.org/definition-consensus-project/.
Jaon, Santriani Bohari. "Beyond 'Pink Brain, Blue Brain': Gender Differences in Neurodiversity and Their Consequences." *The Karyawan*, January18, 2023. https://karyawan.sg/beyond-pink-brain-blue-brain-gender-differences-in-neurodiversity-their-consequences/.
Jones, Carolyn. "Parents' Guide to 504 Plans and IEPs: What They Are and How They're Different." EdSource, March 29, 2022. https://edsource.org/2022/parents-guide-to-504-plans-and-ieps-what-they-are-and-how-theyre-different/669493#:~:text=A%20504%20plan%20is%20geared,have%20one%20or%20the%20other.
Kaiser Permanente. "Kaiser Permanente Study Finds Children Exposed to Complications Before or During Birth at Higher Risk of Developing Autism Spectrum Disorder, Department of Research and Evaluation, Southern California." n.d. https://www.kp-scalresearch.org/kaiser-permanente-study-finds-children-exposed-to-complications-before-or-during-birth-at-higher-risk-of-developing-autism-spectrum-disorder/.
Kennedy Krieger Institute. "Children With Autism Twice as Likely to Report Suicidal Thoughts, According to New Research from Kennedy Krieger," Baltimore, MD, October 21, 2022. https://www.kennedykrieger.org/stories/news-and-updates/research-news-releases/children-autism-twice-likely-report-suicidal-thoughts-according-new-research-kennedy-krieger.
———. "New Research Shows Alarming Number of Suicidal Thoughts Among Young Children with Autism Spectrum Disorder." Baltimore, MD, April 4, 2024. https://www.kennedykrieger.org/stories/news-and-updates/research-news-releases/new-research-shows-alarming-number-suicidal-thoughts-among-young-children-autism-spectrum-disorder.
Khan, Tasleema. "Epilepsy and Autism: Is There a Relationship?" Epilepsy Foundation, University of South Florida, Tampa, March 21, 2017. https://www.epilepsy.com/stories/epilepsy-and-autism-there-relationship.
Kuschner, Emily. "Autism and Food Aversions: 7 Ways to Help a Picky Eater." *Autism Speaks*. n.d. https://www.autismspeaks.org/expert-opinion/autism-and-food-aversions#:~:text=If%20you%20have%20a%20picky,)%20and%20meal%2Drelated%20tantrums.
Kuypers, Lea. *The Zones of Regulation Digital Curriculum*. First edition, 2011; second edition 2024. https://zonesofregulation.com/.
Kytzidis, Pagona. "In Loco Parentis: The Role Schools Must Play to Provide Mental Health Resources." *Columbia Undergraduate Law Review*, August 30, 2017. https://blogs.cuit.columbia.edu/culr/2017/08/30/in-loco-parentis-the-role-schools-must-play-to-provide-mental-health-resources/.

Learning Differences Aotearoa Trust. "Specific Learning Disabilities." Dyslexia Support South, 2024. https://www.dyslexiasupportsouth.org.nz/school-toolkit/specific-learning-difficulties-and-processing-disorders/#:~:text=These%20include%20dyslexia%2C%20dyscalculia%2C%20dysgraphia,common%20ones%20we%20come%20across.

Lemle, Laura. The NVLD Project. n.d. https://nvld.org/.

Maples, Alicia. "Recognizing Glass Children: What It Means to Be a Sibling of a Child with Special Needs." TEDx San Antonio, YouTube video, 2010. https://tedxsanantonio.com/2010-speakers/alicia-arenas/.

Medaris, Anna. "Brain Breakthroughs, How High Energy, Hyperfocus, and Little Tolerance for the Mundane—Hallmark Symptoms of ADHD—Affect Sports Performance." *Women's Health*, November 4, 2024. https://apple.news/AB6NSFtFrQC2iqsF7_3fL-w.

Michaels, Margaret, and Qi "Susie" Duong. "Neurodivergent Individuals Can Make Significant Contributions at Work When They Feel Included." Institute of Management Accountants, April 2, 2024. http://www.imanet.org/blog/2024/04/neurodivergent-individuals-can-make-significant-contributions-at-work-when-they-feel-included.

Möller, Hans-Jürgen, Borwin Bandelow, Hans-Peter Volz, Utako Birgit Barnikol, Erich Seifritz, and Siegfried Kasper. "The Relevance of 'Mixed Anxiety and Depression' as a Diagnostic Category in Clinical Practice." *European Archives of Psychiatry and Clinical Neuroscience* 266, no. 8 (2016): 725–36.

Morris, Monique Q. *Pushout: The Criminalization of Black Girls in Schools*. New York: The New Press 2016.

National Association for the Advancement of Colored People (NAACP). *Dyslexia Resolution*. 2014. https://naacp.org/resources/dyslexia.

National Institute of Mental Health, "What Is ADHD?" *Attention-Deficit/Hyperactivity Disorder: What You Need to Know*. US Department of Health and Human Services. 2024. https://www.nimh.nih.gov/health/publications/attention-deficit-hyperactivity-disorder-what-you-need-to-know.

National LGBT Health Institute. *An Affirming Approach to Care 2020*. August 2020. https://www.lgbtqiahealtheducation.org/wp-content/uploads/2020/08/Neurodiversity-and-Gender-Diverse-Youth_An-Affirming-Approach-to-Care_2020.pdf.

New York University Langone Health. "Common Neurological Tests." New York University. n.d. https://nyulangone.org/care-services/neurosurgery/common-neurological-tests#:~:text=Neurological%20Examination,orientation%2C%20mood%2C%20and%20cognition.

North Shore Pediatric Therapy. "12 Ways to Help Your Child Who Is Sensitive to Textures (tags, socks, sand)." February 1, 2024. https://www.nspt4kids.com/specialties-and-services/occupational-therapy/12-ways-to-help-your-child

-who-is-sensitive-to-textures-tags-socks-sand#:~:text=Add%20cooking%20 oil%20and%20boiling,Fun%20activities%20to%20try.

NVLD Project. "What Is Non-Verbal Learning Disorder?" n.d. https://nvld.org/non-verbal-learning-disability/#:~:text=People%20with%20Non%2DVerbal%20Learning,social%20barriers%20throughout%20their%20lives.

Perler, Seth. "Executive Function is the Key." *Is My Child Twice Exceptional or 2e? [The Ultimate Guide]*. n.d. https://sethperler.com/child-2e-twice-exceptional-ultimate-guide/.

Relevance, "Suicide Crisis Response: Connection, Collaboration, and Choice." September 15, 2023, last updated January 8, 2025. https://relevancerecovery.com/blog/the-significance-of-suicide-prevention-awareness-saving-lives/#:~:text=Suicide%20Crisis%20Response%3A%20Connection%2C%20Collaboration,feel%20understood%20and%20not%20isolated.

Salley, Brenda, Joy Gabrielli, Catherine M. Smith, and Matthew Braun. "Do Communication and Social Interaction Skills Differ Across Youth Diagnosed with Autism Spectrum Disorder, Attention-Deficit/Hyperactivity Disorder, or Dual Diagnosis?" *Research in Autism Spectrum Disorders* 20 (2015): 58–66. doi: 10.1016/j.rasd.2015.08.006.

Section 504 of the Rehabilitation Act.

Shaywitz, Sally. *Overcoming Dyslexia*, second edition. New York: Vintage, 2022.

———. "Shaywitz DyslexiaScreen" Yale Center for Dyslexia and Creativity. n.d. https://dyslexia.yale.edu/resources/educators/instruction/shaywitz-dyslexiascreen/.

Short, Crystal, Crystal Short, Kathy DeOrnellas, and Robert Walrath. "Draw-A-Person Test." In *Encyclopedia of Child Behavior and Development*, edited by Sam Goldstein and Jack A. Naglieri. Boston: Springer, 2011, https://doi.org/10.1007/978-0-387-79061-9_894.

Shultz, Brooke. "Nonverbal Learning Disorder, Explained." *Education Week*, August 27, 2024. https://www.edweek.org/teaching-learning/nonverbal-learning-disorder-explained/2024/08.

SSM Health Cardinal Glennon Children's Hospital. "Understanding Glass Child Syndrome." October 2023. https://www.ssmhealth.com/newsroom/blogs/ssm-health-matters/october-2023/understanding-glass-child-syndrome#:~:text=Glass%20child%20syndrome%20isn't,with%20chronic%20illnesses%20or%20disabilities.

Stevens, Laurie. "QUESTION: What Does It Mean to Be 'Neurodivergent-Affirming'?" Help Group. n.d. https://www.thehelpgroup.org/question-what-does-it-mean-to-be-neurodivergent-affirming/#:~:text=In%20essence%2C%20being%20neurodivergent%2Daffirming,about%20our%20schools%20and%20programs%3F.

Still, George F. Still. "Some Abnormal Psychical Conditions in Children: The Goulstonian Lectures." *The Lancet*, April 12, 19, and 26, 1902. https://wellcomecollection.org/works/ydzjmfqe/items?canvas=5.

Thrower, Emily, Ingrid Bretherton, Ken C. Pang, Jeffrey D. Zajac, and Ada S. Cheung. "Prevalence of Autism Spectrum Disorder and Attention-Deficit Hyperactivity Disorder Amongst Individuals with Gender Dysphoria: A Systematic Review." *Journal of Autism and Developmental Disorders* 50, no. 3 (2020): 695–706.

Tomassi, Alexa. "New Study Highlights Potential Missed Diagnoses of Dyslexia in African American Students." Yale School of Medicine, February 8, 2024. https://medicine.yale.edu/news-article/new-study-highlights-potential-missed-diagnoses-of-dyslexia-in-african-american-students/.

The Trevor Project. "Facts About Suicide Among LGBTQ+ Young People." LGBTQ+ Mental Health Resources, December 15, 2021, last updated January 2024. https://www.thetrevorproject.org/resources/article/facts-about-lgbtq-youth-suicide/.

United States Department of Education, Office for Civil Rights. "2017–18 Civil Rights Data Collection." 2021. Last updated March 4, 2025. https://civilrightsdata.ed.gov/estimations/2017-2018.

United States Department of Education. *Protecting Student's Privacy*. Family Educational Rights and Privacy Act (FERPA). n.d. https://studentprivacy.ed.gov/ferpa.

United States Supreme Court, John and Jane Parents 1 vs. Montgomery Board of Education. No. 23-601. https://www.supremecourt.gov/DocketPDF/23/23-601/294860/20240104101635975_23-601%20Amicus%20Brief%20of%20Professors%20S.%20Ernie%20Walton%20and%20Eric%20A.%20DeGroff.pdf.

University of California, Los Angeles (UCLA) School of Law. "Ilan H. Meyer, Distinguished Senior Scholar of Public Policy." The Williams Institute. n.d. https://williamsinstitute.law.ucla.edu/experts/ilan-h-meyer/.

University of Michigan. "Dyslexia Myths and Facts." *My Dyslexia Help*. n.d. https://dyslexiahelp.umich.edu/dyslexics/learn-about-dyslexia/what-is-dyslexia/dyslexia-myths-and-facts.

University of Michigan. "Tests for Dyslexia and Learning Disabilities." n.d. https://dyslexiahelp.umich.edu/dyslexics/learn-about-dyslexia/dyslexia-testing/tests.

van der Miesen, Anna I. R., Hannah Hurley, Anneloes M. Bal, and Annelou L. C. deVries. "Prevalence of the Wish to Be of the Opposite Gender in Adolescents and Adults with Autism Spectrum Disorder." *Archives of Sexual Behavior* 47 (2018): 2307–17. https://doi.org/10.1007/s10508-018-1218-3.

Virginia Department of Education. "Individualized Education Plan." 2022. https://www.doe.virginia.gov/programs-services/special-education/iep-instruction/individualized-education-program-iep#:~:text=An%20IEP%20is%20comprised%20of,the%20child%20can%20meet%20the.

WalletHub. "Public School Rankings by State 2024." *Word Population Review*. 2024. https://worldpopulationreview.com/state-rankings/public-school-rankings-by-state.

Weil, Bettina. "IEP and 504 Plans: Differences and Similarities," *Niche*, April 23, 2021. https://weilcollegeadvising.com/iep-and-504-plans-differences-and-similarities/.

Wilkins, Faith, *Why Do Black Children with Autism Get Diagnosed Late?* Child Mind Institute, April 10, 2024, https://childmind.org/article/why-do-black-children-with-autism-get-diagnosed-late/#:~:text=According%20to%20one%20of%20the,autism%20during%20their%20medical%20education.

Wilkinson, Gary S., and Gary J. Robertson. *Wide Range Achievement Test*, fifth edition Bloomington, MN: Pearson Assessments, 2017.

Winkelmann, Dawn. "Sensory-Based Feeding Issues: Food Can't Touch." ezpz blog, n.d. https://ezpzfun.com/blogs/feeding-challenges/sensorybased-feeding-issues-my-child-cant-have-food-touch?srsltid=AfmBOopU14y5-SPPw_3R-C2fDCxuwYFIvIbSVNvkndm4i0HCvG34AO6x.

Woodcock, Richard W. *Woodcock Reading and Mastery Tests*, revised edition. Circle Pines, MN: American Guidance Service, 1998.

Yale Center for Dyslexia and Creativity. "Dyslexia FAQ." 2022 www.dyslexia.yale.edu/dyslexia/dyslexia-faq/.

Zettler-Greeley, Cynthia. "Understanding Dyslexia." Nemours Teen Health. May 2022. https://kidshealth.org/en/teens/dyslexia.html#:~:text=You%20probably%20will%20read%20slowly,remembering%20what%20you've%20read.

INDEX

#ABAIsAbuse 98
Abraham, Dayna 148
absence seizures (non-epileptic spells) 131
  impact 131
  zoning out 131
ADDitude Magazine 79
adoption 4, 9, 118, 121, 145, 169
  information about first parents or other relatives 16
  trauma and birth trauma 12
adoptive parents 5, 9, 12, 16, 39, 43, 46, 107, 156, 169
agitation 90, 93, 130, 133
American Academy of Pediatrics 160
American Chiropractic Neurology Board (ACNB) 68
American nuclear family 14
anemia 10
anxiety 4, 11, 19, 35–7, 40–1, 44–5, 66, 74, 76, 81, 90, 99, 110, 112, 123–32, 134, 136–7, 141, 154, 167, 176
  and depression 127–9
  nyctophobia 127
  pre-and post-COVID-19 pandemic issues 127
  social media 127
Apgar score 10
applied behavior analysis (ABA)
  inclusive play-based approach 98–9
  proponents of 98
  tenets of 97
  treatment plan for autism spectrum 99
art therapy 66
  certified art therapist 67
  trauma or have behavioral challenges 66–7
Asian Pacific Islander Desi American (APIDA) 38, 45, 106, 161
assessments
  behaviors, comparing 49
  clinician, role of 51
  discussion and reapproach 52
  504 Plan or Learning Accommodation Plan (LAP) 78
  HTP technique 50
  IDEA 56
  misdiagnosis 59
  personality traits and psychological problems 50
  profile of 51
  psychoeducational evaluation 78, 80–1
  PTSD 51
  quality of life 53
  results 52
  Support Team Education Plan (STEP) 78
  tests 49–50
  time of the test 56
  transparency 51
  value of 53

attention deficit disorder
 (ADD) 12, 17, 26, 34–5,
 37, 115
attention-deficit/hyperactivity
 disorder (ADHD) 1, 5,
 12, 26, 33–7
 asphyxia and 10
 behavior modification techniques
  using reward system 109
 cisgender stereotypes 106
 coping mechanisms 35
 DSM-V definition 110
 similarities and
  differences 128–9
 girls 109
 inattentive, hyperactive/impulsive,
  or combined 106–11
 in-school/out-of-school
  suspensions 108
 lying 35–6
 mixed-race and adoptive
  parents 107
 negative attention 37
 out-of-character risky
  behaviors 110
 shaming 36
 stealing 35–6
 teens with 34
 types of 64
auditory processing disorder 42,
 62, 174
*Autism and Food Aversions: 7 Ways
 to Help a Picky Eater*
 (Kuschner) 92–3
autism spectrum disorder (ASD) 5,
 12, 18, 26, 37–40, 111–13
 Asperger's syndrome 112–13
 bias, racism, and parental
  mistrust 38
 categories of 101
 cheat sheet 112

 hereditary 18
 high-functioning autistic 113
 low-functioning autistic 113
 masking, coping strategy 113
 Rain Man stereotype 111
 subcategories for specific
  symptoms 100
 super version of supporting
  kids 111
 symptoms 136
 symptoms, eight to twelve
  months 37–8
 wheel, categories 101–2
 young adults with ASD 112

baby boomers 14, 46
Baudino, Lori 31–3, 67, 87, 185
behavioral or medical
 interventions 51
Black, Indigenous, person of color
 (BIPOC) 12, 62, 77, 89,
 114, 122, 160, 185
Black 106
Boston, Latoya (on parenting of
 neurodivergent kids)
 advice for adoptive
  parents 156–7
 joint effort 156
 LGBTQ+ community 157
 on parenting a neurotypical
  child 155–6
 social media 157
 treatment plans and therapy, role
  of 156
Brack, Jenny Clark 26
Bryant, Kobe 88, 206
bullying 39, 53, 66, 131, 160

California Department of
 Health Care Services
 (DHCS) 121

Calm the Chaos (Abraham) 148
caregivers 2–3, 5, 7, 11–12, 14, 35–6, 44–5, 49–53, 56–8, 63–5, 70–1, 73, 75, 77–8, 80–1, 83, 85, 91, 93–4, 96, 98, 102, 109, 112, 117–18, 121–3, 125–6, 131, 133, 136, 139–41, 147, 149, 151, 154, 160, 164, 167, 173–4, 178–9
Cassandra affective deprivation disorder (CADD)/Cassandra syndrome 149
Centers for Disease Control (CDC) 38
Centers for Disease Control and Prevention 109
child assigned female at birth (AFAB) 117
child-centered play therapy (CCPT) 38, 66
Child Mind Institute 38, 106
children with special needs 46
Child Success Center 26–7, 81
chiropractic neurology 68–9
cisgender 98, 117, 139
  notions 4
  stereotypes 109
cognitive and emotional development 16–17, 27, 62, 67, 91
cognitive behavioral therapy (CBT) 66, 132
communication 72
  barriers 131
  intermittent 55
  open and honest 137
  poor/impaired 66–7
  text/direct messages (DMs) 127
comorbid symptoms
  absence seizures (non-epileptic spells) 131
  antisocial and/or criminal behavior 126
  anxiety and depression 127–9
  cognitive behavioral therapy (CBT) 132
  COVID-19 pandemic issues 134–6
  depression 130
  interventions for 132–3
  missed comorbid cues or dismissive advice 125
  obsessive-compulsive disorder (OCD) 131–2
  oppositional defiant disorder (ODD) 130–1
  side effects 133
  333 rule 132
  2e or twice exceptional 133–4
Comprehensive Test of Phonological Processing 50
Conners4 Feedback Handout for Parent Ratings 50
Consortium on Reaching Excellence in California (CORE) 115
counseling services 96
COVID-19 pandemic 69, 88
  communication, text or direct messages 127
  comorbid issues and social delays 127, 135
  telehealth appointment 145
CTOPP-2 50
cyberbullying 160

dance/movement therapy 31, 67
  integrative therapeutic approach to movement 67
  movements (rituals, patterns, preferences) 67
Democratic National Convention 43

denial 14, 45, 50–1, 64, 95, 126, 140
   delays 45
depression 4, 10, 14, 16, 35–7, 41, 45, 66, 76, 81, 89–90, 93, 99, 110, 112, 116, 124–5, 127, 130, 134, 136–7, 140, 154, 160
   with anxiety 4, 36–7, 41, 76, 81, 99, 110, 127, 130, 136, 154, 193
   maternal 14
   signs and symptoms 130
   simultaneous symptoms 130
developmental success 11
diagnosis. *See also* misdiagnosis
   auditory processing 62
   emotional IQ, open-ended questions 61–2
   H-T-P test 62
   psychoeducational evaluation 62–4
Diagnostic and Statistical Manual of Mental Disorders (DSM) 3, 64
Diagnostic and Statistical Manual of Mental Disorders, fifth edition *(DSM-V)* 65, 110
Diagnostic and Statistical Manual of Mental Disorders, fifth edition *(DSM V-TR)* 115
differentiated instructional strategies/differentiated learning 71
Disabilities Education Act (IDEA) 56, 71
disabled student programs and services 90
Disneyland 90
disorganization 32, 35, 109
disparities
   in Black children treated in school 23
   in health care 45
   in suicide rates of BIPOC youth 160
disruptive behavior 38, 42–3
dopamine 37
Draw-a-Person test 62
drug addiction 27, 45, 147
DSM-VI 110
dyscalculia 6, 41–2, 73, 165
dysgraphia 6, 41–2, 44, 165
dyslexia 5–6, 12, 17–18, 28, 34, 37, 41–3, 113–15
   with ADHD/ADD symptoms 115
   BIPOC, delays in assessments 114
   consequences of illiteracy 114
   and developmental disability 115
   language-based impairment 41
   language-based learning difference 113
   memorization skills 42
   negative or overtly shy behavior 114
   processing disorders 42
   Shaywitz DyslexiaScreen 50
   signs, attention to 43
   stereotypes 113
   study of inmates in maximum-security prisons 114
dyspraxia 41–2, 44

education(al)
   IEP (*see* individualized education program [IEP])
   NAEP 43
   public 24
   settings 70–3, 183

special   2, 6, 7, 16, 54–6, 59, 64, 71, 115, 165–6, 168, 173–5, 179–81, 186
trauma   164, 165
educators' reader guide and discussion   197–201
Eilish, Billie   112
emotional IQ   61, 184
   open-ended questions   61–2
emotional IQ, open-ended questions   61–2
empathy   15, 36, 66, 74, 153
executive functioning strategies   63, 90, 111, 124, 154

Fagell, Phyllis (on parenting of neurodivergent kids)
   being a counselor   157
   growing with kids, adjust and support   159
   impact and increased rate of suicide   160–1
   language issues   158
   neurodivergent child in middle school   158
   parents of neurodivergent child   158
   risk factors   160
   stigma and mistreatment   160
   suicidal ideation in young children   160
   3 Cs of suicide prevention (connection/collaboration/choice)   161
   warning signs   159–60
family
   adult partnerships   148–9
   Cassandra syndrome   149
   couple's therapy   148
   educational environment, supportive   140
   home-proofing process   140
   impact of neurodivergence   149
   reactions to food   140–1
   sensory processing disorder (SPD)   140
   siblings   141–8
Family and Educational Rights and Privacy Act (FERPA)   178
family play therapy   66
fear of missing out (FOMO)   127
fetal alcohol spectrum disorder (FASD)   39–41
   FAS   41
   neurobehavioral model   40
first-generation children   185
504 Plan (Section 504 of the Rehabilitation Act of 1973)   58–9, 78
   free and appropriate public education (FAPE)   58
   tailored special education services   59
Frederick, George   17
free appropriate public education (FAPE)   71, 173

gender identification and neurodivergence, intersection of
   access to care   121
   common in the LGBTQ+ community   116
   co-occurring issues   116
   gender identification and sexual orientation   116
   minority stress theory   118
   rejection and violence to LGBTQ+ youth   118
   and sexual orientation   116
genetic and environmental factors   11

Gen Z 4, 97, 117, 127, 136
German, Vanaman 176
grandparenting 184
group play therapy 66
growing with child
  racial awareness 151
  stimulant and non-stimulant medication 153
  unconscious bias, role of 151

Hilton, Paris 112
home and school overlap
  board games 74
  card games 74
  incentives 75–6
  organization 74
  positive reinforcement 75
  quiet corner 75
  role play 74
  validation of the feelings 75
homelessness 45
house
  family configuration 139
  members in 94
  stressor for caregivers 94
  tension 94
H-T-P test 62
hyperactivity 1, 5, 12, 18, 25, 67, 106, 110, 126
hypothyroidism 10

Idelson, Melissa 26
immigrants 45
impulsivity 25, 34–5, 39, 110, 126, 141
inattention 25, 34, 110, 152
inattentive-type attention deficit disorder (ADD) 12, 17, 26, 34–5, 37, 115
incarceration 3, 45

individualized education program (IEP) 6, 39, 54–60, 71, 78, 173–5, 177–8
  blind 57
  children on the autism spectrum 57
  educational opportunity program (EOP) 58
  federal document 57
  recommendations for public or nonpublic schools (NPS) 57
Individuals with Disabilities Education Act (IDEA) 56, 71
insomnia 35, 38, 93
integrative approach 31
Irlen Syndrome or visual processing disorder 42

Jackson, Willie Jamal 24

K–12 education systems 57, 71, 73, 99
Kennedy Krieger Institute 160
Koocheck, Claudia (Head of School, Westmark School)
  adverse childhood experiences or trauma 169
  emphasis on child's strengths 170
  inclusive environment 171
  insight to parents and caregivers 167
  learning environment for neurodivergent kids 169–70
  neurodiversity, understanding of 168
  parents being preventative 168
  predictability 167

right language by teachers 167
special education, inspiration to work with 166
special education methodology and pedagogy 168–9
survival mode of parents 169
teaching special education 166
tight partnership 169
trust in education system 168
Universal Design for Learning (UDL), guidelines 170
Kuschner, Emily 92

labeling 13, 42, 125, 130
Latine 45, 68, 77, 105–7, 114, 125
Learn to Move, Move to Learn! (Brack) 26
LGBTQ+ 4, 12, 62, 65, 69–70, 106, 117–18, 128, 139, 154, 157, 160, 179, 186
Los Angeles Unified School District (LAUSD) 24

Magrid 73
Martin, Areva 13, 15, 79
maternal depression 14
Medicaid 65, 98
Medi-Cal 65, 68, 121
members in the house. *See* family; house
messiness 32
microaggressions 84
micromanaging 32
millennials 97
  parents 184
  props to 117
minority stress theory 118
misdiagnosis 18–19, 59, 125, 129, 133, 135
misophonia 92
ModMath 73

Morris, Monique W. 23
Motherhood So White: A Memoir of Race, Gender, and Parenting in America (Austin) 1, 15, 86
multistep directions, avoiding 39, 72

National Assessment of Educational Progress (NAEP) 43
National Institute for Mental Health 25
negative self-image 127
negative side effects 93
neonatal intensive care unit (NICU) 10
neurodivergence/neurodivergent children 1, 4–5, 12, 27
  aggressive behaviors 3
  anxiety and depression 4
  barriers to treatment plans 3
  easy-to-follow books 2
  gender 3
  genetic and/or a result of birth trauma 29
  invisible differences 33–4
  language, importance of 122
  LGBTQ+ Gen Z teens 4
  meals challenging 92
  parenting 2
  preparation for 46
  recognizing signs 31, 46
  spectrum issue 46
neurodiverse-affirming educational environments 184. *See also* education(al)
neurofeedback or biofeedback 67, 91
  computer-based immediate feedback 67
  covered by insurance 67
neurologic differences 26, 41, 52, 90, 96–7, 111, 133

non-Black therapists   68
nonpublic schools (NPS)   57, 165, 173–8
   assessment from the school district   173
   description   174
   experienced with neurodivergent students   174
   psychoeducational evaluation   174
   special education class or special day class (SDC)   173, 175
nonverbal learning disability (NVLD)
   impacts focus and motor skills   18
   interpretation of nonverbal social cues   44
nonverbal learning disability/disorder (NVLD)   12, 18–19, 28, 34, 37, 43–4, 49, 99, 106, 115–16, 141, 173, 180
   barriers to learning   115
   DSM V-TR   115
   great with words   44
   intellectual ability   19
   mimics ASD, ADHD   115
   neurodivergent adults   19
   signs of   115
   symptoms   18, 115–16
nyctophobia   128

obsessive-compulsive disorder (OCD)   123, 131–2
   fears and obsessions   131
   impact   132
occupational therapy (OT)/therapist   26, 28, 31, 52, 67–8, 87
oppositional defiant disorder (ODD)   123, 130–1

Osaka, Naomi   89
ostracism   160
OT plus therapy   27
out-of-pocket costs   94
outright neglect   45

parent-child relationship   26
parent education   46, 79
parenthood (authoritative, gentle, or a laissez-faire)   13
parenting   2, 66, 98, 185
   ability to shift perspective   185
   books   4–5
   education classes   9
   experience   183–4
   good   14
   grandparenting   184
   handbook   91
   logic   16
   poor   38
   strategies   4
   styles   13, 15, 33, 68, 151–2, 185–6, 189
   successful   13
   trends   13
   websites   11
parents
   FERPA   178–9
   LGBTQ+ rights   179
   local rights   180
   metrics, public education by WalletHub   179
   national rights   178–9
   Office of Special Education Programs   179
   reader guide and discussion   202–5
   role of   94, 124
   special education rights   179
   state rights   179
parochial schools   54, 164

pathological demand avoidance
  (PDA) 40
Perler, Seth 133
personality
  activities matching 86
  girl-boss 1
  HTP technique to measure 50
  traits 50
  Type A 32
phenylketonuria 10
phobias 128
physical therapy (PT) 51
post-traumatic stress disorder
  (PTSD) 10, 51
private education, sensory-motor
  and phonological
  processing 178
progressive curricula 91
psychiatrist 28, 52, 65, 77, 93, 115,
  124, 132, 176, 184
Psychic Friends Network 188
psychologist 2, 4, 26–8, 31,
  33, 52–7, 62–4, 68,
  81–4, 92–3, 107, 111, 115,
  120–1, 126, 132–3, 148,
  173, 176, 181
psychotherapy 65–6, 97
  one-to-one sessions 65
  play therapy, types of 66
  two-way relationship 66
public schools 54, 57, 71, 165, 173
*Pushout: The Criminalization of
  Black Girls in Schools*
  (Morris) 23

racial and socioeconomic
  diversity 175
racial identity 70, 154
racism 3, 45, 106–7, 122, 160
Real Moms Live 154–5
Regional Center services 99

Reiss-Davis Child Study Center 25
remote learning 88
request, making
  IDEA 56
  insurance company 55
  pediatrician and
    psychoeducational
    evaluations 54
  referrals from friends 55
  schools for reassessment 54–5
results, interpreting
  in-person meeting 63
  interpretation of child's self-rating
    scale 63
reward system 37, 85, 109, 125
Rock, Chris 18, 43–4, 116

schools, change of 171–3
  comorbid challenges, knowledge
    of 173
  emotional labor for parents 172
scotopic sensitivity syndrome 42
Screen for Child Anxiety Related
  Disorders (SCARED)
  rating scale 40, 129
self-determination plan
  (SDP) 101–2
self-harm 6, 45, 110, 136
self-regulation 35, 44, 67, 84, 86,
  87, 92
sensory processing disorder
  (SPD) 1, 19–20, 26, 64,
  81, 84, 86, 92, 123, 140,
  151
  activities 21–2
  behavior as disruptive 20
  categories (tactile, proprioceptive,
    auditory, vestibular, arousal
    and attending, vision,
    social consciousness, and
    olfactory/gustatory) 26

food aversion   92
social and emotional
    development   23
social skills   21
student-centered and experiential
    learning with teachers   20
sexual violence   45
shadow (para-educator or
    co-teacher)   72
shaming   36, 45
Shaywitz, Sally   43
Shaywitz DyslexiaScreen   50
short-term memory   36, 57, 87, 167,
    171
sibling relationship   26, 146. *See also*
    family
sleepiness   93
Snapchat   4, 127–8
snowplow parenting style   152
social emotional training   85
social marginalization   160
social media   6, 14, 70, 98, 122,
    127–8, 137, 139,
    157
spatial awareness   32, 67, 81
special education training   186
Special Needs Network   79
stealing   34–7, 126
step-down in services
    access to care   121
    free health insurance   120
    free OT   120
    intimate relationship with a care
        provider   119
    UCLA Ties for Families   118–19
stereotype tightrope walk   12
stimulant medication   77
suburban life   14
Suicide and Crisis Lifeline   159
suicide/suicidal   4, 13, 45, 110,
    159–62
    ideation   93, 133, 160

impact of   160–1
3 Cs of suicide prevention
    (connection/collaboration/
    choice)   161
of youth   13
Support Team Education Plan
    (STEP)   78

therapeutic interventions   33, 79
therapies
    art therapy   66–7
    child-centered play therapy
        (CCPT)   66
    chiropractic neurology   68–9
    cognitive behavioral therapy
        (CBT)   66
    dance/movement therapy   67
    family play therapy   66
    group play therapy   66
    neurofeedback or
        biofeedback   67
    occupational therapy (OT)   67–8
    psychotherapy   65–6
    therapeutic models, options   69
    yoga   67
three Rs—reading, writing, and
    arithmetic   41
tiger moms   15
TikTok   4, 81, 89, 111, 127, 146, 206
Tourette's syndrome   123
trans youth   12, 65
treatment plan   2–3, 44, 63, 65, 71,
    76–81, 83–5, 87–8, 91,
    94–9, 102, 111–12, 117,
    123–5, 136, 148–9, 153,
    156, 173, 176, 186
2e or twice-exceptional student   135
    misdiagnosis   135

UCLA TIES (training, intervention,
    education, and services)
    46, 118–19, 134

undiagnosed neurodivergence   160
US Department of Education Office for Civil Rights   108

video games   88, 134, 142, 144, 146
Vista Del Mar Child and Family Services   25

Wide Range Achievement Test 5 (WRAT 5)   50
withdrawn affect   93

Woodcock-Johnson III Tests of Cognitive Abilities   49
World Wide Web   26

Yale Center for Dyslexia and Creativity   17
yoga   10, 67–8, 72
YouTube   4, 73, 127–8, 146, 148

zones of regulation   85, 136

ABOUT THE AUTHOR

Neferiti Austin, author and memoirist, writes about the erasure of diverse voices in motherhood in the number one Amazon bestseller *Motherhood So White: A Memoir of Race, Gender, and Parenting in America*. Nefertiti's work around this topic has appeared in the *New York Times*, *Washington Post*, *The Nation*, *Romper*, *Adoptive Families* magazine, *Parents Magazine*, *Vibe*, *SheMedia*, and countless others. She has appeared on numerous podcasts and radio programs including *The Today Show*, and multiple NPR outlets and jokes that adolescence is no match for menopause.

Nefertiti considers herself an accidental journalist, as her goal was to write novels and adopt a baby. Instead, her training, expertise, and mommy-jones coupled with degrees in US history and African American studies from UCLA led her to elevate Black women—mothers specifically—in her work. She is a former certified PS-MAPP trainer, where she co-led classes for participants wanting to attain a license to foster and/or adopt children from the foster care system. An alumna of Bread Loaf Writers' Conference and VONA, her first two novels, *Eternity* and *Abandon*, helped usher in the Black Romance genre in the mid-1990s.

She is the proud adoptive mother of two children and two Shih-Poos: Monsieur Lafayette and Siddhartha. The fivesome live in Los Angeles, California.